TRANSNATIONAL BUSINESS AND CORPORATE CULTURE

PROBLEMS AND OPPORTUNITIES

edited by

STUART BRUCHEY
ALLAN NEVINS PROFESSOR EMERITUS
COLUMBIA UNIVERSITY

T0347860

WEBS OF RESISTANCE IN A NEWLY PRIVATIZED POLISH FIRM

WORKERS REACT TO ORGANIZATIONAL TRANSFORMATION

JENNIFER LYNN RONEY

Routledge
Taylor & Francis Group

LONDON AND NEW YORK

First published 2000 by Garland Publishing Inc.

Published 2013 by Routledge
2 Park Square, Milton Park, Abingdon, Oxfordshire OX14 4RN
711 Third Avenue, New York, NY 10017

First issued in paperback 2014

Routledge is an imprint of the Taylor & Francis Group, an informa business

Copyright © 2000 by Jennifer Lynn Roney

All rights reserved. No part of this book may be reprinted or reproduced or utilized in any form or by any electronic, mechanical, or other means, now known or hereafter invented, including photocopying and recording, or in any information storage or retrieval system, without permission in writing from the publishers.

Library of Congress Cataloging-in-Publication Data
Roney, Jennifer Lynn, 1959–
    Webs of resistance in a newly privatized Polish firm : workers react to organizational transformation / Jennifer Lynn Roney.
        p. cm. — (Transnational business and corporate culture)
    Originally presented as the author's thesis (Ph.D.—David Eccles School of Business, University of Utah, 1996).
    Includes bibliographical references (p.) and index.
    1. Total quality management—Poland Case studies. 2. Work ethic—Poland Case studies. 3. Working class—Poland—Attitudes. 4. Poland—Social conditions—1980–   I. Series.
HD62.15.R66 1999
658.4'013'09438—dc21   99-30104

ISBN 13: 978-1-138-87987-4 (pbk)
ISBN 13: 978-0-8153-3390-6 (hbk)

To Kevin and Delaney.

Contents

Exhibits

Preface

This book is the result of a five-year journey into a world I had previously not experienced. The pages that follow represent thick description, supported by research in organizational studies as well as Polish history, sociology and anthropology, of the perceptions of employees in a single Polish factory. The journey was a difficult and rewarding adventure, on which I often took my entire family, and friends both professional and personal. Along the way I made new friends; people who welcomed me into their world and shared their struggles and their dreams. Many of them work at the factory that is the focus of this study. This factory is experiencing the uncertainties and opportunities of tremendous change in external contingencies and internal operations. The employees in this factory are trying to adjust to a new owner and many new managers, the fear of lay-offs and confusion about the world in which they now find themselves.

To ascertain the trust and thus the openness of the many informants of this study it was necessary to ensure their anonymity. This promise of anonymity was absolute and thus, policies and changes discussed by management were not shared with employees, even if this information may have relieved the stress that the uncertainty often caused. In addition, employees were guaranteed that I would not share specifics about what they told me to their management. To live up to this promise I have used pseudonyms throughout this book. All other facts included herein are truthful to the best of my knowledge. In addition, all quotes are direct from the employees and other Poles who spoke them to me.

As mentioned, I did not complete this journey alone. I had a great deal of help, support and love along the way. I must first thank the many residents of Goria who shared their opinions, fears and lives with me. Many opened their doors to my family and myself and my life is forever enriched by their genuine hospitality. I would like to particularly thank Teresa, who selected her own pseudonym, and who gave much more than I would have dared to expect. I would also like to thank Renata and Agnieska for their assistance that went well beyond interpretation.

Several sources of funding made this journey financially possible. I would like to acknowledge a Fulbright grant, National Security Education Program grant, also a Marriner S. Eccles grant for Political Economy, and funding from the CIBER center of the University of Utah, for funding various portions of the research for this book.

I am one of the few people I know who looks on the process of my doctoral thesis as a wonderful and joyous period in my life. I know it is in great part because of the support from my mentors and friends at the University of Utah. Thank you, to Brooke Derr, Karin Fladmoe-Lindquist, Janeen Costa, Pat Seybolt and John Seybolt for their unending support. I am grateful to Brooke for being willing to take on a student with such an ambitious thesis project and for supporting me through every step of the way. I am deeply indebted also, both professionally and personally, to Karin Fladmoe-Lindquist. Karin helped me through critical periods in the writing of this book, but she was also many times my lifeline to my "other" life while I was in Poland. Karin's emails of encouragement kept me going through the cold Polish winter and I am forever grateful. She continues to be a fabulous mentor and great friend.

To Janeen Costa, I am grateful for the tremendous insight and experience that she brought to the process of ethnography. It is a research approach that is deeply personal, stressful and immensely rewarding. I feel most comfortable with the rigor of this study and it took someone with Janeen's experience to guide me through this process.

To Pat, I am grateful for your support and guidance in many ways; for making the first trip to Poland possible and for your help in preparing me for the trip. I am also grateful for your friendship, which I highly value. Finally, to John, thank you for inviting me along on your trip to Poland, which truly gave me my foot in the door and for chipping in at the end when I needed you.

I would also like to thank Mary Teagarden, Mary Yoko Brannen, David Whetton, Eric Jansen, Susan Chesteen and Russ Belk for assistance on various parts of this project and on my academic development.

Finally, I must include in my thanks, my family. I could not have completed this without them. Delaney is my inspiration, Kevin my rock and my best friend, and Mom and Dad my greatest supporters, I love you all.

Webs of Resistance in a
Newly Privatized Polish Firm

CHAPTER 1

Introduction

The globalization of our world, partially brought on by rapid improvements in information flow capabilities, increased competition from emerging economies, and newly opened markets, has transformed organizational life (Thomas, 1996). All fields of organizational study are faced with the new complications this international dimension has generated. The ways in which people from different cultures transact business have become varied and complex. Multinational corporations, cross-cultural joint ventures, international consulting and marketing have all provided vehicles for this interaction.

In management, we are faced with a growing set of issues of how to manage and motivate individuals from diverse cultures who hold very different assumptions about work, time, and the world. Costa and Bamossy (1995) address the increased importance of cultural understanding brought by the globalization of business. They write,

> the tremendous advances in global travel, communication, and media reach have led to suggestions that cultures are converging . . . observed commonalities in behavior, [however] remain superficial . . . there continue to be clear differences in what these behaviors mean to the individuals and groups of different cultures (Costa & Bamossy, 1995:4).

As different cultures cross paths more frequently and more profoundly these differences in meanings applied to products, behaviors and shared experiences are becoming an increasingly important issue for study.

In an effort to become efficient and flexible to the changing business climate, countries and companies across the world have entered a phase of management information sharing. This transfer of management "know-how" has included intact management philosophies aimed at increasing competitiveness and reducing costs. Total Quality Management (TQM) is one of these management philosophies. Introduced to Japan by American statistician W.E. Deming, TQM helped transform the Japanese economy after World War II. With its focus on the processes that generate quality and its "quality is free" assumption, TQM provided a competitive advantage for Japanese companies in the world market. As Japan became a legitimate threat to the West in the 1980s American businesses embraced and studied every element of the Japanese success story, particularly the Total Quality Management philosophy. TQM has struggled to find its place in American management philosophy ever since, and in this process it has become Americanized.

This dramatic transformation of business practices occurred concurrently with a major political phenomenon, often symbolized by the crumbling of the Berlin Wall. The demise of European communism has introduced several neglected economies to the realities of capitalism and the competitive world. One of these struggling economies is Poland. One result of the communist regime and socialist policies, within the Polish context, was a virtual collapse of the Polish economy. In addition, organizations in Poland were operating under management practices that were inefficient and ineffective. In order to compete in the world market, many managers working in Polish businesses are currently introducing Western business approaches to their Polish workforces; TQM as practiced in the US, is one of those approaches. This transfer of management practices represents a wave of US culture washing across the fallen iron curtain in Poland.

THE RESEARCH QUESTION

What occurs when a management philosophy, like TQM, is transferred intact across cultural borders, in this case to Poland? In addition, to what extent does TQM contain the values of the American people, and how does this impact transfer to a new culture? Finally, how will the Polish people invoke their stored cultural "tool box" to adapt to a management philosophy that comes from the United States, where the culture and life experiences are quite different? These three questions frame the direction for this study. To adequately explore these questions in depth it was necessary to select one component of the

TQM philosophy to study. The decentralized control structure of TQM was selected because it was assessed, on the basis of prior research, to be the most interesting and important within the Polish context. To identify this particular component for study, I turned to Polish history (a detailed review is found in Chapter 2) for a sense of the behaviors and attitudes of the Polish people during previous times of major change or crisis.

Poland's recent experience with communism institutionalized the connection between power/status and position. Massive hierarchical structures became the organizing mechanism for government and social institutions alike. In addition, communist party membership was a prerequisite for any position of power or influence. Only those individuals who held positions of authority, usually party members, held official power within the political structure in communism. This served to centralize societal power around the party and the individuals who held positions of authority. Though Poles have become accustomed to this centralization of government, they have often rejected it. This is a pattern continued throughout the communist period, the preceding period of foreign power domination, and even back to the period of serf labor in Poland. Preference for local government, promotion of individual interests, along with recent contempt toward communist party rule, suggests that a conflict related to control systems, particularly those applied by the communist government and other official institutions, exists in Polish life. This is contrary to what might be expected after 50 years of socialist ideology that promoted egalitarianism and "collective" interests. This study will focus on the meaning of changing control systems, influenced by TQM, to the Polish worker, therefore, exploring this history of Polish conflict over control systems within a new set of circumstances.

Organizational studies have hitherto largely neglected the role of culture in the study of global management change. In addition, the study of the success and appropriateness of the transfer of management approaches across cultural borders has been ignored. Hofstede contends:

> Not only values and practices, but even theories, are products of culturally determined socialization. This should make us modest when we try to transfer, for example, Western types of education and management or training packages to people in a third world country.

Not only the tools but even the categories available for thinking may be unfit for the other environment (1992: 152).

Many within the realm of international management have called for the investigation of the basic assumptions and values that cultures utilize to deal with their environment (e.g. Boyacigiller & Adler, 1991; Van Maanen & 'Laurent, 1993; Parkhe, 1993; Wright, 1996). They suggest that international management studies have reached a point of parochialism and stagnant theory development. This study will endeavor to redirect this trend by examining the topic of international management from a different perspective; exploring the complexities caused by the juxtaposition of culturally imbedded management ideas within a traditional Polish context.

THE MEANING OF CULTURE IN THIS STUDY

Scholars across a wide range of academic disciplines have defined "culture" differently. Thus, it is important to clarify its meaning for this book. For our purpose culture is defined as:

> a set of assumptions commonly-held by a group of people. The set is distinctive to the group. The assumptions serve as guides to acceptable perception, thought, feeling, and behavior, and they are manifested in the group's values, norms, and artifacts. The assumptions are tacit among members, are learned, and are passed on to each new member of the group (Phillips, 1990: 10).

Culture represents the "fabrics of meaning" (Geertz, 1973) that are common for the individuals in a given environment. Ong captures the essence of culture:

> Culture is taken as historically situated and emergent, shifting and incomplete meanings and practices generated in webs of agency and power. Cultural change is not understood as unfolding according to some predetermined logic (of development, modernization, or capitalism) but as the disrupted, contradictory, and differential outcomes which involve changes in identity, relations of struggle and dependence, including the experience of reality itself (1987: 3-2).

Key to my usage of culture in this study is that it is forever changing, and in cases where two cultures meet it is "negotiated" (Brannen, 1994; Giddens, 1979). Cultures are created as distinct groups of people find different ways to adapt to the specific circumstances that they encounter. They are assumed here to be changing especially during times of major external upheaval. In these cases societies use stored cultural characteristics that they have developed, and react to the changing environment. This process serves to change the culture either by strengthening pre-existing norms or by altering those norms as a by-product of the encounter.

In addition to living in a changing cultural environment, we also live out our lives as simultaneous members of many different groups. Rosaldo claims that individuals exist in "a plurality of partially disjunctive, partially overlapping communities" (1993: 182). Meaning comes from the symbolism and experience of several social worlds for each person. Research is emerging that addresses this multiplicity of cultures, and it is reviewed in Chapter 3. This study will focus on the influence of the multiplicity of norms, values and assumptions, which define the culture. *Norms* are the accepted behavior of individuals within the cultural group. *Values* designate a shared sense of what "ought" to be, and distinguish the difference between what members view as "right" versus "wrong." Finally, *assumptions* are the shared belief in what "is," the assumed "reality" of their world. This study explores the norms, values and assumptions held by the individuals in a particular factory in the southern region of Poland where the research was performed. In addition, I endeavor to uncover the impact that communism has had on this culture, and the extent to which a "communist culture" has been assimilated in this context.

WEBS OF RESISTANCE—MEANING BEHIND THE TITLE OF THIS BOOK

The title of this book "Webs of Resistance in a Newly Privatized Polish Firm: Workers React to Organizational Transformation" was inspired by Geertz's view of culture. He said "believing, with Max Weber, that man is an animal suspended in webs of significance he himself has spun, I take culture to be those webs" (Geertz, 1973:5). As is the case in all cultural contexts, I believe the political, religious, economic, and social history of Poland has produced an intricately woven web of culture. This web has been painstakingly constructed over centuries. It has changed over time, yet it has remained the same in many respects. This web now presents a resistance to the latest attempts to change Poland and her people. The resistance is substantial, yet it bends and gives against extreme pressure, to a point. At that point the web will repel the pressure or remold itself to accommodate it. It is at this pressure point that I will tell the "tale" (Van Maanen, 1988) of the Polish workers in this factory in Poland. The catalyst for the "pressure" is the first major change in management philosophy since the company's inception 25 years ago. The pressure further represents a meeting of two distinct "national" cultures, the Polish culture of the people that work in the factory and the American culture introduced by the implementation of TQM, through a new Polish-American owner.

THE CASE[1]

The former communist Polish State presents an excellent environment in which to assess the relationship between culture and the adoption of new management practices. Poland has implemented drastic policies and initiatives to "kick-start" her economy, borrowing heavily from Western economic, financial, and managerial techniques. While undergoing these dramatic changes, however, the historical and cultural legacy of this country and her people has been apparent and has influenced the very nature of the changes themselves.

This research study was performed at Lockem, a manufacturer of locking mechanisms (not its real name or product). Lockem is located in a farming village with 5,000 residents, in southern Poland. The company was privatized in early 1994 through a lease/buy plan. Approximately 700 individuals were employed at this facility at the beginning of the study. This company previously employed the majority owner, a Polish-American, in the 1970s. He subsequently moved to the United States and started a successful manufacturing company where he implemented TQM. He is currently attempting to do the same in his Polish factory.

I chose this particular factory because it is at the extreme of cultural tension that I wish to study. The cultural background of the new majority owner, American yet Polish, presents a important and visible contrast in management ideology. In addition, this factory is located in a farming community, where approximately half of the factory employees work two jobs (they work in the factory and they farm their own land for personal use). The peasant past of the Polish people in general makes the examination of this particular group of people, who still maintain the traditional way of life, a particularly appropriate point of study (Gorlach, 1995; Hann, 1985).

RESEARCH APPROACH AND ASSUMPTIONS

This project used field-based ethnographic techniques to study a Polish manufacturing organization in transition from a state owned enterprise to a privately owned company. The approach was employed to uncover the values and assumptions, impressions and attitudes of the cultural members. Understanding of the meaning of the changes to the employees and their proclivity to accept these changes was the result.

The meaning in this setting is unveiled through the symbolism that informants give to events and experiences. This symbolism is interpreted through analysis of patterning in their shared stories, actions, and communicated values. This required a separation of the cultural constructions that are historically generated and the societal demands that are imposed through managerial dictate, whether in policies, procedures, or informal edict (Archer, 1988). The management and formal institutions are assumed in this setting to have influence on behaviors in the organization. The cultural values and norms, however, have also shaped this interaction regardless of the managerial approach. Meaning and an understanding of behavior in this context were assessed through the interaction of the historically generated cultural constructions and the managerial dictates, which are also culturally constructed, but may conflict with the general culture.

ETHNOGRAPHIC AUTHORITY

I approached this research with few preconceived notions about Poland or her people. The impetus for this project originated from my interest in the study of the transfer of TQM across national and cultural borders, not from any connection with Poland. It is precisely this detachment of predetermined personal interests coupled with immersion in the culture that I felt would provide a basis for discovery. Visker (1993), a postmodern philosopher, indicates:

> Real knowledge is knowledge of who we will never understand in the other, of that in the other which insures that he is not himself. It is because there is something in the other thanks to which he stand

outside of himself, that the transcendental hymen separating him from me does not prevent me, but precisely allows me to know him.

To begin the process of "knowing" the people that were to be the focus of this study, it was necessary to undergo extensive Polish language instruction, study of Polish history and culture and to make several preliminary trips to Poland.

The process of inquiry brought my family and me to Poland for 14 continuous months. We lived in Krakow, 50 kilometers from the factory which is the focus of this study. Throughout those 14 months I spent 2 to 3 days a week in the factory, as well as additional days in the town and the surrounding region. I stayed in a farmer's house one night a week throughout the most intensive period of data collection. Living in Krakow gave me a broader frame of reference within which I could place my research findings from the small farming village. This viewpoint became invaluable in differentiating those aspects of what I experienced that were generated by the rural life style and unique history and those that were more generalizable to the overall Polish mentality. An interpreter was used for collecting most of the primary data for this study.

I entered the field with what I will call an academic interest in the project, and a growing respect for the Polish people. What I found required many periods of discussion with Polish and American colleagues and friends. The process of discovery, analysis, reflection and questioning became the cornerstone of my study protocol. The end result of this experience is discussed in Chapter 7. It is accurate to say that the process of getting to know people, who are so different from myself, different in lifestyle, education level, and experience will forever change me. Yet I cannot ignore the fact that we are basically alike in the most important ways. We value our lives, family, beauty, peace and freedom. It is this juxtaposition of the very different with the very similar that, I think, allowed me to touch the hopes and fears that the changes in the lives of these people have created. I hope that it has allowed me to sift through the insignificant and the presentation of a collective representation (Goffman, 1959) and to present the important and the interesting so the reader can determine truth in this setting for himself or herself.

THE ORGANIZATION OF THE BOOK

In this opening chapter I provide a brief narrative of the topic of this book, the research focus and its importance to the study of organizations within a changing global environment. The case and the epistemological approach are introduced. The next chapter situates this study in three major streams of research: culture, TQM, and Polish peasant history. Within the first stream, the topic of culture in management literature and the growing inquiry into the multiplicity of cultural influences within a given setting is explored. National/regional and communist culture are reviewed in this chapter focusing on the individualism-collectivism dimension of culture. Within the second stream of research, the Total Quality Management philosophy, I briefly review the literature on the topic in its entirety and then concentrate on the decentralization of control as the primary focus of this research. After addressing these two literature streams, I examine the literature that has addressed both the culture and TQM within the same context. Finally, in the third stream of literature, I look at the history of the Polish peasant. This literature presents the economic, social and political changes that the peasantry has endured since medieval times. This section concludes with a review of the current literature on the impact that communism has had on the Polish shared values and assumptions. Chapter 3 describes the case from three angles: the country, the community and the company. Each takes the reader deeper into the lives of the people under study, exposing different layers of their world.

Delacroix describes the experience of uncovering culture in this way.

> each culture forms an integrated whole; its parts hang together with some degree of coherence, like the furniture in a tasteful home. The lay observer senses the coherence before he recognizes the parts. [Yet, ordinarily] . . . we don't know enough about contemporary modern cultures to avoid arbitrariness in selecting what is essential to this coherence (1987: 7).

The complexities inherent in selecting the essential elements of this culture were tackled through a systematic process of inquiry and discovery, which has involved several years of literature review, advance trips to Poland, and a detailed methodological approach.

Chapter 4 outlines this methodological approach. First, I discuss the epistemological assumptions that frame my choice of a case study and ethnographic methods for this project. I then describe the specific methods used, and conclude with a preview of the ethnographic tale, the technique employed for the presentation of the results chapters (Chapter 5 and 6).

Deciding how to pare down the voluminous notes of experiences, observations, stories, impressions, assertions and subtleties of an intense field experience such as this one was the most difficult task in completing this study. I have decided to allow the data to tell their own story, framed in the relevant literature. By this I mean that I have presented those things that simply wanted and needed to be told. Throughout the course of my field experience the themes that are presented here caused questions, frustrations, and unending wonder for myself, my family, other foreigners living in Poland, and for the Poles themselves. They represent those things that, though not obvious, are just under the surface of everyday life in this region of Poland. Constructing the meaning, applications, and idiosyncrasies of each of these themes was the challenge of this task. The issues presented here, however, are the ones that almost had a life of their own; they appeared so frequently, they could not be ignored.

Chapter 5, 6 and 7 represent differing levels of results from this study. Chapter 5 describes the social organization that is found in this region of Poland. It discusses three influences on this social organization; historical, political and religious. Chapter 6 explores the "fabric of meaning" that is creating the web of resistance to change in this factory. It tells of four themes that emerged in this factory which represent the shared view of the world as it is enacted. This view is intensified and brought to the surface in the turbulent environment in which the workers find themselves. Each theme is presented by taking the reader onto the factory floor or into the village and contextualizing what the workers say and do. Chapter 7 offers a view of the impact of the changes that have occurred in the factory in relation to the desired results, as framed by the TQM philosophy. This chapter takes each of the elements of the decentralized control structure of TQM and represents the progress thus far, through the eyes of the workers, toward achieving those goals.

Chapter 8 concludes the book with a discussion of lessons learned in this process of discovery. It maps out the contribution of the present study and areas where future research can build from that, which has been experienced here. Finally, it explores some critical issues that have become apparent in attempting to tackle an ethnographic study of management change in a foreign country, and some recommendations for those who might choose to tackle a similar project.

CHAPTER 2

Culture, TQM and Poland

CULTURE

Within the field of international management research, a growing number of scholars are expressing the belief that a multiplicity of dynamic, shared mindsets exist (Martin, 1992; Phillips, 1994; Phillips & Sackmann, 1991). These shared mindsets represent the perceptions, thoughts, feelings, and behaviors of a group of people which distinguish them as distinct "cultures" (Fisher, 1988; Phillips, 1994). Cultures have been studied, for example, at the level of subgroups (Sackmann, 1992), organizations (Ouchi & Wilkins, 1985; Sackmann, 1992; Schein, 1984,1991,1992; Wilkins, 1989; Wilkins & Dyer, 1988), industries (DiMaggio & Powell, 1983; Grinyer & Spender, 1979; Phillips, 1994; Spender, 1989), and nationalities (Hall, 1959; Hall & Hall, 1990; Hofstede, 1983a, 1984; Stewart & Bennett, 1991; Trompennars, 1994). Cultural pressures originating from each of these sources complement each other and often compete for dominance in influencing the behavior of individuals within firms.

Communist culture is a new idea in the study of organizations. Sztompka (1992,1995a) recently introduced this concept in his explorations of the sociological impact of the 1989 political and economic revolution in Eastern Europe. Communist culture denotes the similarities in behaviors, attitudes and approaches among the previously communist countries of Europe. Prior to 1989 only limited contact was made between Western and communist scholars. Exploration of the communist social influence was not examined rigorously for political and ideological reasons. This phenomenon, therefore, has been virtually ignored in the management literature.

Here, however, it is a critical factor in assessing shared values, and it is reviewed in this section.

Cultures tend to exist as "separate, overlapping, superimposed or nested" (Boyacigiller, Kleinberg, Phillips & Sackmann, 1996: 24) within a particular organizational setting. The various forms of culture studied in organizational literature have been treated as if they were separate and distinct. It is important to emphasize that these cultural forms (e.g., national, industry, organizational) do not exist in a "pure" form in reality (Boyacigiller, Kleinberg, Phillips & Sackmann, 1996). National/regional culture and communist culture (cultural assumptions and behavior shared by peoples who have lived under communist government systems) are described below since they are the focus of this book. Many influences, however, are subsumed under the cultural titles that are presented. For example, religious culture is incorporated under the title of national/regional culture. This is not to suggest that any given region or nation holds a mutually exclusive or all-inclusive religion; instead it assumes that the region or national culture holds shared meanings that are formed in part by the religious influences that exist in the area. As Hofstede (1991) implied in his assertion that cultural assumptions of people delineate "central tendencies" this book endeavors not to section off separate and distinct cultural forms. Instead I focus on the ways these various influences interact within a given organizational setting.

Organizational and industry culture have been shown to be critical determinants of organizational behavior in a wealth of empirical work (e.g., Fombrun & Shanley, 1990; Gordon, 1985; Grinyer & Spender, 1979; Meyerson, 1991; Ouchi & Johnson, 1978; Van Maanen, 1973; Wilkins, 1983) but they are assumed to have only a minimal impact in this study. This is because the organizational culture in this factory was the product of a shared set of procedures handed down by the centralized state until 1994. These procedures are the product of the communist culture as it was enacted throughout the country. Kostera (1995) discusses the state influence on Polish organizations. She draws from the work of Obloj and Kostera (1994) and Kiezun (1978) ; she said:

> [Polish] enterprises seemed to be copies of each other, tiny elements within a big mechanism . . . all important goals were imposed by a central plan—and the communist party . . . the communist party

controlled managers in such areas as motivation and appointment (Kostera, 1995: 682).

In addition, Czarniawska states "the concept of 'organizational culture' proves to be fruitless when applied to organizations in socialist economies" (1986: 313). The current organizational culture at Lockem is being shaped by the majority owner who has brought with him American management practices and procedures. His influence in the company and how it is received by management and the workers is a focus of this study. Because of the relative newness of this influence, however, it is not studied as an unmediated factor of the organizational culture (for an examination of organizational culture literature see Ouchi & Wilkins, 1985; Sackmann, 1991; Schein, 1984). The industry culture influence is relatively new, given the nature of the communist market system. Currently many of these norms are being introduced by the new owner, who has worked within the global locking device industry for many years (for an examination of industry culture literature see Gordon, 1991; Phillips, 1994; Spender, 1989).

National/Regional Culture

Finding a definition for national culture separate from the definition for the broader term *culture* is difficult in organizational literature. The dominant trend in organizational literature has assumed that nations represent the culture of people (Boyacigiller, Kleinberg, Phillips & Sackmann, 1996). As I discussed earlier, there is a growing body of literature that identifies a multiplicity of mindsets within a given setting (Boyacigiller, Kleinberg, Phillips & Sackmann, 1996). In Chapter 1, I defined culture as "a set of assumptions commonly held by a group of people." When shared mindsets distinguish those individuals who are citizens of a national state or reside within a given geographical border, share the same language, common childhood practices, religion and philosophy, early education and educational systems and attitudes about work and life (Derr & Laurent, 1989), organizational literature generally has termed these commonalties as national or regional culture.

Boyacigiller, Kleinberg, Phillips and Sackmann (1996), in their review of international cross-cultural management research, have identified problems in looking at culture as representative of a nation state. The homogeneity of a given nation varies across nations and is dynamic within nations. Therefore, research in this area has begun to turn to a study of regional commonality that is embedded with other factors, including religious, political, language, tradition, and rituals. For this reason, in this book, the "regional" definition will be adopted over the "nation state" definition for national/regional culture.

Differences have been found between regional cultures in the way the members view the world (Stewart & Bennett, 1991), how they deal with uncertainty, the degree to which individuals are integrated into groups, in the way roles are distributed between the sexes, the extent to which the less powerful members of organizations accept and expect that power is distributed unequally (Hofstede, 1984) how information is processed, conceptions of time (Hall & Hall, 1990), how individuals establish relationships with others, the modality of human activity, what a human being's relationship to nature is, and the character of innate human nature (Trompennars, 1994). Utilizing this research, organizational theorists have sought to identify the managerial assumptions that are strongly shaped by national cultures and appear quite insensitive to the more transient culture of organizations (Laurent, 1992).

Regional culture research has been awash with a need to segregate and classify cultures. This trend has led scholars to develop a full range of dichotomies to explain the differences in behavior across cultural boundaries. Hofstede's (1980) seminal work influenced this trend by succinctly categorizing a nation's people upon each of five scales: individualism-collectivism, power distance, uncertainty avoidance, masculinity-femininity and Confucian dynamism (added in a later work, Hofstede & Bond, 1988). Others have continued in this line, adding dimensions of achievement-ascription, particularism-universalism, man-nature (Trompenaars, 1985), low context-high context, monochronic-polychronic time, past-future oriented (Hall & Hall, 1990), to name a few.

Boyacigiller, Kleinberg, Phillips and Sackmann (1996) point out that the classification of cultures on these dimensions assumes that national culture is a given, single, and permanent characteristic of an individual. This limitation is significant to this study of Poles in a state of change. As the Polish people struggle with the vastly different forces generated by communism, traditions of Polish culture and the "global" culture introduced through the market system the categorizations offered by Hofstede and others seems inadequate to describe the complexities of this context. Communism, for example, espoused a primacy of social collectivity while the traditional Polish response to adversity and the market system both promote individualism as a value. This literature fails to grasp the notion of cultural multiplicity and cultural change generated by the meeting of two distinct and conflicting cultural influences.

Individualism-collectivism, is the most studied of these cultural dimensions. It is detailed here for the purposes of providing an example of the dimensions presented in the literature, and because it is of particular significance in the case of Polish culture. Poles have traditionally acted in somewhat individualistic ways, preferring to govern at very local levels. Their individualistic spirit has been enacted at times as almost a fear of collective behavior (Nagengast, 1991; Topolski, 1974). Yet social classes (nobility, working class, peasantry), and their collectivist dimension, as well as communism and its social ideology of equality, are factors in Polish society. This tendency to prefer individualist organization, coupled with a long history of social class polarity, and a recent history of communism calls into question where Poles lie on a individualism-collectivism scale.

The individualism-collectivism nature of Poland is significantly complicated by the communist experience. Despite the ideological rhetoric of communism which espoused equality for all citizens of the country, the practice of communism sent a very different ideological message. Poles that opposed the communist ideology say that they disliked it because it was not fair and served to differentiate party members from nonparty members. These opponents of communism say that they would prefer a more egalitarian distribution of rewards and resources than the communist party system produced. This is in contrast to those that supported communism for example, party members. Many of these party members have been quick to support the new market driven distribution of resources which is ideologically contrary to communism, seeking the opportunities that this new system presents. Thus, communist dogma is in conflict with communism in practice, and it muddles the lines between individualism and collectivism.

The individualism-collectivism dimension identifies the importance of the individuals in the society as compared to the group (Hofstede, 1983a, 1983b; Kluckhohn & Strodtbeck, 1961; Parsons & Shils, 1951; Schneider, 1992). It represents the level at which the culture tends to prefer to organize, make decisions, structure government, and structure reward and punishment systems. This dimension ranges from, at one extreme, "individualism" which represents a culture that rewards individual effort at the expense of the group, tends to make decisions at the highest levels of the authority structure, and encourages a highly competitive environment. In addition, individualism represents the pursuit of self-serving goals (Morris, Davis, & Allen, 1994). Hofstede states that "individualist cultures assume individuals look primarily after their own interests and the interests of their immediate family" (1984: 390). Employees in individualist societies tend to view their relationship with the organization in a calculated manner, such as in relation to the particular compensation scheme or the status associated with employment (Boyacigiller & Adler, 1991).

At the other extreme is "collectivism" where individual accomplishments that place one person above another are discouraged or severely punished, group decision making is preferred, and authority is decentralized. Through birth right, or other forms of differentiation, individuals assume membership in particular "groups" from which it is difficult to detach themselves (Hofstede, 1984). They subordinate their individual needs and interests to the goals of the larger group of which they are a member. Often intergroup conflict results from a heavy emphasis on intragroup cooperation, sharing, and group harmony (Morris, Davis, & Allen, 1994). Employees in collectivist societies commit to organizations based on relationships with other employees such as managers, owners, or co-workers (Boyacigiller & Adler, 1991).

Research into this dimension has explored the relationship of various organizational characteristics and measures of performance with the individualist-collectivist nature of the culture in which these organizations operate. Trompenaars (1985) explored the meanings inherent in organizational structures in nine countries. He found a significant correlation between collectivist cultures and organizational relationships defined in terms of social status and authority. Conversely, a high correlation was found between individualist cultures and rational organizational positions defined in terms of tasks or functions. Hofstede's (1980) study of 40 countries identified strong correlation between perceived differences in power of organizational actors and collectivism. Earley (1993) and Wagner (1981) each looked at the effects of individualist-collectivist social organization on the effectiveness of work groups. Earley, studying groups in three separate countries, the United States, China, and Israel, found that collectivists have lower performance working alone or in an out-group than they do working with an in-group, and they view themselves has most capable of performing tasks when they are working in an in-group. Wagner found that the individualism-collectivism variable had both main and moderator effects on cooperation in groups when looking at US students. Further, Morris, Davis and Allen (1994) examined the impact of individualism-collectivism measures on entrepreneurial behavior within the firm in four countries, the United States, Australia, Great Britain, and Canada. They found that a correlation exists between individualism and entrepreneurial behavior.

Each of these studies seeks to place groups of people or, in the case of Wagner, individuals concretely upon a singular linear continuum. Once placed, analysis is performed to discover if a relationship exists between where one group is "tagged" in relationship to others with a set of organizational phenomenon. The limitation of this approach is that it does not account for the potential shifts of groups along that continuum as conditions change. Additionally, it does not provide for the possibility of conflicting tendencies within the group toward both individualism and collectivism simultaneously. This limitation makes this research only peripherally relevant to this study. This same limitation exists for all of the dichotomous classifications mentioned in the preceding section. Each was developed through quantitative analysis using survey techniques. Attempts to "pigeon hole" cultures using these dimensions does provide a basis for comparison, but at this point in our quest for the true impact of culture upon organizational life, it appears to suffocate understanding that is desperately needed.

Communist Culture

Sztompka has identified a "peculiar culture-generating setting of vast scope: the communist bloc" (1992: 3). He has equated the impact of the communist bloc to that of the empires of past centuries. Sztompka has called this influence of the communist ideology, which permeated virtually every aspect of economic, social and political life in post-communist countries, a "cultural syndrome." This cultural influence has had a significant impact on generating culturally constructed "obstacles" which Sztompka calls "cultural incompetencies." This strong ideological force has influenced the cultural landscape and affected the way that Polish workers view not only their world in general but specifically the organizations in which they work. In addition, the communist centralized economy dominated the ways and means of doing business in Polish companies during the 50 years of communist rule. This influence has acted in the same manner as the owner/leader influence in organizational culture (Schein, 1992).

Limitations

This review of the *management* literature on culture has pointed to four general limitations: 1) cultures are seen as distinguishable in categories (e.g., nation, organization, industry) not allowing for the changing and overlapping of cultural influences 2) culture is assumed to be a static characteristic of individuals, 3) there is no understanding of the interface of culture and organizational transformation, and 4) the influence of communism on the traditional regional culture of Poland has not been explored thoroughly. These limitations restrict the literature's usefulness as a framework for making sense of the cultural dynamics of my study and in part dictate the methodology used (see Chapter 4).

TOTAL QUALITY MANAGEMENT

Total Quality Management (TQM) is an integrated approach to management that asserts that exceptional quality is essential to maintaining competitive advantage and ultimately organizational survival. It unites a humanistic, systems approach to management, which is organized around processes with powerful statistical techniques and as a result has created a management philosophy that transforms the organization (Crosby, 1992; Deming, 1986; Juran, 1989). TQM involves a corporate state of mind that directs all strategic and operational policies in which the company engages. Deming (1986) sees TQM as a transformation from an inefficient environment of heavy reliance on inspection, autocratic leadership, and hierarchical control, to an environment of teamwork, attention to customer satisfaction, quality the first time, and continuous process improvement. Research on the underlying theory of TQM has been lacking (Dean & Bowen, 1994; Sitkin, Sutcliffe, & Schroeder, 1994; Spencer, 1994). Spencer writes "in practice TQM does not describe an objective reality but instead depicts a somewhat amorphous philosophy" (1994: 468). This philosophical nature of TQM has made it difficult to define it clearly as other than simply a set of practices and techniques. However, it is this definition of the underlying philosophy of TQM that is most important to understanding the values and assumptions it embraces.

Dimensions of TQM

Recent theoretical development of the TQM approach to management, can be summarized by three primary dimensions: 1) process focus, (2) long-term customer focus, and (3) decentralized control structure (Bowen & Lawler, 1992b; Dean & Goodman, 1994; Roney, 1994; Roney & Fladmoe-Lindquist, 1995; Sitkin, Sutcliffe, & Schroeder, 1994; Waldman, 1995) (see Exhibit 1). The literature for the first two dimensions, starting with process focus, is presented briefly in this section to provide a context for looking at the third dimension which is the focus of this study. This section concludes with an review of the literature on the union of TQM and culture.

Exhibit 1. Total Quality Management Dimensions

Process Focus
Continuous Process Improvement
Measurement of Processes
Active Involvement of Suppliers and Customers

Long-term Customer Focus
Expanded Definition of Customer
Long Range Planning
Emphasis on Quality

Decentralized Control Structure
Teamwork
Empowerment
Visionary Leadership

Process focus. This dimension describes an organizational emphasis on the identification and measurement of all steps in the flow of production instead of merely the characteristics of the production output. In addition, process focus embodies measurement for the purpose of continuous process improvement and an active involvement of suppliers and customers in internal process analyses (Anderson, Rungtusanatham, & Schroeder, 1994; Deming, 1986). Dean and Bowen call this the "continuous improvement" principle and describe it as a "commitment to constant examination of technical and administrative processes in search of better methods" (1994: 395).

This dimension requires job redesign and efficient information flow within the organization to encourage visibility of processes that precede as well as those that follow a given job (Waldman, 1994). This principle focuses on the elimination of dependence on inspection to achieve quality products (Deming, 1986). It transfers the responsibility for the quality of every work process to the individual employees that work on that process. The output of each employee should be at a significant standard of quality, prior to transference, so that the next employee is not impeded in adding additional value to the product. This dimension requires the organization to design motivational systems to reward for knowledge about the processes of the job instead of the characteristics of its output (Schonberger, 1992). Individuals need to make decisions and act based on the data obtained from the process analyses that they perform in their jobs. They are required to project into the future, and down the process line, the impact of process variation that is detected (Anderson, Rungtusanatham, & Schroeder, 1994; Dean & Bowen, 1994).

Design-of-experiments (Taguchi, 1990), concurrent engineering (Lee, Luthans, & Hodgetts, 1992), just-in-time inventory systems (Flynn, Sakakibara & Schroeder, 1995; Snell & Dean, 1992), and statistical process control (Bushe, 1988) are techniques that complement the TQM philosophy by assisting the employee with measurement and analysis of the processes of the organization. These techniques are used to systematize the practices of up-front design of quality products, maintenance of quality production without the need for inspection, and continuous attention to improvement. They have frequently been implemented without the quality culture and TQM philosophical principles to support them. Often, however, this has been destructive and has resulted in expensive failures for the companies that have attempted such implementation (Anderson, Rungtusanatham, & Schroeder, 1994).

Long-term customer focus. The second dimension of TQM is integrated into the strategic direction and decision making of the organization (Gehani, 1993). Long-term customer focus changes the ultimate focal point for planning and decision making from the shareholder to the customer and has far-reaching implications for many organizations (Crosby, 1992; Deming, 1986; Juran, 1989). TQM advocates claim that the traditional customer must be of prime concern to every employee as she/he sets about doing her/his individual job, to assure that this customer's expectations are met or exceeded.

Employees should be rewarded for stepping out of the accepted procedures for performing the job when improvements are identified that improve customer satisfaction with the product/service (Anderson, Rungtusanatham & Schroeder, 1994; Deming, 1986; Juran, 1989; Sitkin, Sutcliffe, & Schroeder, 1994).

In addition to this emphasis on the traditional customer, the term "customer" is broadened in this environment. Consistent with stakeholder theory, the customer is any individual or group that maintains a stake in the company's well-being (Freeman, 1984). This definition includes internal customers such as the employee that is next in line in the production process, government agencies, suppliers and community groups (Dean & Bowen, 1994; Sitkin, Sutcliffe & Schroeder, 1994). This expanded definition of customer significantly affects the sense of awareness and focus for the employee and for management. The accepted mode of action changes from adherence to procedures without consideration for the impact on the customer to individual employee authority to amend processes to better meet customer needs. Additionally, the much broader definition of customer requires management to focus on employees as customers, which, in turn, transforms the entire landscape for both employees and management, and creates new expectations (Roney & Fladmoe-Lindquist, 1995).

The three elements that make the TQM's long-term customer focus unique in its strategic planning criteria are: the longer range of this focus, the customer orientation, and the emphasis on quality. Dean and Bowen (1994) identify a conflict between quality theorists and traditional management theorists in the role that quality should play in strategic management of the organization. They point out, however, that when quality is defined as "meeting or exceeding customer expectations" it can be seen as "comprising virtually any source of differentiation" (Dean & Bowen, 1994: 404). This leads to the conclusion that quality is the leading determinant of profitability and thus an essential foundation for strategic planning processes. Daniel and Reitsperger (1994) point out that quality has become an ever increasing factor in sustaining competitive advantage, and is a widely accepted cornerstone of Japanese manufacturing strategy. Hamel and Prahalad (1994) go one step further by suggesting that quality is quickly becoming a competitive necessity rather than a source of competitive advantage.

Decentralized control structure. As was suggested in Chapter 1, this dimension was chosen as the focus of this study because it was expected to be particularly significant to the success of TQM in Poland. It deals with power within the organization, and it is especially sensitive to differences in cultural context. The decentralized control structure allocates control and power within the organization to the most appropriate level. "Appropriate" is gauged as that which is most efficient for the organization as a whole, and "efficiency" is assumed to increase when employees who are closest to the work process have responsibility and authority to make decisions about those processes. It involves an intricate balance of teamwork (Bowen & Lawler, 1992a; Dean & Bowen, 1994; Flynn, Schroeder & Sakakibara, 1994) and empowerment of the workforce (Spreitzer, 1993; Thomas & Velthouse, 1990; Lawler, 1993) with strong visionary leadership (Juran, 1989). Teamwork, and empowerment require that the control of key processes within the organization shift from the executive manager's office to the shop floor. This shift must be balanced with leadership that is knowledgeable and visionary (Anderson, Rungtusanatham, & Schroeder, 1994; Waldman, 1993). The leader must understand her/his employees and their work processes while instilling a sense of trust, fairness, and commitment to the future of the organization.

A *teamwork* approach to decision making and problem solving is a means to change organizational processes toward a focus on collaboration and cooperation. The concept of teamwork is similar to that of self-directed work teams (Orsburn, Moran, Musselwhite & Zenger, 1990; Pearce & Ravlin, 1987). Effectively applied, teams result in products superior to those produced by individuals alone (Deming, 1986). Teamwork includes the identification of cross-functional and cross-level needs and sharing responsibility and credit (Ciampa, 1992). It also advocates rewards based on team productivity (Myers, 1990). In practice, teamwork has been an important and consistently applied implementation tool in TQM (Harris, 1995). It is less internally competitive, produces results that would be difficult without collaboration, and creates buy-in from the participants that would not exist if decisions were made by a manager and dictated to employees (Deming, 1986).

Instilling in the employee the desire to accept an increased level of responsibility is a key to the success of this dimension; *empowerment* is an approach frequently cited for accomplishing this in the TQM literature (Dean & Bowen, 1994; Deming, 1986; Waldman, 1994).

Empowerment has been studied from two perspectives in the current organizational literature (Seybolt & Roney, 1994a). The first relates to the transfer or sharing of power from a superior to a subordinate. This transfer of power assumes that power is maintained by particular individuals in the organization and is transferred at their discretion to other individuals (March & Simon, 1958). The second definition of empowerment relates it to internal task motivation. Thomas and Velthouse have focused on this second approach to empowerment. They claim:

> intrinsic task motivation involves those generic conditions by an individual, pertaining directly to the task, that produce motivation and satisfaction (1990: 668).

This perspective is cognitive in nature and implies that empowerment is a much more personal condition determined primarily by the relationship between the individual and the task as opposed to the delegation or transfer of power from a superior. The internal task motivation perspective of empowerment has been studied by Spreitzer (1993), Thomas and Velthouse (1990), and Conger and Kanungo (1988). They suggest that empowerment is multidimensional. Spreitzer (1993) has reviewed the literature and developed four related but distinct constructs for empowerment: meaningfulness, competence, self-determination, and impact. A brief review of each follows.

Meaningfulness involves the perception that the relationship between the task an individual is performing and one's beliefs, attitudes, values, and behaviors are congruent and fit well in the individual's judgment (Kahn, 1990; Spreitzer, 1993). Meaningfulness occurs when individuals "feel worthwhile, useful, and valuable—as though they made a difference and were not taken for granted" (Kahn, 1990: 704). An individual's sense of meaningfulness is shaped by a combination of a person's values and beliefs coupled with the organizational and task construction (Seybolt & Roney, 1994b).

Competence is the perception that one can perform a task effectively. This is the individual's general sense of his or her ability to accomplish goals within the specific situation. An individual who feels a high level of competence in a given assignment will not necessarily feel that same level of competence in another assignment, however (Seybolt & Roney, 1994b). Success or failure influences an individual's feelings of competence and, therefore, directly impacts the assessment of empowerment (Spreitzer, 1993; Thomas & Velthouse, 1990). Self-determination is the extent to which an individual perceives autonomy and choice in various job-related situations (Spreitzer, 1993). When a self-perception exists that involvement in a given activity is intentional and volitional, the level of self-determination is considered high (Deci & Ryan, 1989). High self-determination has been linked to higher levels of initiative and self-regulation (Deci & Ryan, 1989), internal motivation (deCharms, 1968), and sense of autonomy which allows individuals to perceive themselves as "origins" rather than "pawns" in determining specific behaviors and actions (deCharms, 1968).

Finally, impact is viewed as the level of influence an individual has on the immediate task environment (Thomas & Velthouse, 1990) or on the organization as a whole (Spreitzer, 1993). Impact is similar to the concepts of control studied by Rotter (1966) —locus of control—and Paulhus (1983) —spheres of control. Paulhus looked at the perception of control in three behavioral spheres: personal achievement, social relationship, and the political and social system. This construct, as with the other three, relates solely to an individual's perception of the condition, and not the actual *impact*, for example.

The balance between strong leadership and the focus on teamwork and empowerment is very precarious. Senior managers in organizations that are hierarchically structured and maintain an autocratic leadership will have difficulty relinquishing control while maintaining a motivational presence (Spencer, 1994). The purpose of a *visionary leader* is to foster the mutual respect that is a cornerstone of the quality culture discussed (Deming, 1986; Juran, 1989). A cultural environment that insists upon respect for all individuals will be far more open to the ideas of its participants and will foster a sense of trust (Deming, 1986; Ford & Fottler, 1995; Whitney, 1995). Employees will be willing to voice their opinions and to provide suggestions for improvements even without being asked. This sense of trust promotes many benefits that are attainable only through the voluntary actions of employees who feel respected and appreciated (Bromiley & Cummings, 1993; Coleman, 1990; Cummings, 1983).

Transformational leadership (Avolio & Bass, 1986; Bass, 1985; Burns, 1978) has been equated with the visionary leadership that TQM prescribes (Anderson, Rungtusanatham & Schroeder, 1994; Waldman, 1993, 1994). Articulation of the company's vision, communication and enhancement of self-efficacy are all characteristics that are shared by both transformational leadership and TQM advocates. In addition, the emphasis on promoting teamwork and continuous improvement of processes is found in both the visionary leadership and the transformational leadership literature (Waldman, 1993).

Culture and TQM

A body of literature on the TQM approach to management has slowly developed over the last three years. Still, very few empirical studies have been performed and little theory exists surrounding this established management system (Waldman, 1995). Harris (1995) outlines three foci of TQM research: the degree to which quality management is dependent on the culture of the workforce, information system requirements, and appropriate measurement and assessment of performance. The first of these provides the closest connection to the focus of this study.

An emerging theme within the TQM literature is that TQM represents a shift in thinking and organizational culture (Beyer, Ashmos & Osborn, 1997; Cole, 1993; Mitki & Shani, 1995; Sashkin & Kiser, 1993). Rarely has compatibility of the cultural environment with the TQM approach been analyzed. Bushe (1988) provides an exception to this lack of integration of technique with implementation environment. Bushe used an ethnographic approach to assess the cultural roadblocks to successful implementation of statistical process control in one large US corporation. He found three cultural themes that impede Statistical Process Control (SPC) : learning versus performing, the meaning of information, and holism versus segmentalism. Each of these themes represents a "set of norms" in the organization under study that created an incompatible climate for the implementation of SPC. In the first, SPC's focus on learning was incompatible with the company's focus on performance at any cost. In the second theme, the author found that the company historically had used a vastly different form of "public information" than the control charts produced, which either created uncomfortable reactions to the information, or on the other hand, were virtually ignored by employees. Finally, the holistic approach that Statistical Process Control takes was countercultural to the functionally organized company that was studied.

Bushe's work addressed the interdependence of TQM and organizational culture. International management researchers, however, have only begun to study the relationship of TQM with national culture. The research suggests that TQM harbors in its basic philosophical framework a set of values and assumptions that may or may not be consistent with those held by the national cultures into which TQM is introduced (Roney, 1994). The research on national culture and TQM has taken two paths. The first is the evaluation of the factors that have differentiated TQM in Japan and in the US. These studies have shown that Japanese firms put a greater emphasis on quality in their strategic decision making (Ebrahimpour & Johnson, 1992) and management control systems (Daniel & Reitsperger, 1994) and that this emphasis favorably impacts cost and productivity advantages (Feigenbaum, 1986; Schonberger, 1982) and a product's market appeal (Barksdale, Perreault, Arndt, Barnhill, French, Halliday & Zif, 1982).

The second stream of research uses case studies and qualitative techniques to understand the implementation of TQM within foreign contexts. In one of these studies Osland (1995) defined the national culture in a Central American plant as being characterized by high power distance and strong collectivism. He found that these cultural characteristics made self-determination (one of the four empowerment constructs found by Spreitzer) irrelevant. Specifically, this study called into question the importance of self-determination within any cultural environment with these characteristics.

Using semistructured interviews, Mitki and Shani (1995) examined the successful implementation of TQM in two Israeli firms. These authors suggest that this specific cultural climate might hinder integration of TQM. The nature of the Israeli management culture is one of improvisation and short-term perspective, and Mitki and Shani suggest that this is a result of a people who have undergone significant struggles of survival over a long period of time. Their results, however, show success in two firms, a paper mill and an insurance company, despite their varied approaches to TQM implementation. This leads these authors to suggest that TQM may contain a "universal set of management practices and principles that goes beyond cultural boundaries" (Mitki & Shani, 1995: 169).

Limitations

we probably believe that although much of Japanese management is not transferable to the American culture, their emphasis on groups and teamwork should be transferable and, in any case, we need to

consider the possibility in spite of our penchant for individualism
(Burke, 1995:167)

Burke's "intuition" highlights the lack of knowledge we have about the transferability of management approaches. As scholars, we suppose and speculate, but little actual research has been done to support these numerous contentions. The TQM literature to date has remained largely prescriptive or descriptive of implementation only (Harris, 1995). The limited systematic studies reviewed above leave many gaps in the exploration of TQM within multiple cultural contexts. Specifically, the studies are either limited in scope, exploring only one element of the TQM approach, or they are all-inclusive, looking at TQM as a generic "whole." The first set of studies ignores the philosophical nature of TQM and risks being a study of techniques rather than a study of management approach. The second set is so general, encompassing all elements of the organization as a complete unit, that it lacks enough detail to be illuminating. Though both these types of studies provide valuable empirical insight into the issues discussed, they leave a great deal of room for further exploration. Much more must be done empirically and theoretically before assertions about the universality of TQM, such as that made by Mitki and Shani (1995), can be substantiated.

POLAND

Whenever a Pole wants to explain some aspect of his work he starts by talking about Polish history.[2] History has played an important role in shaping the Polish way of thinking. Therefore, I will endeavor to present the relevant history of the Polish peasants[3] in this section to provide a basis for the study (for a complete review of Polish history see (Davies, 1982a, 1982b).

The focus of this book is an organization located in a region of Poland that has a predominantly peasant population. The agrarian way of life has existed in this region of Poland since it was settled in the middle of the tenth century. This section explores the relevant history, economic environment, and culture of the Polish peasant. Attention is paid to those aspects of peasant life that represent their relationship with dominant exterior groups and their reactions to these dominant influences. Peasant life is, in many respects, dependent on the differentiation of power from nonpeasant groups. Lewis argues:

from the beginning peasants as a social group have been in contact with urban societies, they have had to provide them with food in return for tools and commodities though they have lived beyond the pale of its most obvious social forms . . . one of the distinguishing marks of a peasantry in contrast to a tribal society is its awareness of belonging to a society ruled by other groups and of its own low status in relation to them (1973: 29-30).

This section concludes with a review of the literature on the impact that communism has had on Polish culture.

Polish Peasant History

From the medieval period (sixth century) through the late 19th century the people that farmed the land of Poland were predominantly serf labor for a group of very powerful, and wealthy family landowners (Topolski, 1974). Periods of emancipation and refeudalization occurred throughout this period. In the fourteenth century, feudalism waned as peasants gained increasing rights all over Europe and towns were on the rise. However, the 15th and 16th centuries saw huge profits for the Polish landowners from growing and exporting wheat and wood. The push to expand production drove these landowners to severely exploit the peasants who worked for them. Peasants responded by fleeing to colonize available lands or to towns. Landowners secured legislation to force the peasants to stay on their land, and a period of refeudalization followed. During this period the Polish bourgeoisie declined as landowners began to exploit their privileged tax status and transported their products without the assistance of Polish middlemen. This had the benefit of eliminating the bourgeoisie as a political threat to the landed gentry. Landowners, needing these services, encouraged Jews, Germans and Armenians to assume technical positions, since the foreigners' economic prosperity did not pose a political threat. The population of Polish towns declined as the bourgeoisie diminished, and the power and tax base of the king fell. Landowners during this period became increasingly tied to specific German and Dutch bankers for capital. This left the landowners relatively powerful while they developed an increasing dependence on what Wallerstein (1974) calls the "core" of the European economic system (north-western European states). Some peasants did own the land they worked during this period, but those that did remained primarily subsistence farmers using the means to farm that had been passed down for many generations (Taylor, 1952). The technology used in Polish agriculture remained primitive to a great extent because of the ample supply of serf labor.

The Polish state during this time was run by a parliament that consisted of members of the Polish gentry who selected the king. These wealthy landowners were successful at maintaining their independence and wealth through their employment of the "liberum-veto." This procedure gave all members of the parliament the power to defeat any legislation with a single vote. It helped maintain a balance in Polish politics and it defined the strong individualistic values of the Polish gentry. It did also, however, prevent Poland from amassing strong collective behaviors that were required to fend off foreign invaders through political means (Taylor, 1952).

The partition of greater Poland that began in 1772 sliced off segments of this country and incorporated them into Russia, Prussia and Austria. This action ushered in an era of great power domination for Poland that lasted through the end of World War I. The result was the complete elimination of the Polish state. During this period, controlling governments attempted to break the power and wealth of the gentry. A history of political activism by these landowners was a threat to each of these foreign governments (Taylor, 1952). As a result the power of the landowners was virtually destroyed, though several maintained significant land holdings. Pressure throughout Eastern Europe during this time forced the abolition of serfdom and redistributed land to foreign parties and to the peasants themselves (Okey, 1986; Walters, 1988).

With the conclusion of World War I Poland was a free country, and the distribution of land ownership to the peasants (land reform) was a primary political objective (Taylor, 1952). A soaring population growth rate (29.9% in the 20 years that separated the wars) coupled with the tradition of land endowment involving partible inheritance, which divided land among all living children upon the father's death, prompted the economic failure of land reform (Roszkowski, 1991). The process resulted in lower production and lower profits from agriculture during the interwar period.

This was a period of significant economic change, but Poland was still predominantly rural (72.6% in 1931) (Lane, 1973). The Polish peasants' life at this time was dominated by familial and church tradition and doctrine. The nuclear family was the basic unit for production and consumption and the fundamental social institution

(Lewis, 1973). The peasant lived a primarily subsistence agrarian life that was steeped in ritual that was Christian in symbolism, although its roots are found in pagan tradition. These rituals served the purpose of guiding farming practice, providing justification for times of deprivation, and establishing a sense of security within the community (Benet, 1951). All property and the center for all peasant life were determined through the nuclear family. Land and all other valuable property are passed down through the nuclear family unit through inheritance that required equal division to all male children. The life of the peasant rarely strayed outside the confines of the village (Lewis, 1973). Contact outside the peasant community was limited to trade for select items from traveling merchants or the occasional return of a son who had moved to an urban area for work or compulsory military service. Sons who moved to urban areas usually maintained strong ties with their families and generally intended their work outside of the village to be temporary (Benet, 1951).

The aftermath of World War II brought a division of the spoils between the victors, the Western allies and Russia. War devastated Poland became a pawn in this process. Polish communist supporters were elevated to positions in the government aided by the communist Russia government which was in the process of developing the "Soviet Union." Agreements between the victors of World War II (primarily Russia, the US and Great Britain) in 1945 assured the Soviet government that there would be no Western interference with the external pressure on Polish politics. Communism was adopted as the official state ideology in 1948, and despite is lack of general support among the Polish populace, Soviet government support made it impossible to sustain significant resistance (Davies, 1982b). Economic rebuilding and a change in government focus prompted the postwar Polish leaders to divert resources from traditional sectors, such as agriculture, to industry (Rosati, 1991). Sweeping land reform was reintroduced after a brief period of repopulation; the remaining large estates were divided for private cultivation, removing the last bit of control that the gentry had over the land (Lane, 1973). The Polish government also created a government-run direct distribution system for agricultural products.

The immediate actions taken during this postwar period were motivated by the political and social objectives of the new Polish government, a Soviet based communist regime. This massive redistribution of wealth was described by the finance minister in 1950 as "the completion of the process of shifting part of the capital held by capitalists to the masses of workers and peasants" (Taylor, 1952: 185). The net objective, however, was to take control of all property out of the hands of private citizens and to place it into the waiting arms of the government bureaucracy. The Polish government developed comprehensive economic plans in the decade that followed the war to establish centralization and socialization of the Polish economy. These plans highlight the dual objectives of the communist government. The first objective was to reestablish Poland as an economically viable country. The second objective, which was equally important, was the establishment of a socialist society (Eysymontt, 1989). The first economic plan called for an even distribution of rural and urban population throughout the country, the development of industry, the creation of a homogeneous system of agriculture, and the linking of the old and new territories by a uniform transport network (Taylor, 1952). Points one and three of this plan establish the ideological objective of the communist regime. Phrases like "even distribution" and "homogeneous systems" are indicative of the socialist agenda. Points two and four highlight the economic elements of the communist plan. In the emphasis on "industry" and "transport networks" the desire to become economically strong is apparent. This plan laid out the framework for collectivization of farming in Poland.

In a speech given to the United Polish Workers Party Congress in 1948, Hilary Minc of the Ministry of Industry and Commerce, described the primary objective of the second plan:

> Basically the plan is designed to lay the foundation of socialism in Poland. . . . Since industrialization is the basic goal of the Six Year Plan, it is obvious that the scales will gradually tip in favor of industry as against agriculture. Although agricultural production will increase as such, the tempo will be slower than in industry (Taylor, 1952: 16-19).

These plans highlight the emphasis that the communist government would place on industry at the expense of agriculture. They set the stage for the neglect of agricultural needs and for the discriminatory policies that followed (Hann, 1985). During this time in manufacturing, mining, service and construction industries grew, while agriculture declined (Dawson, 1989). Though both of these plans were relatively successful initially in accomplishing the prescribed objectives, the end result was a worsening economy and growing social discontent (Myant, 1989; Socha, 1989). Collectivization of farming took place in Poland in the years 1949-1956 (Lane, 1973). The monetary and property ownership policies initiated by the government were effective to some extent, because they forced some farmers to join farming collectives due to their dependence on state credits and supplies of machinery and fertilizers (Lane, 1973). In addition, high investment outlays were made in collectivized farms by the government during these years. The dualistic government policy that combined land reform with collectivization resulted in farming plots that were too small for efficient agricultural production (Polonsky & Drukier, 1980). In addition, the direct distribution system proved to be inefficient.

At its height only 8.6% of total cultivated land was collectivized (Lane, 1973). Hann (1985) suggests that the powerful peasant commitment to the land and often to a specific plot of land was the reason for the failure of collectivization. He said:

> This personal involvement with the means of production is severed by collectivization. Contrary to those who might interpret this as perhaps no more than a formal change to 'administrative' domain, I shall contend that collectivization necessarily inaugurates the demise of the peasantry (Hann, 1985: 11).

In fact, those who did collectivize their farms were primarily individuals rather than families.

For the peasant, the farm was as much a social as an economic unit. Its output was produced for the satisfaction of family needs. Market pressures that run counter to family consumption needs and demanding production increases were often perceived as oppression, disrupting the peasants' way of life. The reaction to these pressures was often to reject increased production and to produce only enough for family subsistence (Lewis, 1973). Government agricultural policies had succeeded in reinforcing the essential features of peasantry (Hann, 1985). This gave peasants power that could significantly disrupt the government systems, and they were seen as a threat. As the state required greater and greater levels of agricultural production, the peasant farmers tended to resist through delaying tactics. This highlighted their power over the government system, which initiated greater pressure from the state, creating a vicious downward spiral of lower levels of production. In the 1950s this process hit a crisis point where peasants lost their pride of ownership in their farms and became reluctant to improve or even to maintain them, resulting in low productivity and workforce apathy (Lewis, 1973).

During the communist era the agricultural workforce aged significantly. Polish youth pursued nonagricultural occupations because of the incentives that the government placed on transition from agriculture to other professions, and because of the growing inability of Polish farmers to subsist on the very small plots that were allocated to them (Lewis, 1973; Polonsky & Drukier, 1980). In addition, these young peasants were more vulnerable to the pressures of modernization because they were exposed at a young age to the radically different worldview expressed by communist ideology. The low status that the peasant held in society was also a motivating factor toward movement into urban areas to increase social status. The lack of urban housing, however, prompted these young peasants to maintain ownership of their rural homes, which impeded consolidation and more rational utilization of agricultural land (Hann, 1985).

The Catholic church and the symbols of Catholicism were not outwardly diminished by the communist attempts to condemn them. In fact, commitment to Catholicism may have been reinforced by the condemnation, as were other aspects of Polish life. Polish peasants continued to abstain from meat on Fridays, name their children after saints, and marry, baptize and administer communion in religious ceremonies. The Catholic church also occupied an active role in the political life of the peasant. Much of the opposition to government policies in Poland was openly sanctioned by the church (Nagengast, 1991). In addition, the church provided the structure to aggregate and articulate peasant interests. The devout Polish peasants were able to collectively oppose communism through their religious affiliation.

The theory and legitimacy of the communist regime was based on the working class. Rural citizens generally rejected communism because of its emphasis on internationalist and pro-Russian values in the countryside where Polish nationalist feeling was very strong (Lane, 1973). In general, peasant communities suffered less than urban areas from the war, and many peasant traditions which formed the foundation for the more general Polish sense of national consciousness survived (Lewis, 1973).

In the late 1970s, despite full employment, there was no improvement in the efficiency of the Polish worker. The socialist policy to eliminate the disparity between peasants and the bourgeoisie mandated a yearly increase in the purchase price of agricultural products despite their stagnant yields (Socha, 1989). The population's basic distrust of the government systems produced an unwillingness to make sacrifices to turn the economy around (Myant, 1989). The socialist ideology on which the Polish social and political system was built trained Poles to believe that it was the states' responsibility to provide for the household. When the state could not provide adequately for the Polish people, they became resentful. To compensate for the growing unrest, general price increases, and wage competition, the government increased the workers' wages five fold in the years 1979 to 1986 (Socha, 1989). The Polish government was close to proclaiming state bankruptcy when it declared martial law in 1981 to quell the growing unrest and the calls for reforms by the Solidarity movement (Czarniawska-Joerges, 1989).

Polish peasants were a major force in the resistance to the Soviet-style communist regime. Lewis states that peasant masses have "more than once acted as a moderator of social progress, blocking excessively radical impulses, tempering the effects of radical and revolutionary activities" (1973: 38). Peasants resisted expansion and innovation, not because they were opposed to progress, but because it was a natural response to discriminatory policies against the private sector and agriculture (Hann, 1985). Through the 1980's peasants remained suspicious of authorities and continued to produce just enough to satisfy immediate family demands for food products, and perhaps sell small quantities to generate a minimum cash flow.

Polish peasant society has undergone significant change as a result of communist rule. The ideology that is embedded in communism and the unique current and historical variables that influenced governmental policy resulted in an inconsistent and unsuccessful agrarian policy. It is precisely because of the peasants' ability to adapt well to their environment that the change that has occurred has not been pervasive, or universally evolutionary. Lewis writes:

> [it is] the very fact of peasants' capacity to adapt to change in the greater society that has enabled them to survive as a group for such a long time and to emerge in modern society as 'conservatives'. There is a difference between a group's capacity to change in order to

perpetuate tradition and to conserve certain values, and its undergoing transformation involving the adoption of new sets of norms and values (1973: 71).

The Impact of Communism on Polish Culture

Whether the infusion of communist ideology and culture was absorbed into the Polish mentality is a matter of current debate. Sztompka (1992) claims that "real socialism" infiltrated Polish life in every respect. He says that it broke down the social systems that had preserved the Polish way of life. Wnuk-Lipinski (1987), however, agrees with Lewis. He believes that the church, the family unit, and the communities in Poland preserved the basic values and beliefs of the Polish people. He points to the impact of the Catholic church on Polish life during the communist era. Even though religion was considered unnecessary in public rhetoric and even threatening to the state, the Catholic church was extremely popular. The church served as a collectivist mechanism that established a collective "us" against the collective "other," the communist state (Nagengast, 1991). Czarniawska (1986) points to attempts by the government after the economic crisis of 1980-81 to change the ideology of the Polish people through the promise of better times ahead. This process, though initially successful at curbing the unrest, eventually failed because the leaders were unable to maintain a belief in their commitment to change or to produce tangible long-lasting results.

Questions Generated by this Review of Polish History

Poland's history has been turbulent and laden with periods of foreign domination. This submission to exterior control has changed the landscape of Polish economic, political and social life. The peasants have remained throughout this period an ever-vigilant stabilizing force of resistance, aided by the Catholic church, and strong family traditions (Benet, 1951; Lewis, 1973; Hann, 1985). These structures served to maintain the social values, traditions, and beliefs of the Polish peasant people throughout this era. Evidence seems to now point toward the perseverance of the Polish peasants and the preservation of the traditional Polish culture. However, this is primarily speculation at this point. This body of research points to a need to explore the theme that runs through Polish history of submission to foreign powers or influences. For example, the following questions are relevant. What impact has this had on the Polish people's view of power, control and authority? How do they view responsibility? Will the Polish people view the influx of western ideology as simply an additional foreign power influencing and controlling their destinies? Finally, how will resistance to this latest wave of domination manifest itself in the Polish context?

CHAPTER 3

Concentric Circles of Polish Life[4]

THE COUNTRY

Poland is a land, and a people of perpetual inconsistency. Frustration and delay remain a part of the Polish everyday experience. Yet as they have done for centuries in times of difficulty, the Polish people press on with their lives and their individual pursuits. In Chapter 2, this book reviewed the literature on Polish history, economy, and culture. Here we will explore the current state of the Polish people, country, and political climate. The next section of this chapter will describe the community where this research was performed, and the final section will detail the company.

Poland occupies an area of 120,400 square miles, approximately the size of New Mexico. Yet Poland has the population of New Mexico, Arizona, Utah, and California combined, between 38 and 39 million people. Approximately 95% of that population is Roman Catholic, and only 2 % are of an ethnic origin different from Polish, the largest minority group being Ukrainian. This relative ethnic homogeneity is the result of the depopulation of Jews (9% of the Polish population in prewar Poland) during World War II and the movement of other ethnic groups, Ukrainians (15% prewar), Byelorussians (4-7% prewar) and Germans, Czechs, Russians and Lithuanians (3 % prewar) afterwards. This movement of people was partially a result of the major changes in land that was considered "Poland." Specifically, western borders were extended into land that has been considered German for centuries and approximately 1/3 of eastern Poland was transferred to the Ukrainian, Lithuanian and Byelorussian states under Soviet control. Massive migration occurred as Polish, German, Lithuanian and

Ukrainian nationals moved west as a result of negotiations after the war.

Sixty-eight percent of the people of Poland live in towns and cities and 32% in villages. Unemployment rates were at 10.4% and dropping in 1998. The average farm size is 6 hectares, about 15 acres. The average monthly income in the enterprise sector is 1,000 zloty ($ 370) but in the agricultural sector it is 729 zloty ($ 270) (Pawlik, 1996).

As remarkable as the dramatic overthrow of the Polish communist regime was in 1989, even more remarkable, perhaps, has been the quick return to power of the communist party that was hastily voted out. Former communist party members now hold the presidency (Kwasniewski) and a controlling interest in the parliament (sejm), though both were brought to power by slim margins (Kwasniewski was brought to the presidency with 50.3% of the second vote). This apparent change of heart of the Polish electorate is reflective of the great state of indecision and conflict brought on by economic hardship coupled with ideological principles that currently divide them as a people and a country.

THE COMMUNITY

Lockem is located in the small farming community of Goria about an hour south of Krakow. This is an area where the people refer to themselves as "simple people," and they regionally identify themselves as "highlanders." The highlanders have a rich tradition, and they form a very important part of the Polish identity. Visitors to Poland are proudly directed to this region to partake of the clean air, beautiful scenery, and regional traditions that have remained intact.

The area is sprinkled with little villages such as Goria. They are of various sizes, but most are too small to accurately be called a "town." In this region of Poland these villages take on a characteristic look. Farmhouses of various sizes, often unfinished on the exterior or on entire floors, are distributed along the main roads. Land stretches out behind each home, reaching up to the forests that line the ridges of the hilltops. The forests sit on top of each rise in elevation like moss growing on a rock. People tend to live with nuclear families, but one child typically assumes ownership of the family home and remains in the home after marriage. The modern practice of the inheritance tradition dictates that, at a point determined by the parents, ownership of the home and land is transferred. The child that receives the farm must give land or money to all other children as their inheritance. If possible, the farm is given to the youngest male of the family. The parents typically live in the home until their deaths. They do not do this because they prefer it, but because of the shortage of housing in Poland throughout communism and to the current time. The center of the smaller villages typically consists of a grouping of homes of varied age with very little land around each, a small store, a post office, and several other businesses.

In every village, a church sits in a prominent location and serves as the focal point of town activity. The churches are the beneficiaries of much of the village money and attention. Some are very old, as old as 500 years, and others were built since the demise of communism. The exterior architecture of the old and new churches alike is simple. New churches are large, bearing brick or lightly painted stucco exteriors. The old churches are rustic, made from meticulously matched split logs with steep curved metal roofs. They are simply adorned with wood crosses and rosebud shaped steeples. The inside of these old churches is like the inside of the Polish people; filled with color, attention to detail, wealth of spirit and surprise. The church exterior hides the riches of golden altars, antique wooden carvings, and hand painted-walls. The churches are not gaudy, but simply elegant and rich with years of protecting the unfulfilled souls of the peasant people.

During the planting, growing and harvesting months of April to October, the land looks like a patchwork quilt with small plots planted with various crops. Potatoes, sugar beets, and cucumbers are intermixed with hay and several varieties of berries. Years of Polish peasant estate practices, which often resulted in the land being divided among all the children in the family, accompanied by a steadily rising population have resulted in very small individual land holdings. Recent practice allows for one child to assume ownership of the land and the house but the recipient must compensate other siblings for their portion of the inheritance. In some cases land has been redistributed to single owners, but the plots are located in various locations spread out over miles in the surrounding region. The result of this practice is very small-scale farming, usually below subsistence level.

Other sources of employment in Goria include government jobs (e.g., healthcare, postal service, teaching, and transportation), local small businesses (e.g., retail, lumber, and construction), what remains of a small clothing manufacturer, and Lockem. During communist times, this was a relatively prosperous area. The problems of the communist era were muted by the self-sufficiency of the peasant people and the independence from government control that they enjoyed. In addition, jobs such as nursing, road service, and technical farming advisors were abundant. The technical farming experts, for example, were hired by the state, during communist times, for each little village (now they hire only one for every twelve villages). The sewing factory was a thriving concern, and a guitar manufacturer, which has recently closed, helped maintain virtually full employment. Finally, residents frequently went to other East Bloc countries for short-term construction and other work. Those jobs have virtually vanished now because of difficult conditions in all the East Bloc countries. Some work can be found in the Western European countries like Germany and Italy, but they tend to be lower status like cleaning houses and baby-sitting. Local residents may take these jobs for a year or two so they can bring the money back to the area.

Lockem draws its workers from a very small radius of villages. Goria is the largest village in the area (5,000 residents). The other villages that support the factory are smaller and fit the description drawn above. The center of Goria sits on the top of a hill where two main roads and two secondary roads meet. A park sits at the apex of the hill, with benches, planted shrubbery, large trees and several religious shrines. The park is divided into four sections by the roads that meet in the center of the town and line the perimeter of the park. In one of the four sections of the park sits the town hall. A large Catholic church assumes its position at one corner of the village, towering over all other buildings.

Various retail shops are lined up along the perimeter of the park. They are located on the first floor of two- or three-story buildings that are occupied by families. On Monday mornings the town is flooded with people who come from the surrounding towns to buy from the open air market that closes off two main sections of road in the center of Goria. In this market you can buy fresh vegetables and fruits, clothing, children's toys, household items, and even fur pelts. The center of Goria is always active, children going to and from school, mothers doing the daily shopping, workers sharing a beer with colleagues, teen-agers talking on sidewalks, and elderly people visiting with friends.

Goria is a town that also supports many recreational activities. Several small lakes draw people from the surrounding area; one of them, located just outside of town, has a hotel and a restaurant. In addition, Goria has an extensive labyrinth of hiking trails that criss-cross the fields and forests of the area.

The opening of the factory (Lockem) was accompanied by the construction of a neighborhood of high rise apartment buildings (blocs) just outside of Goria's center. The blocs are large, rectangular, dirty buildings that are visible from the main inter-city road when entering town. They look out of place in this region of green hills and individual farmhouses. These buildings were built to support the new factory 25 years ago, and they attracted many residents from outside of the local area. Housing was scarce in Poland during the communist period. In addition, it was centrally maintained and controlled. When people were in need of housing they would have to take from the limited offerings that the government would present. These blocs attracted particularly young people into this small farming village who were looking for their first homes and jobs. Many of these new residents were far better educated than the existing inhabitants of the area. This diversity has served as a symbol of social status polarity to this community throughout the last 25 years, and it remains a factor in the factory and in everyday life today.

Goria has a quaint atmosphere, the epitome of a European village, yet it has a cold feeling as well. My first exposure to the people of Goria was when I made my first visit to a local shop. It was an extremely hot early summer day. I had been collecting data at the factory, where there is no air conditioning, for many long hours and desperately needed a cool drink. I entered a large (by Polish standards) grocery store. It was laid out in the traditional way, with a counter around three sides of the interior of the store with all the food stored behind the counters. A large amount of floor space in the center of the store provided room for people to line up to get their food. It was empty this day, except for two employees of the store, one on either side. I waited for several minutes while an employee stood directly in front of me behind the counter and unloaded boxes of food, never offering to assist me. I could see that there was a shelf full of warm drinks behind her, but I really wanted a "cold" drink. After what seemed like a very long time, the woman asked me what I wanted. I asked her if they had any cold drinks for sale. In an over-dramatized way, she chose to answer me with a huge sigh as she raised her hands above her head in disgust, and then grunted as she went back to work. I did not get my cold drink, nor did I return to the shops in Goria for several days after that. The scene was never repeated, in the exaggerated fashion, but I frequently dealt with sales people who would not move to serve me when I entered their shops or restaurants, and impatience was a common reaction to my requests. I learned over time that this reaction was not reserved for foreigners and was a common way to respond to many inquiries made by local residents as well.

That experience in the grocery store seemed to typify the general feeling in the village. Smiles and hellos are uncommon, and eye contact is rarely made as people go about their business. After several months in the factory I began to develop relationships with workers. As I saw these people in the village they would greet me with shy smiles and hellos. On occasion someone would welcome me with enthusiasm, but this was rare. This was in stark contrast to the reaction I received when I met people in their homes. The warmth and generosity were seemingly unbounded. I was offered cakes and tea on every occasion, and depending on the time of day sandwiches or whole meals. They were gracious and warm and very giving. I learned that the loyalties of the people in this community lie with the very immediate family (and those they invite to join them) and with their church.

Church events are compulsory, and failure to attend is viewed by neighbors as unrespectable and blasphemous. During holy periods, such as Christmas and Easter, residents attend the many church services held every day of the week. Services like the Easter Resurrection ceremony the night before Easter pack the church, and the people overflow into the street. Men congregate outside the church as the women, children and elderly people file in. The men and older boys gather around the entrances to listen and to participate in the service in reverent silence. Church personnel have adapted to these circumstances by sending a priest outside the church to administer the communion rituals at the appropriate time.

THE COMPANY

Lockem is a locking mechanism manufacturer. They have supplied locking devices to the construction industry for 25 years. The plant exemplifies the typified East Bloc factory. The buildings look as if communism failed them, along with the Polish people. They are drab and run down, and the architecture "functional." Long single story "hangar-like" buildings make up the main production areas. Administrative offices occupy a large six story bloc-style building at the factory entrance.

The factory was built in this location by the communist government to utilize the abundant peasant workforce. In addition, this location was selected because it was hidden within the forests and hills of the region. Lockem was built in 1970, at the height of the Cold War, to be convertible to a military armaments factory in the event hostilities were to break out. To this end, railroad tracks were installed alongside the buildings to facilitate easy transfer of products to the front lines.

Lockem was privatized in early 1994 through a lease/buy plan which gave a single person 56% interest in the company. Management and several individuals that were brought in from the outside by the majority share holder obtained a lion's share of the remaining interest in the company. The 700 employees at the time each received a very small percentage. The 10-year lease with the government expires in the year 2004, at which point ownership of the company will transfer to these individuals.

Lockem has remained a profit-making enterprise throughout the pre and post-communist periods. Increasing competition from other European suppliers and a difficult struggle to generate new customers for the product have threatened their previously secure financial picture (see Appendix A for 1994 and 1995 financial statistics).

The Owner

This company employed the majority owner, Mr. Andrzej Sroka, in 1974-1976 (at that time, state-owned) following his graduation from a Polish university. Mr. Sroka worked as a quality inspector during the first years of the factory's operations. He then moved to the United States when he was 26 years old and started a very successful locking mechanisms company there. He is a nationalized American citizen, and a single parent of three teenage children. Upon completion of the lease-buy agreement with the government, Mr. Sroka was named CEO and chairman of the board of Lockem at the time of the privatization. He owns an apartment in Krakow, but lives in Poland only about 20% of the time. He is very involved in an organization for ex-pats that are investing in Poland, from all over the world. He considers himself American. He says he will die in America. "After all" he said " I have three American children."

Mr. Sroka is a dedicated and very driven man. His life is complicated by responsibilities that include both of his organizations and his children. His style is direct and at times confrontational. He rarely does just one thing at a given time. He moves and talks at a very rapid pace, continuously combining either thoughts or words and actions. He likes to deal with big ideas but cannot seem to avoid the details of his organization, even though he has little time or patience to adequately address them.

Mr. Sroka speaks frequently of communication and empowerment as the focus of his management philosophy, but he maintains a touch of autocracy in his inclination toward management. During one interview I had with Mr. Sroka, I asked him about his empowerment plans. He said that first he needed to empower his managers and supervisors; that it needed to come from the top. He said, "I told them (the managers) that they are apostles, but I am Jesus Christ. I will tell them how it should be."

Mr. Sroka implemented TQM in his American company and intended to do the same in his Polish company from the beginning. He speaks of TQM with understanding and commitment, and he says that he believes that the TQM philosophy is the best way to manage people in both the US and in Poland.

In one of my earlier interviews with Mr. Sroka I asked him what were his top three objectives for the company in the short term. He answered me while in motion, as he frequently did. He took his laptop computer out of a computer bag and turned it on. "I rely so much on the computer now," he said, "I have my notes in there about my priorities." He then read the list off:

- To improve the skills of the employees

- To increase the norms by 10%.

- Reduction of office people

- Reduction of absenteeism

- Good employees from the "back-up" areas will be put into production jobs

- Supervisors that are or were union members will be told it is not acceptable for them to be union members

This list of priorities became the impetus for many of the changes that occurred in the factory throughout this study. Yet they are inconsistent with the basic tenets of TQM which Mr. Sroka frequently discussed. Mr. Sroka was continuously frustrated by the implementation of these priorities. He expressed to me that he did not think that the management at the factory understood these priorities in the way that he thought they should.

Management

The management at Lockem can be placed in two distinct categories, those who have been with the company for over 20 years and those who have been with the company for less than 2 years. The old guard is primarily educated youth from other regions of Poland that had connections and were given opportunities to join management in the new factory when it was constructed 25 years earlier. They represent the core of the "foreign" invasion that impacted this farming community at that time. In most cases they entered the company in management, and they have remained in management throughout the life of the company. The new guard, who were hired directly by Mr. Sroka, are in key management positions, Marketing, Quality, and Finance.

The president of the company changed during the course of this study. The first president was Mr. Tadeusz Gadomski. He held either the presidency or the vice-presidency for the entire 25 years of the company's existence, up to 1995. His entrenchment in the company included the employment of most of his immediate and extended family in various "support" positions throughout the factory. He championed Mr. Sroka's efforts to privatize the company, but did not stand by his approach to management change. Mr. Sroka claimed that Mr. Gadomski simply did not see the urgency with which they must move in order for the company to remain profitable in these changing times. Mr. Gadomski accepted early retirement at 63; subsequently, all his family members quit or were asked to leave the company as well. The agreement was not friendly, and instructions were given at one point to bar Mr. Gadomski from entering the premises.

Mr. Piotr Bylica, who was recruited from Krakow and continued to live there throughout this study, replaced Mr. Gadomski. Mr. Bylica is a man of about 50 years old with gray hair and a "political" smile. He wears expensive suits and drives a foreign sports car. He had spent much of the last 20 years working as a manager in the oil fields of Iran. This experience provided an opportunity to work with people from various nationalities and it is one of his most valuable qualifications, according to Mr. Sroka.

Tremendous distrust exists between the management staff (old and new) and Mr. Sroka. Loyalties for the old president coupled with a fear of displeasing Mr. Sroka and losing their jobs, have generated confused and inconsistent management from the old guard. Old managers tend to perpetuate previous management policies, while attempting to "look" as though they are making changes in their management approach. All the while they avoid direct questions about the suitability of the changes and particularly the management approach of Mr. Sroka. The new guard struggles with gaining acceptance by workers and other management and successfully implementing uncomfortable and unpopular directives by the majority owner. For example, the new marketing, quality and finance managers each expressed doubts about the decision to hold wages at their present level for 12 months, despite 20% annual inflation. These managers express an understanding of the need to hold down costs, but each of them struggles with the productivity of their staffs, who are extremely unhappy with their pay. Management holds a patriarchal and almost condescending view of their relationship with the workers. They believe that they know what is best in almost all affairs given their superior education, experience and status.

Workers

The employees in the factory are hard working people with a strong dedication to their land, their heritage, and their families. Ninety percent of the workers I spoke to in the course of this study had lived within a 10-km radius of the factory for their entire lives. They are 77 % male, the average age is 38, and the average number of years with the factory is 15 years. The factory workers take home an average of 459 zloty ($170) per month. For nonproduction and management workers the rate is 1, 018,17 zloty ($377). Groups of workers that were formed during the company's start-up years have tended to stay intact, with only infrequent adjustments made to work groups as workers left for retirement or medical leaves.

With 50% of the workers farming for personal consumption, land ownership is a divisive factor among the workforce, as is previous communist party membership. Discussions of either of these issues are not open, but the problems among workers are often rooted in jealousy about land ownership or resentment over past party membership and the favoritism that it brought.

The climate for the workers in the factory grew worse as the period of study progressed. In the early stages of the study, only one year after the privatization of the factory, discontent had grown due to the layoffs that had recently begun, but glimmers of hope for the promises that Mr. Sroka had initially made still remained. Though suspicious, the workers desperately wanted to believe that prosperity was around the corner for them and the company. A year later the climate had changed. Frustration and anger had replaced hope. Workers began to suspect and accuse each other of receiving special favors and unfair treatment. The strained order that marked their relationship with management in the early stages of this study was supplanted by hatred for the chaos and fear these same managers were now creating.

Union activity was changing as well. The "communist" union that had gained membership from the disintegrating Solidarity Union during the first half of the study was losing members once again to Solidarity. New members were being recruited from the previously unaffiliated ranks of workers as well. Calls for protests and even strikes were growing, highlighting the general disquiet in the factory.

Customers and Suppliers

During the communist period Lockem maintained a monopoly on the manufacture and sale of its product in Poland. Demand was great during this time, inside Poland and in Cuba, the former Soviet Union, and other East Bloc countries. Company folklore tells of the long lines of trucks and other vehicles that lined up at the company gates for their locking devices. These buyers would take whatever parts they could get, regardless of the quality. Today, the demand from the traditional customers outside of Poland has disappeared due to significant financial problems within these countries. In addition, competitors from western Europe have entered the Polish market. The Western Europeans in 1996 were competitive, even with a 20% tariff on all foreign goods, on several of the major products. Due to Poland's application for EU status, however, these tariffs will be eliminated in January of 1997. Currently, Lockem is attempting, with only minimal success, to sell its products to American, Canadian, and Western European customers. The major reasons for the minimal success are that costs for Lockem locks remain high compared to the competition due to old equipment and inefficient work processes.

Supply lines are also changing for Lockem. All of the past suppliers that were used by Lockem were state owned. Some of these companies have privatized, some have closed and others have remained state owned. The suppliers that have stayed state owned have produced the greatest problem for the company. Mr. Sroka stated that these companies have maintained a "socialist idea of a customer." He said, "we cannot continue to deal with companies like this, they are too slow to react, and they do not see the advantage to them of innovation and change." Thus new suppliers from Western Europe are supplying products to Lockem, and some of these products are now being made in-house.

The Changes

Technological changes. The technology used in the production of the locking mechanisms in this factory is obsolete. It is old, inefficient, slow, and unable to produce consistent quality parts. Much of the machinery has undergone successive modifications to maintain basic operations over many years. Many require continuous adjustments to function. One of the first steps in the organizational transformation of Lockem was to purchase several new machines for the production and assembly processes. Because the problem of obsolete machinery was pervasive throughout the factory, only a few machines were purchased. I was told by management that the machines purchased went into the areas that were the slowest and most critical in the production process—the bottlenecks. This created a whole series of new problems when the new state-of-the-art machines required high precision input parts in order to work effectively. Old and unreliable machines, however, were still producing the input parts. As a result, the new machines were highly unproductive in the early stages, and the company was forced to run parallel processes.

In addition to the production machines, computerized purchasing, marketing and engineering systems were introduced. The introduction of all the machines and technology prompted numerous changes in production and support processes and reduction and re-deployment of personnel. For example, the machine purchased for final assembly of one of Lockem's highest volume locks required only two people for its operations. It was computerized, and the individuals chosen to operate it were chosen because they had technical degrees. When in full operation, this machine would replace 10 low skilled workers, 5 on each of two shifts. Those workers were moved to a variety of jobs working old machines, packing boxes, hand polishing, or they were laid off. *Personnel changes.* The introduction of technology was only one of the reasons for a major restructuring of personnel. The new technology and the changing market required better and differently educated personnel. Several new employees were hired with skills ranging from computer experience to English language competency. In addition, the majority of the senior management of the company, who had held these positions for 20 or more years, had difficulty making major changes. Their management philosophy and techniques were based in the communist experience, and they failed to adapt to the changing business climate. Thus the senior management team was restructured, including early retirement for the president and hiring personnel from outside of the region. Finally, the past socialist policies of guaranteed employment had produced significant bloating of most state-owned organizations. The new owner estimated the head-count in this organization to be 100% above the required manpower needs. This overstaffing condition, brought on by the communist policy of guaranteed employment, induced a reduction in force through a steady stream of layoffs.

The reshuffling and hiring generated a whole series of problems in the factory. One example was the hiring of workers that have English language competency in jobs that interface with the public. These workers were given higher wages than the existing employees were in these departments, even in cases where they had less education and experience. Resentment is high among the other workers, especially given the current circumstances of high inflation and relatively stagnant pay raises in the factory.

Exhibit 2. Lockem Personnel Change Statistics

June 1994	June 1995	June 1996
approx. 700	604	561

The layoffs also generated serious fear and unease (see Exhibit 2). Group layoffs were ruled out because of the serious impact that this would have on the community. Therefore, a strategy of dismissing one or two workers at a time was implemented. The criteria for selection of employees for layoffs were not made clear. Workers cited issues of sick leave and favoritism as reasons for the choices. Not knowing, and not believing what management said, made the fear of layoffs loom great in the hearts of the workers. Virtually every worker expressed a fear of losing her or his job. This situation was compounded when the managers and first line supervisors used the threat of layoffs to exert control over workers. Many requests or complaints were met with the response "if you don't like it, just leave. There are plenty of other people who would like to have your job." (See Appendix A for Lockem organization chart.)

Quality changes. The production focus within the planned economic system of the past was quantity rather than quality. The third change that was initiated in this organization was the improvement of the quality of the products. The first step was a company-wide awareness program of the new quality focus. Through the hierarchical chain of command, this focus was verbally conveyed to the workers. The result was an instantaneous improvement in the quality of the products produced. Universally, all employees agree that quality in the factory has markedly improved, and they claim the reason for this was simply awareness that the quality of the product is important.

The next step was to apply for ISO 9000 certification (European standard of quality), which required measuring quality processes, and extensive documentation of quality procedures. The application process was in a start-up phase throughout the period of this study. The quality manager, Mr. Stanislaw Litwa, first told me, in the early months of this study, that the official application would be made within a month. Upon follow-up conversations throughout the course of this study, he repeatedly claimed the same thing. As of the end of 1996, application had not been made for ISO 9000 certification.

"The quality is not going to come from heaven," Mr. Litwa said, and they were striving to make a number of changes toward their quality goals. Employees were made accountable for quality, and quality improvement training began. It took the form of a two-phase training program. One phase was intended primarily for managers and office staff and was a two "partial-day" program on the new quality approach. The second phase was given in one-hour sessions to all production personnel and focused on the general technical aspects of improving quality in the factory. This emphasis on training had broken down in the factory when it came to on-site quality training, however. Personnel changes had eliminated positions that were previously responsible for training employees and this had generated a climate of confusion. The training positions were rarely needed in the past since workers had performed the same tasks for many years. The major personnel moves, described above, however, forced workers to learn new jobs frequently, and training on the proper procedures and the quality requirements was nonexistent. Workers were forced to rely on co-workers, who were already involved in working their own jobs and who feared punishment for talking with workers while demonstrating the job tasks.

Mr. Litwa also talked of a series of new suggestion forms which had been developed and were available throughout the course of the study to all employees in the factory at their work sites. These forms were to be used if employees discovered a quality problem, or if they had a suggestion for improving quality or efficiency within the factory. Inquiries of a large sample of workers uncovered a complete lack of awareness about these forms or their purpose.

Finally, a quality improvement team had been created. This team was comprised of technical employees who were assigned the task of resolving the quality problems that had arisen from the factory floor. They had solved 21 problems in 9 meetings and had left only 3 problems to be solved since they required more time and money. Quality teams were not anticipated for the production workers until there was a significant expenditure on new machines. In addition, the quality manager feared problems with implementing teams at this level given the nature of the employee-supervisor relationships there. He said "it is still not in the hearts of people to accept this type of approach to working . . . It is not so much a problem with the workers but more with the Mistr [the first line supervisors] . . . Now it is up to the Mistr and the manager to decide who works together." He suspected that this policy would remain the means by which team membership was determined, undermining the effectiveness of the teams and their acceptance by nonmembers.

Thus, the new focus on quality, and attempts to gain ISO 9000 certification generated a speedy initial improvement of quality, but only a sluggish attempt at making further improvements. A series of preexisting relationships and views in the factory hampered even the beginnings of a full-scale quality improvement effort in this factory. Exhibits 3 through 8 depict locations within the Goria region and the Lockem factory.

Exhibit 3. At Lockem with a group of workers. The author is in the center.

Exhibit 4. Exterior of village church, 500 years old.

Exhibit 5. Interior of same village church seen in exhibit 4.

Exhibit 6. Goria village center.

Exhibit 7. Lockem factory entrance.

Exhibit 8. Lockem production buildings, in the winter.

CHAPTER 4

Research Design and Methods

Making the decisions surrounding the appropriate design to address the research question described in Chapter 1 was a complex and often personal process of analysis and self-reflection. Morgan and Smircich state that

> the choice and adequacy of a method embodies a variety of assumptions regarding the nature of knowledge and the methods through which that knowledge can be obtained, as well as a set of root assumptions about the nature of the phenomena to be investigated (1980: 491).

An evaluation of my personal assumptions about the foundations of knowledge and scientific inquiry was necessary in the process of developing a research design. In addition, I had to factor in the reasons for choosing this particular topic and the practicalities of the project. The single case study emerged as the best approach to reach the depth of meaning and the holistic view that was inspired by the research focus.

The most appropriate methodological technique (s) within the case approach emerged as the specific site was selected and an understanding of the source population was developed. A holistic understanding of relationships among the workers and events, processes, patterns, and the immediate sociocultural contexts in which the changes in this factory unfolded was needed (Jorgensen, 1989). This would require a period of intense immersion in the culture (Barrett, 1991). Ethnographic methods were determined to be the most effective approach, employing participant observation[5], formal and informal interviewing, and secondary source data. This chapter will first explore the many reasons for selecting the case study as the approach and ethnography as the method of collecting data in this study. It will also describe how ethnography was used to uncover underlying assumptions of the workers in the setting. The methods for data analysis used to form and organize understanding from the vast quantities of data collected are presented. Finally, a discussion of the text presentation technique used in this book will conclude this chapter.

RESEARCH DESIGN: CHOOSING ETHNOGRAPHY AS METHOD

> . . . once one relaxes the ontological assumption that the world is a concrete structure, and admits that human beings, far from merely responding to the social world, may actively contribute to its creation, the dominant methods [quantitative] become increasingly unsatisfactory, and indeed, inappropriate (Morgan & Smircich, 1980: 498).

General Assumptions

The approach employed for this study has its roots in the interpretivist tradition. Interpretivism assumes that individuals approach their world with a set of representative symbolic knowledge, which is taken for granted, that reflects their place in the economic, ritual, and moral society in which they live. Ontologically, this perspective maintains that knowledge is symbolically mediated. Meaning is sought through the symbolic representations that are shared by the members of a given community. Truth is uncovered through these meanings. Therefore, there are multiple truths to coincide with the multiple realities (Barrett, 1991). In the interpretivist tradition subjectivity is the means by which meaning is determined. Objectivity will not uncover truths; rather it will provide description. Interpretivism also asserts that all meaning is changeable for a given individual and within a given context (Lincoln & Guba, 1985; Morgan, 1980).

Truth, therefore, is assumed to exist only within a given set of circumstances. Epistemologically, truth is uncovered through communication between individuals. Meaning is communicated through language, and truth is what people make of a given connection. Therefore, there is no truth outside of the human experience. Morgan and Smircich argue that interpretivism has "an epistemology that emphasizes the importance of understanding the processes through which human beings concretize their relationship to their world" (1980: 493).

Methodologically, interpretivism uses a hermeneutic approach. Close, direct interaction with the subjects under study is crucial to this methodology. Fabian (1983) contends that this means that truth can be achieved only when the two (ethnographer and other) meet in the same temporal space. Location in the here and now of everyday life situations and settings is the foundation of inquiry and method.

Reasons for Choosing a Single Case Approach

The reasons for using ethnography to uncover meaning in this setting are discussed in detail below. A brief mention must be made, however, of the selection of the single case method. The case study strategy is a superior approach for the development of theory especially in preparadigmatic fields (Dyer & Wilkins, 1991; Kuhn, 1970; Marshall & Rossman, 1989; Parkhe, 1993; Wright, 1996; Yin, 1994). Advocates of the single case study cite the holistic nature and rich description as the primary reasons for selecting this method. Dyer and Wilkins state that "theory that is born of such deep insights will be both more accurate and more appropriately tentative because the researcher must take into account the intricacies and qualification of a particular context" (1995: 615). It is the getting "close to the action" (Parkhe, 1993: 248) that makes the case study the most appropriate for this research study.

Reasons for Choosing Ethnography

The choice of ethnographic method for this project was made for four primary reasons: (1) the early paradigmatic development of the field and the lack of general theory (2) the focus on "culture," (3) the exploratory nature of the research questions and the lack of specific theory, and (4) the specific case factors.

The preparadigmatic development of the field—Lack of general theory. International management (IM) research finds itself in a period of early development, what Kuhn (1970) calls a pre-paradigmatic state of development. This state is characterized by a lack of coalescence of empirical research into a collective body of work, represented by insufficient theoretical understanding. We are still assessing the right and the most important questions to ask (Hayek, 1978; Wright, 1996).

IM research, epitomizes what Parkhe (1993) calls "messy" research (Wright, 1996). In the past it has been based primarily on North American social science with its dependence on traditional positivistic strategies and a reliance on quantitative techniques and internal validity. Boyacigiller and Adler (1991) argue that these theories lack fit with the nature of international studies that is dependent on contextualization and high levels of external validity.

Recently, a ground swell has developed within the IM field that points to the lack of appropriate theoretical foundation and a need for better methods to acquire this needed theory (e.g. Adler, 1983; Boyacigiller & Adler, 1991; Parkhe, 1993; Ricks, 1993; Wright, 1996). Further, leading scholars have advocated, for years, the utilization of qualitative methods when theory generation is desired (Burrell & Morgan, 1979; Glaser & Strauss, 1967; Weick, 1989). Qualitative methods allow us to address the broader, more complex issues that are the important areas of consideration in international management. Therefore, scholars such as Boyacigiller and Adler (1991) and Parkhe (1993) have called for a shift in the traditional methodological approaches in international management research toward the ethnographic field research expressly for the purpose of building a base of theoretical work in this field.

To address these issues, this book reflects the results of an ethnographic field study. The objective of this study is to understand the change processes in a Polish factory inspired by the diffusion of management practices from the West. A great deal of literature exists on organizational change and the adoption of new managerial techniques. This literature has focused almost exclusively, however, upon Western European and American organizations. Applying the results from this plethora of research to a Polish factory would be an act of misplaced concreteness. The reality of the settings where the data were collected for this body of research does not exist in a Polish organization. The meaning in this setting is in the employees and their cultural foundations. Using measurement instruments that were generated in Western organizational settings is ethnocentric and would undoubtedly generate inaccurate understanding.

The focus on "culture."—Fetterman states that "culture is the broadest ethnographic concept" (1989: 27), and Brannen points out that ethnography is simply "the study of culture" (1996:116). The study of culture has traditionally been the domain of anthropologists. Their preference for ethnographic techniques is based on the need to understand a great deal about a small number of people (Barrett, 1991). In-depth understanding requires examining the meaning that the members of the society apply to events, relationships, people, and traditions.

Ethnography is well suited to the discovery of these issues because it takes a holistic perspective, which contextualizes to give a broader and richer understanding. In addition, it assumes an emic perspective which implies that multiple realities exist within a given context. Informants are used because they are members of the society, have been socialized, and have hence learned the customs, rules, and behavioral norms of the society (Barrett, 1991). The ethnographic approach, therefore, encompasses specific characteristics that make it uniquely appropriate for the study of culture.

The exploratory nature of the research—Lack of specific theory. Two factors highlight the exploratory nature of this research. First, the scarcity of reliable and current information on Polish culture and organizational life in Poland, and second, the lack of adequate theory and data on the impact of culture on major organizational transformation, particularly TQM.

Both the lack of data transfer across the "iron curtain" over the 50 years preceding the 1989 round table accords, and the lack of support for detailed studies of Polish culture during that period, have contributed to the dearth of recent studies on contemporary Polish life. While the American and West European scholars were developing theories about the modern organization, the communist political establishment acted to subvert any study of organizational behavior or the transfer of information that was collected. Communism was viewed (and arguably enacted) as a unified culture, upon which Polish culture was a threat (Sztompka, 1992). Conformity was emphasized, and diversity was suppressed. Research funding went to studies that were designed to promote the ideology of communism, and tended to be superficial and general. These factors contribute to the lack of any clear understanding of the nature of Polish workers' attitudes about work and change.

As I pointed out in Chapter 2, relatively little work has been done on the impact that cultural assumptions have on acceptance of change within organizational settings. Particularly the TQM philosophy is lacking important understanding of the impact that various cultural assumptions may have on the acceptance of its tenets.

The juxtaposition of these two factors, the introduction of a major transformational force, TQM and the Polish cultural landscape, leaves a gap of theoretical development. As was discussed above, the processes of data collection and analysis and theory generation are much more closely linked in qualitative than in quantitative research (Glaser & Strauss, 1967).

The specific context. The people who work in the organization in which this study was performed have lived for several generations under an unpopular and very oppressive political system. All individuals who held positions of official power were either members of the communist party and thus received special favors for their loyalties, or they had paid bribes to members of the party to get those same favors. The individuals who work in this factory are still very wary of authority. The uneasy environment of frequent layoffs and even more frequent threats of dismissals compounded the workers fear of anything that might give management an excuse to make them the next "victim."

Anything official in form or structure is looked upon with suspicion. It is assumed that anything written down would somehow make it to management with negative implications. Thus, written surveys were rejected as a means for data collection, even in tandem with the ethnography. In addition, care was taken to not single out members of work groups for individual interviews within the factory. Social norms of this culture serve to sanction any individuals who are singled out, even if it is not of their choosing. Ethnographic techniques of participant observation and informal group interviewing were chosen, therefore, as the dominant means for data collection.

Issues of credibility. Much has been written about the issues of rigor, generalizability, reliability and validity in connection with ethnographic research. Morgan and Smircich state:

> the epistemology involved here [interpretivism] does not hold that the
> findings thus obtained would be universally generalizable, but it does
> regard them as providing nonetheless insightful and significant
> knowledge about the nature of the social world (1980: 497).

Ethnographic case study research does not attempt to produce generalizable findings. Instead it seeks to produce thick description that takes the reader so deeply into the setting of the study that it becomes easy for the reader to determine whether or not the findings and themes are easily transferable to other contexts (Geertz, 1973). Descriptions and quotations from field notes and interviews are used to document for the reader what is occurring in the factory, and how the informants are assigning meaning to those events. In this way, the reader will have enough first-hand evidence to judge the validity of the conclusions of the study for herself or himself.

Credibility checks were placed throughout the research process to assure reliability and construct validity of the data. These checks took the form of multiple procedures and forms of evidence, including use of a research protocol and meticulous documentation, triangulation of data, member checking and peer reviews. Issues of reliability and validity are discussed further in the data analysis section of this chapter.

DATA COLLECTION METHODS

The data for this study were collected through an inductive process of inquiry over the course of two years, 14 months of which was spent living in Poland. This period can be broken into four stages which are detailed in the research protocol (Appendix B). In this section I will look at my role in the research environment, the methods used to collect data inside the factory, including sample selection, and finally methods used to collect data outside the factory.

My Role

An overt strategy (Jorgensen, 1989) was used to enter the site. I met the owner through an organization that places retired American business people in Polish companies for purposes of consulting on a number of business topics. He had requested support from this organization. I was invited for a visit to the factory, which entailed a tour, several meetings, and extensive discussions about the history of the factory and plans for the future. This visit was followed by several communications with the owner which culminated in an agreement to perform my study in the factory. I was given free access to any or all employees and to any data I requested that is not technologically sensitive.

The owner and all informants were made aware of the true purpose of my presence. Assuming a role other than researcher was never seriously considered for this project, nor was it desirable. I was entering a relatively closed society, I did not speak the language well enough to blend in, and my background and education level were quite removed from that typical of the employees at the factory. Consulting for management was rejected for two reasons. First, consulting would put me into the role of change agent, which presented a range of compromising issues. These issues included the potential for significant researcher bias in the interpretation of the data, ethical considerations, and a possibility of creating distance between myself and the workers. Second, issues surrounding my association with the owner were always questioned throughout the course of the study. It was imperative that I distance myself as much as possible from management and particularly the owner to gain the trust and openness I required from other informants. Thus it was not appropriate for me to become a participant. I maintained an outsider role, but an unbiased and independent one within the site. Advantages of this approach are that I was able to view the entire scene, noting major and distinctive features, relationships, patterns, processes, and events, while not compromising my self-concept, nor raising ethical problems. Gaining acceptance in the field was a challenge. It was necessary to provide enough plausible information about myself and act in a way that would reduce the inevitable label of "spy" which Poles frequently assign to both insiders and outsiders in many situations in their daily lives. My American heritage was helpful in that it distanced me from the entire management staff and any potential Polish government agencies that might spy on the workers, but it gave me a close connection with the owner of the company who was a naturalized American citizen and who currently lives primarily in the United States. Time and routinization of my schedule were the equalizers in this situation. Employees who came to know me simply did not believe the spy explanation to be plausible, and they generally rejected the idea. The extent to which I was able to break down these barriers varied among people in the factory, however. With some I was able to gain complete and enduring acceptance, while others maintained various levels of suspicion, which tended to ebb and flow often concurrent with unrelated but threatening changes in the factory.

Data Collection Inside the Factory

Preliminary data collection. Data were collected inside the factory through daily observation, interviewing (both formal and informal), and secondary source data. During the initial visits to the factory I conducted a series of brief (approximately one hour) exploratory interviews with the owner and a few key management personnel (for example the marketing, quality, and finance managers). This was done to gain a general understanding of the structure, organization, and history of the company and the changes that were taking place. In this stage I also gathered all available documentation about the product line, the quality program and the financial status of the company.

In addition, from the first day in the factory I began talking to the workers in the various departments. I explored the entire factory, walking through the various departments, observing the work, and engaging people in polite conversation. I watched and took notes, drew the layouts of offices and work areas, and read all the material that I could acquire. I asked questions about what things were, how they were used, who was involved in various things, and where certain things were located. I asked the workers about their community, the changes in the political system and the weather. We talked about holiday traditions, children, and living in Poland. They asked me about the United States, the cost of living and the average salary. Conversations were generally short and friendly. I avoided direct discussion of the factory and the changes there, unless the workers brought it up themselves. The strategy was to allow them time to get used to me, my presence, my questions, and my role there.

Sample selection. After several months of generally getting a sense of the factory and its workers, I began a judgmental or theoretical sample selection process (Jorgensen, 1989). Three groups of five to six production workers were selected. They worked on virtually the same jobs, but under different immediate supervisors and in different locations or shifts. The criteria for selecting these informants were sixfold. First, I wanted to sample workers who had worked together for a long period of time so that I could observe established social groups. These workers averaged 15 years with the factory, working in these same jobs during their tenure. Second, it was important to select a work area that was most likely to undergo change during the course of this study, since the purpose of this study was to evaluate the response to the changes that TQM imposed in the organization. These workers were completely displaced during the study period. Third, I wanted to talk to workers who performed jobs that were critical to the success of the company, since they would have the greatest impact on the success of TQM in the factory. This was the case with much of the direct labor production jobs. Fourth, traditionally in the US and Western Europe, the areas that receive the first changes in implementation of TQM are the production area, another reason for selecting employees from the production area. Fifth, care was taken to select individuals who worked primarily in stable groups. I was able to engage multiple people this way, and to reduce the stress of the exchange. In addition, it was critical to the TQM philosophy to understand how teamwork functioned in the organization prior to making changes. Finally, I selected groups that were easily accessible to the researcher. Many employees work on large noisy machines in the factory. Engaging these individuals in conversation during work hours on a regular basis would be difficult and dangerous. Thus, I selected as my primary work task the assembly areas, since the workers were able to work and to talk to me at the same time.

These workers became the "core" sample group. I spoke with each of the members of this group on a weekly basis. In addition, I used the snow ball[6] approach to select additional informants. These informants often approached me out of curiosity during the time I was talking to my core groups or they interfaced with core group members in the course of their jobs. By using this approach I was able to talk to workers in a wide variety of work functions including quality assurance, transportation, and engineering. These workers provided data on a semi-regular basis.

I then extended informant selection from the core group to all levels of supervision in their reporting line, including senior management and the president of the company. In addition, I selected two non-production groups from which to sample. These workers were office staff in the marketing and purchasing departments; I talked with their management as well. Each of these individuals was interviewed at least once and many of them on multiple occasions. All senior management personnel across all functions and representatives of the Solidarity Union were interviewed over the course of this project. The sample thus included workers from all levels of the hierarchical structure within the organization. They all represented the most critical functions from a theoretical perspective as well as a comparative sample, to assess functional and professional differences.

This sampling approach is highly effective for obtaining a great deal of data on a cross-section of the target population. It is limited, however, by the judgmental nature of the selection. As the researcher, I used my judgement to select the employees that I would sample. Thus, the process and therefore the data are limited by the accuracy of the judgements used through the sampling process.

Primary data collection. Informal interviews were conducted during the study with the core and secondary informants. The repetitive interaction with the informants involved a logical process of inquiry that was open-ended, flexible, opportunistic, and required constant redefinition of what was problematic, based on facts gathered in the setting (Jorgensen, 1989). Questions concentrated on topics of power, leadership, control and responsibility both in the factory and outside. Additionally, discussions of current situations were framed in the past. As topics arose, questions were asked about how this topic has changed since the times of communism. It was a procedure of questioning and observing daily work relationships and then exploring relevant topic areas. For example, trust became an emergent theme as the study progressed. At one point I asked a series of questions about whom the informants trusted, why they trusted some more than others, and what trust meant to them. Thus data collection was an iterative process which worked in tandem with the analysis of the data.

Formal interviews were semi-structured, taking advantage of relevant and interesting courses that the answers took, while maintaining a continuity of questioning. The questions asked depended on the job level of the individual being interviewed and the functional area they represented.

I also taught English to 25 employees of the company over the course of several months. These employees were primarily engineering and other technical workers. This interaction provided an additional opportunity to engage in conversation (before and after class) and it gave me a window into behavior and norms within a different context for comparison.

Brief notes were taken during most informal interviews, all formal interviews and observation periods. Detailed research notes were created from these hand-written notes. I chose not to tape record the interviews due to the high level of fear, distrust, and suspicion that was prevalent among all informants at this research site.

Data Collection Outside the Factory

Living alongside the target community when culture is a focus of your research makes virtually every experience relevant data. Therefore, I tried to participate in any and all cultural and social events possible. After these events, which included Easter basket blessing ceremonies and services, bon-fires, grave visitation traditions, social visits in people's homes, Christmas tree hunting, and visiting a sick employee, I documented and analyzed each experience.

In addition to the factory workers, I taught English to the local high school students and asked questions that arose from the themes that emerged at the factory. I also interviewed village people of all ages (early 20s to 70s) to assess where differences lie with working aged members of the community.

Secondary data were collected in the various reference locations in Poland. Legal, economic, political, historical and social references were collected and used to provide perspective to the direct data collected. Popular press reports, jokes, legends, songs and folklore were also used to provide a frame of reference.

DATA ANALYSIS

Diverse types of data were consolidated and analyzed with the purpose of creating the detailed case study, the tale of the factory. The data were used to support comprehensive theory development (based on an extensive literature review) of the relationship between the specific culture and TQM issues under study (see Chapter 2).

The process of data analysis was an iterative one. Because the nature of this study was to establish the framework for developing theory, the analysis became a process of discovery, which involved continuous redefinition based on new information collected in the field. The results of the analysis, in turn, generated new lines of questioning for subsequent field visits. The focus was on generating an account of the meaning and symbolism found in this context which would provide enough contextualization to make it easy for the reader to transfer the experiences from this setting to other contexts and with other studies.

Every set of research notes was submitted to repeated, close, readings, with several questions in mind: How is (are) the informant (s) assigning meaning to this situation? What is that meaning? How does it relate to what was said by this person (s) in the past? How does it relate to what others have said? How does it relate to the literature review and other sources of data I have collected outside of this context? The answers to these questions produced a set of codes which were used to mark and then gather similar themes for further analysis.

Reliability and Validity of Data

The strength and credibility of the conclusions drawn in this study depend in great part on the integrity of my understanding the attitudes, beliefs, and assumptions of the workers in this factory. Care was taken in preparation for the trip to Poland, and during the data collection process to increase the potential that my interpretations are trustworthy. A research protocol (see Appendix B) and detailed and extensive database were generated to assure reliability of the data (Yin, 1994). A field audit was performed by Dr. Janeen Costa, which involved a visit of several days to the field, including one full day at the factory. In addition, she reviewed field notes throughout the course of the field experience.

Multiple data collection methods were employed throughout the study to establish construct validity. Triangulation of data sources went across various forms of data, and within these forms of data. Informants, for example, were chosen from both within and outside the organization (Denzin, 1978; Erlandson, Harris, Skipper & Allen, 1993; Yin, 1994). Within the organization, triangulation occurred across vertical and horizontal lines (hierarchical position, and functional responsibility). Outside the organization, data collected both within the local area and in other regions of Poland were triangulated. The means of collecting these data also varied with the same informants. Semi-structured interviews were coupled with informal conversations (both alone and in group contexts) and observation of the informants to assess similarities and differences. Informant data were triangulated with secondary source data, which was triangulated within itself (for example government reports with newspaper articles).

Peer reviews with Polish and American academics and Polish business leaders occurred throughout this research project. In addition to the field audit, respected Polish scholars[7] were consulted to ensure a proper host culture perspective of the data, while also maintaining a sound theoretical foundation for these results (Erlandson, Harris, Skipper & Allen, 1993). Member checking was employed by discussing various preliminary findings with key informants inside the factory and Polish individuals outside the organization to further assure validity of the data (Erlandson et al., 1993).

THE ETHNOGRAPHIC TALE

The tale generated by this study endeavors to paint the picture of this factory in broad strokes to establish underlying cultural themes and value systems, and in fine intricate detail to put definition and meaning to the broader themes. The approach in the creation of this text was to identify and then go beyond what Erving Goffman calls the "collective representation,"

> a given social front [that] tends to become institutionalized in terms of the abstract stereotyped expectations to which it gives rise, and tends to take on a meaning and stability apart from the specific tasks which happen at the time to be performed in it name (1959: 27).

Ethnographic text, which is designed to tell the "tale," uses a series of rhetorical devices that assist the ethnographer in establishing credibility, legitimacy, and authoritative stature in the presentation of the "other" (Atkinson, 1990; Van Maanen, 1988). The presentation of this study uses several of the techniques discussed by Atkinson for creating a persuasive ethnographic text. The first technique is to establish a "privileged stance" in relation to the facts of the setting under study. This permits the creation of a textual order, selection and arrangement of elements, and the establishment of cause-and-effect relationships between the elements. Second, exemplars are used extensively to present the major social themes (Atkinson, 1990). Finally, confessional accounts and periodic shifting of the representation of my role between "insider" and "outsider" were used throughout the text (Van Maanen, 1988). Atkinson states that "the authority of the text rests on the premise that a stranger has become intimate with the culture in question" (1990: 163). This presentation of the results seeks to create the detail and patterned themes that generate a synergy, thus revealing this Polish factory to the unfamiliar reader.

CHAPTER 5

Social Organization

Societies develop mechanisms for maintaining control and order in different ways. The people of the Goria region of Poland have responded to a unique set of economic, political, and social conditions to shape their own system of social organization. This chapter will explore "social organization" in Goria by examining three major influences: traditional, political and religious. In addition, I will discuss the values and assumptions that guide the pattern of shared mindsets, which is the topic of chapter 6. By investigating these more general factors impacting life in Goria, I will lay the groundwork for a discussion, in chapter 7, of the specific interaction of these factors with the TQM management philosophy at the Lockem factory. To begin chapter 5 I will describe a specific event that occurred at Lockem during the course of this study. This event, and particularly the reaction of the employees to it, presents a set of questions that the discussion that follows will begin to answer.

SPIES WITH TELEVISION SETS

The entrance to production hall #4 is through a set of tall and heavy gray metal doors. The doors can be opened, with great effort, to allow forklifts and other motorized vehicles, as well as pedestrians, to enter. The workers in department P4 have walked through this entrance each day for many years, some for as long as 25 years. Hall #4 is one of eight halls that make up Lockem's production area. The buildings are configured in a way that resembles four dominoes laid face up side-by-side, two halls making one domino. A shared covered corridor that cuts down the middle of each hall connects the four buildings. Hall #4 is typical in size and exterior appearance of the other seven, but each is set up a bit differently inside to accommodate the specific work performed.

Just inside these large metal doors is a concrete ramp that leads to the large production area. This particular hall is split into three sections with two large square archways dividing them. A long roadway runs the length of the building. This roadway is kept clear for motorized vehicles and pedestrian traffic. The entire hall has an appearance of "bigness," yet not the spaciousness that often comes with large spaces. The ceilings are high and windows line each side. Several of the windows are broken, and others have been painted over. The feeling in the hall is empty and dark.

On the left is a new chicken wire fenced-in enclosure. Attempts to streamline the movement of parts throughout the large factory had prompted several changes to the stocking and movement procedures. This enclosure represents the latest decision—to securely store parts within each hall. In the past these parts were left in unsecured areas. Just prior to moving the parts to their present location, the production manager tried to centralize the part storage, but this experiment was not successful. The current storage area is not full. Large metal boxes stacked two or three high contain partially completed parts.

On the right side just inside the hall is an enclosed office area where all the supervision from the first line-supervisors through the director of production have their offices. These rooms are very basic in decor and furnishings. Most of them are furnished with mismatched pieces of furniture that are old, but not quite falling apart. The large open space just beyond these offices is used as a staging area. It is set up to allow for additional assembly work when necessary.

Beyond the storage area on the left side of the hall is a row of large green machines which perform various production tasks. One worker operates each machine while sitting high upon a platform that makes it appear as if the worker is sitting inside the machine itself. Their jobs include placing parts onto, and removing parts from, moving arms of the machine. These arms transport the parts inside the machine for various processes to be performed and move them back out again. The workers also inspect parts using visual and other tests which have been developed over the years, such as screwing a part into another completed part. The machines are noisy and the work is dirty. The workers frequently deal with machine malfunctions or difficulties with getting the machines to consistently produce quality parts.

Past the first square archway is the second section of the hall, which used to be exclusively a manual assembly area. Two assembly areas, one on either side of the hall have been set up. Each has two long makeshift tables that were simply constructed by the workers from whatever was available—metal structures with wood over the top, or storage containers. Others have metal tabletops with linoleum covering the top surface. Certain sections of the tables have various manual tools built into them. The introduction of a new assembly machine recently changed this area dramatically, and only one assembly area remains.

Workers in assembly work in groups of five or six. The groups have remained relatively stable for many years, with some workers performing the same work processes since they began working in the factory 20 or more years before. This area is usually busy with work.

Workers typically look up only briefly as I enter the room, and then quickly place their heads back down to their work. On one day in late March when I entered the hall there was a feeling that something was "up." Small groups of people were talking, standing away from their worktables. Their brief looks were more like stares this day, accompanied by additional conversation.

As I made my way through the first square archway I saw Alicja[8] (see Appendix C for a brief description of informants) working at the end of the assembly table alone. Alicja is the youngest of this group of workers. She has been working for this company for eight years, assembling the same doorknobs for the entire time. She has a round friendly face with short dark brown hair. When in her work group Alicja has frequently shied away from controversial questions. Questions about politics or anything that requires her to formulate and express an opinion are usually deferred to her co-workers. She always listens intently when others are speaking, but she chooses only to agree with the rest of the group rather than to voice an independent opinion. When Alicja is alone, however, she is much freer to acknowledge that she has an opinion and to speak openly about a wide variety of topics.

This day Alicja wore the same smile that I had come to know; it is warm and captivating. I had only a chance to complete my "hellos" to her, when she told me that Mr. Sroka, the new owner, had walked through their work area the day before. This was a newsworthy piece of information which she was eager to share with me. Just as Alicja had begun telling me about Mr. Sroka's visit, Agnieska walked up next to us and began listening to the conversation. Agnieska tends to rove around this hall. Her official job is to manage the subassembly parts and to assure that they get to the appropriate locations for assembly. She has claimed on numerous occasions that she is swamped with work and that she even needs to solicit help from other workers. My observations, however, indicate that she is always available to join in a discussion about the conditions in the factory and the problems they are facing. The others workers call her "mom" because she is always making coffee and preparing snacks for the workers to eat. They have also referred to her as "lazy" in joking terms that were probably a case of more truth than joke. Agnieska has been with the factory for 23 years. She has spoken frequently about her desire to take early retirement. "The young people who cannot find jobs now should work," she said, "and we, who have worked hard all our lives, can go home and rest."

Alicja continued the conversation by telling me that Mr. Sroka had walked around the factory and had even talked to some people. She said that he was "very polite." It was rare for Mr. Sroka to walk through the factory. In the two years since he acquired majority ownership in the factory, these workers had only seen him two or three times. The workers told me that he had never spoken with them during his infrequent walks around. I asked Alicja if his visit had gone well. Alicja said, "Yes, it went rather well." But just at that point, Agnieska burst into the conversation. She looked at Alicja with almost an accusing look, and said "Now tell the truth, Alicja. It didn't go so well." She laughed uncomfortably and said, "Well, yes, this was true." She smiled, paused for a breath, and then said, "Some of the employees were awarded television sets yesterday." She took another breath and then stopped as if she had given me the whole story. When I did not say anything, she continued "those employees that were not ill for the entire year (1995) were given the television sets." She said that there was a problem, however, because there were 40 people who had met the criteria but there were only 10 television sets awarded. She said:

> Now there are many rumors, and lots of jealousy. People are saying 'Why you and not me?' They think that they were also not absent for the whole year, and they were not given the television sets.

I asked various employees over the course of the next several days who had received the television sets. Some, like Alicja, told me that it was mostly the supervisors and the technicians who fix and set the machines. Others like Agnieska told me that it was only those who were "close to the heart of the manager" (meaning Sroka) that got the award. When I asked the employees over the next several days on what "basis" the awards were given, a trend emerged. Most of the employees did not answer the question directly, which was unusual. In addition, they seemed to turn away from me and turn to my interpreter to explain the situation.

One such discussion depicts the general trend. I had asked Jerzy, a male quality inspector about 30 years old, how he thought management decided who would get the television sets. He coyly smiled at the question. The facial expression and gestures that accompanied his answer were clearly directed toward my interpreter, and not myself. Jerzy looked deeply at her and said, "You know." His voice inflection emphasized the message he was trying to convey. My interpreter, who recognized Jerzy's meaning, said "Yes I know, but you must explain it to Jennifer." Jerzy lowered his head at this point and said "This is just my opinion, but I think the ones who received the awards were favorites of the manager." I asked him what he meant by favorites and he said, "I don't know anything about this for sure, I can only guess." Jerzy then turned away for a moment, looked back up at me with the coy smile again and changed the subject. My interpreter later told me that she thought that he was referring to bribery that was paid by workers to their bosses for favors. The workers seemed, during my discussions about the television sets, to be hiding something. The "something" was a secret that they seemed embarrassed to discuss with me.

None of the employees told me directly the "secret" they were harboring. I began to understand, however, as I was told the same story by several of the workers about Joanna. Joanna is one of the youngest of the assembly workers with only six years at the factory. She loves to laugh and make jokes with her co-workers, but she had an equal ability to express anger and frustration. Her temper apparently exploded in reaction to the awarding of the television sets.

The televisions were awarded on a Thursday at the beginning of the second shift at 2 p.m. This was done so that all the workers could attend the ceremony in the cafeteria if they wanted to. However, attendance was not mandatory. All the employees who had met the criteria as well as those who would actually receive the awards were informed either the day before, for the second shift employees, or the morning of the ceremony. After telling all the employees who were assembled about the importance of perfect attendance, the owner of the factory called the 10 recipients up to the front of the room and awarded the television sets. At this point he took questions for a short while and then he asked them to return to work. Joanna, who had been working the second shift this week, was furious about what she had determined was a terrible injustice. She had decided not to attend the ceremony and had gone to her work area instead. As the workers returned from the ceremony, one of the recipients, a technician who repairs the machines, walked by Joanna's work table. She turned to him and yelled "Get out of here, you spy! You are what is wrong with this company!" The story was told to me, with little admonition for Joanna. Her fellow employees seemed to think that it was a perfectly justified thing to say. They spoke about Joanna simply reaching the end of her patience. When I asked Joanna about it several days later, she waved her hand, expelled air from her mouth, and took the opportunity to move a box of parts to the other side of the table. She clearly did not want to talk about it with me.

Many of the employees referred to the television recipients as "spies" or "favorites." Zygmunt, who works on the production machines, told me that the owner of the company had his "own people." "To be a Sroka person" he said " you must be a supervisor or above. Or maybe it has to do with family connections I don't know." He continued "Sroka's people are more educated, not ordinary, and they were threatening the people."

The accusation of favoritism spread among the office workers as well. Tomasz and Adam, who work in the marketing department, were discussing the television set distribution between them. They said that it was "unofficial," but that they had heard that there were spies, "Sroka's people," who were telling what is going on in the factory. These spies are telling Mr. Sroka who is doing what and who is loyal to him. Tomasz said that there was a lot of jealously in the factory.

When I asked Teresa, a 40-year-old assembly worker who had worked at the factory for 20 years, if she really believed that Mr. Sroka had spies at the factory, she thought for a moment, and then said,

> Actually, no. I do not believe that Mr. Sroka has spies. He probably does not have enough time to have spies in the factory. But, I do think that the managers that are there from the old days do have people who were telling on what the other workers were doing and saying (spies).

A second theme emerged in the discussions of the "television incident." The accusation of spying was coupled with the charge of injustice. One worker laughed at his unintended joke when he said "It is a 'sick' idea; it is unjust." The charge of injustice was leveled at the management, particularly the owner. Agnieska said at one point "Some people have said that Sroka thinks if you are ill, you should die; if you are not ill you should come to work. We are not allowed to be ill at work." Maria, another assembly worker who had been working for the company for over 20 years, complained that it was unfair to mothers who had to attend compulsory teacher-parent meetings at the schools. A third accusation of injustice centered around the low work load they had been experiencing in recent months. On several occasions, many workers had been asked to take sick or vacation time and go home because there was not enough work for them. Anna, who had been with the company for 10 years, stated that she felt evaluating perfect attendance was not fair under these conditions. Finally, Tomasz told me of several workers who were required to work in the open air when it was really cold the previous year. He said that they had gotten sick and had to take time off, but it was the company's fault that they were sick. Therefore, Tomasz indicated that it was unfair to use this basis of awarding television sets.

The issue was divisive across the company. In one case, Beata, the wife of one of the television recipients (Grzegorz), did not receive one herself, even though she had met the same criteria. Beata commented that she did not think this was a good plan because there was a lot of jealously among the workers. She said that Sroka had said that they had to pay 4 million zloty ($160) for each worker who was out sick and he thought it was better to give the workers who were not out sick some money. Beata said, however, that she thought it would have been better to have divided the money among the employees who qualified rather than giving out television sets to only some of them. This sentiment was echoed by almost all of the employees that I spoke to about this event. They felt that an equal distribution of cash would have been more appropriate than giving television sets to only a few.

Management reaction to the incident was peculiar and seemingly inconsistent with the events. One of the two vice presidents, Mr. Wtorek, told me that the awards were part of a new incentive system that was being introduced. He was very nervous in talking about this topic. He said that the television sets were given to the workers that had been suggesting innovative ideas for improving their production processes. The managers of the production areas, however, were not eager to talk to me about this decision. They simply told me that they chose the workers based on the criteria that were given to them by Mr. Sroka, and then each of them changed the subject. The Solidarity Union representatives told me that the award recipients were decided by the supervisors who submitted names of people in their departments. Mr. Sroka, however, said that he had told his executive staff to buy television sets for those people that were not sick the year before. When they told him that there was not enough money to buy one for every person, he told them to decide how to pick who would get them.

The same Solidarity Union representative told me of the inevitable backlash of this decision. He said that he had a colleague in his department who had received the television set. The colleague was in a horrible position because his co-workers wanted to know why he got the award and they did not. He said, "What can I do to help this man? He has received a television, but all of his co-workers hate him. I can tell you one thing. He won't have a perfect attendance record next year."

What would generate a climate in which the participants turn on each other with accusations of "spying" for the management in a case like this? The Lockem employees blamed the management for making "unfair" decisions, but their anger was equally directed at the beneficiaries of those decisions, their fellow employees. This chapter will explore the context in which the series of events just described transpired.

INFLUENCES ON SOCIAL ORGANIZATION

The responses just described to the "television set" incident were remarkably consistent, and where inconsistencies arose they can be easily understood by organizational position. After observing and gathering the reactions to a series of events like this one over the course of a year of research, the consistencies began to form a pattern. This pattern, which reflects the regional culture[9] discussed in Chapter 2, showed three primary influences: traditional, political, and religious. These influences have helped shape the "rule book" of how to survive and adapt for this culture, and they provide a context within which the workers in this factory make sense of the changes that are occurring.

I have chosen "social organization" as the focus of this exploration of Goria regional culture. Social organization here refers to the way the society makes order out of chaos; provides access to power, information and other resources; and ensures control. This is a particularly pertinent cultural focus for studying the impact of the decentralized control structure of TQM that will be explored in Chapter 7. Therefore, the examination of influences and values and assumptions will focus on the social organization within the regional culture. Communist culture is embedded in this discussion, particularly the political influences, and I will explore the relevance of this term at the conclusion of this chapter.

Finally, by traditional influences I mean the prevailing customs, rituals and practices which grew out of the centuries of living an agrarian lifestyle and learning to cope with external factors. These are separate from political and religious influences. There is a force that is external to the political and religious institutions, doctrine, and rhetoric that is influencing the traditions of the Goria people. Political influences refer to the ideology, institutions and practical applications of the communist system. The religious influences refer to the role that the Catholic church has played in regional life. The communist government and the Catholic church are the focus of this discussion because of their recent impact on the Polish people and the strength of these influences in this context.

Traditional Influences

> Swept by converging streams of economic, political and social events, Poland has been affected by all. Yet she has remained stubbornly unique . . . she has absorbed much, resisted much, and remained very much herself. In many respects, Poland presents a remarkable example of continuity not often met within history (Benet, 1951: 26-27).

This "uniqueness" of Polish culture is reflected in the many rituals and traditions which are specific to Polish life. Modern day traditions can be traced to a centuries-old process of assimilation of the old with the new. One example of this assimilation process is the incorporation of pagan rituals with Catholic religious rituals. Many of the pagan traditions practiced prior to the 11th century have remained in practice but have taken on religious meaning. For example, the harvest rituals have turned into an opportunity to appease the saints as opposed to the gods or demons.

In Mokarszy, a village five kilometers from Goria, the 1995 harvest ritual was filled with religious symbolism mixed with the practicalities of everyday life. The women's song group, which meets periodically to pass down traditional songs, had composed something for this occasion. This year they had gone to a nearby town as a part of the festivities to celebrate the building of a new church there. A section of this song (Exhibit 9) reflects the mood. Issues of change, new churches and a new disco are interspersed with "old" problems and foci, the lack of lighting in the village and the fertility of cows. This demonstrates how the harvest celebration represents a time for reflection, on the "new" and the "old" in village life.

Exhibit 9. Harvest Day Celebration Song

All the nice guests are cordially welcome
Now we, from Mokarszy village, are going to sing a song
We welcome you for such a wonderful moment
We thank you for inviting us to your harvest day celebration
Harvest day is a time of great joy in Bialem Targ
Otherwise we would not be in this new church
Soon we will need to build new parks
Because our sons don't want to stay on the farms
Boys and girls would take to the fields
If ham grew on them
People in the city say we are rich
Young people from the country say it does not pay to stay here
On Saturday teenagers run away from the farm
Because today there is a disco in Goria
And you mayor count your budget well
And don't forget those that sing to you now
But you have other problems
In the middle of Mokarszy you need cat's eyes
Because in the middle of Mokarszy there are no lights at night
Our bull, however, is not doing bad
When he impregnates a cow she has twins
We gather here and there is a big choir
Because we have harvested grains from the field
And now we're finishing our song
In a while we'll go dancing
Our village administrator will soon be taking taxes
If you don't pay you'll not get away with it.

Traditions play an important role in defining cultural identity and unity. One such tradition, that of land inheritance, (see Chapter 2), has had an increasingly detrimental impact on rural life. Rather than change the tradition of bequeathing land to all surviving children, farmers have adapted by establishing new social systems to accommodate their changing needs. After World War II, particularly after the dust had settled from a massive migration of people, it became increasingly impossible for farmers to support their families on the smaller and smaller plots of land. Employment off the land was sought to supplement farming. The Goria region inhabitants started to take on multiple part-time jobs to support their families and to buy seed and necessary farming equipment. Schneider (1969) identified a similar pattern in Sicily after the break-up of powerful clienteles in the period following World War II. Schneider writes:

> The patrimonies are incomplete: the breadwinners, or family heads, who hold them are continually forced into a variety of contractual arrangements, whether to make up for the assets which they lack or to employ those which they have in excess . . . in life 'si arrangia'—one makes the best possible 'arrangements.' The arrangement most always implies the action-set; the temporary coalition of supporters which ego constructs in order to protect his position in critical negotiations (1969: 116).

The Gorians, also, have developed a system of temporary coalitions of supporters. These networks represent the unofficial and informal connecting of all social members to power and resources through dyadic relationship, or "action-sets." Access is granted through a barter system of services that connect one person to another through a past exchange. The action-sets provide information about who to go to for services, how much money must be paid "unofficially" and when to repay favors.

The term "action-set," as it is used here, originates from Mayer's 1966 study of election-making in India (Schneider, 1969). Action-sets are different from patronage as Silverman (1965) describes it. Traditional patronage is an informal contractual relationship between persons of unequal status and power, which imposes reciprocal obligations of a different kind on each of the parties. In addition, these relationships are face-to-face and continuing (Silverman, 1965). Action-sets can be temporary and fluid or for only a specific purpose, and they can be and quite often are what Wolf (1966) calls dyadic-singlestranded horizontal (between equals) relationships (Schneider, 1969). In Goria, as Hann (1985) discovered in Wislok, a Polish village in the Carpathian mountains, these relationships are based first on familial ties and second on economic or social standing, as opposed to occupation.

This form of social organization is not only a response to a long-standing Polish tradition, it is also a necessity caused by the difficulties associated with the socialist state. The end of World War II brought a period of frustration and difficulty for the peasants of the Goria region.

They were subjected to a government that was ineffective and illegitimate in the eyes of most of the Polish people (Kennedy, 1992; Marody, 1987). This government system subjugated peasant (agrarian) interests for the benefit of rapid industrialization and growth in the cities. Polish peasants needed to find a way around the system that *officially* desired to collectivize their farms, which they viewed as tantamount to stripping them of their identity. They relied on their traditional values of individualism and their attachment to the land to guide their approach to dealing with their environment. Hann identified this attachment when he wrote:

> A necessary condition for peasantry, is psychological. . . . there arises a powerful commitment to the land, and very often to a specific plot of land that becomes the property of the family, or its patrimony (1985: 11).

In addition, the communist government *unofficially* hampered the farmers by creating a massive bureaucracy, with minimal government support applied to things that were important to these farmers.

Therefore, in Goria and the surrounding community some of the most important manifestations of social organization are these structures of personal networks which have formed chains of two-person ties throughout the community. Ties with a given individual through an action-set provide access to all the ties that that individual maintains.

> Such bonds may be expressed by symmetrical or asymmetrical exchanges. By definition they join the network of ego to the respective networks of other, ensuring for him a potentially endless range of contacts. The complex web of overlapping two-person ties which is the sum total of countless personal networks has, in fact, no absolute physical boundaries. (Schneider, 1969: 110).

Today, these action-sets provide access to the Goria regional power structure, which is comprised primarily of the remnants of the communist order, and to supplies, jobs, education, services and entertainment. As is the case in the Sicilian study, these networks transcend traditional boundaries of geography or organization. Thus, the networks of the community play an important role in the true power structure in the Lockem organization. The action-sets compete with the formal organization of the company, but powerful forces that are working to maintain traditional values in this region sustain the action-sets. Examples of the presence of action-sets at Lockem abound. Jerzy told me, "What matters here are connections. If you know the right people, then you can keep your job; if you don't, you will lose your job." Janusz, a 30' year' old worker, told me, "Everything is in the hands of the manager now . . . they are only looking out for themselves. It is good for them if the work with their colleagues so they choose who they want in the right positions." Teresa may have summed it up best. We were talking about the president, who had recently taken early retirement. She said that things would not change now that he was gone and I asked her why. She said:

> The old president was from a branch of something else. He was involved in many things for too long. . . . It is like a tree. You cut off the biggest branch, but the little branches and the leaves are still living. The old president's connections at the factory are the other branches and they are still living off the tree.

Action-sets have become a necessary organizational tool for rural Poles. Cynical obedience, the manipulation of informal networks to obtain good, and a move toward private enterprise were the only means for survival during the crisis in Poland in the communist era (Wesolowski & Mach, 1986). Gorlach (1995) calls the coping mechanisms a "survival strategy game." Those that employ the action-sets for not entirely "legal" or even "moral" activities also give this survival representation.

One poignant example comes from a protector of the moral conscience of the Polish people, a Catholic priest, Father Kazimierz Jancarz. He describes the 1970 efforts to build a church in the community of Nowa Huta, just outside of Krakow. A large steel mill was built there for primarily political reasons, and employees were recruited from all over the countryside. The influx of people to Nowa Huta generated an immediate need for a new Catholic church. The Polish state, which had turned a blind-eye in many situations of church building, saw Nowa Huta as a model city of the socialist ideology and did not approve of the plan to build a church there. The Catholic diocese had to turn to it constituents to help. Father Jancarz describes what occurred when they needed cement.

It is impossible to describe—and frankly, one should not describe—
how we bought those materials. It is sad that it was impossible just to
go to the store and buy things, but everything was rationed. And that
is why we had to use names of different people to buy different
things. It is not my goal to teach you 'Red' arrangement. Officially
we could have material allocated, but these allocations were only
enough to build one column! And besides, for a church there was no
opportunity to buy cement, but an individual citizen could buy 1.5
tons of cement, so people brought their IDs and through connections
(our parishioners worked everywhere), we were able to buy the
necessary cement . . . faith unites people . . . but one also 'arranges.'
It is sad. This is the system—arranging things and giving bribes.
Arranging embraces everything. An outsider cannot understand it.
People go and ask their friends. 'Listen, I need this.' . . . You asked
me to tell you what deals. . . . I won't tell because I don't know
myself. I go to woman and say 'Please arrange this for me.' I don't
know how she does it (1992: 206-207).

The church did not discourage this process of "arrangement" to
accomplish objectives, and it points to the degree to which these action-
sets were, and still are, seen as necessary. Despite the potentially illegal
or immoral nature of the activities that occur through these action-sets,
a tacit acceptance is given because the activities are seen as necessary
and prevalent behavior. In addition, the general view is that no one is
getting hurt, no one, that is, except a faceless state system that is
considered the enemy.

Various members of the society pursue legal, semilegal and illegal
activities with few sanctions applied. The community members follow
the cue of the clergy. Much like the approach of Father Jancarz they
acknowledge that these activities occur but refuse to confess specific
knowledge about them. This was also the case at Lockem. The practice
was acknowledged in general, but never in specific terms.

Action-sets are found in virtually every known society in one
degree or another (Schneider, 1969). In Poland, however, they have
assumed a particularly prominent role because they have filled a void
that existed between the ideological and practical interests of the ruling
class and the needs and practicalities of the Polish peasant life. They
have become a highly appropriate means to deal with the political,
economic, and social realities of peasant existence. In addition, they are
consistent with the deep-rooted values and traditional views of Polish

identity. Action-sets are the organizational tool which allows community actors to accomplish whatever they need to do within environmental constraints. These constraints are imposed by both the traditions of this region and external forces. The action-sets are every bit as important in the confusing times of transition that the Goria residents are now in. The fact that this method is deeply rooted in Polish historical necessity may make it difficult to uproot. My data show that their use continues to be the primary method for getting things done in the new system.

Political Influences—Theoretical vs. "Real" Socialism

Bribery is an ever-present phenomenon in Polish life. It is a source of jokes, folklore, and resentment. Bribery is often the explanation for the "way things are." There are numerous expressions and phrases that describe this practice and many of them are used at Lockem. One example came from the blue group.[10] The blue group was generally a happy group, joking was common; they said it broke up the monotony of the work. Iwona, a 40 'year' old woman who had worked at the factory for 20 years, tended to be instigator of the playful banter. Joanna, employed 6 years with the company, the youngest of the group, was thin and tall; her energy was easily turned from great wit and humor to tremendous anger and uncontrollable rage, as was evidenced in the "television sets" example in the first section of this chapter. Alek (employed 13 years with the company) also demonstrated a willingness to express tremendous feeling about topics. He played a quieter role in the daily banter, but a more dominant role when serious discussions about politics or conditions in Poland, or the factory, came up. Czeslaw (employed 7 years with the company) was more educated than the rest, and he held a more responsible job, adjusting and fixing the many machines that the workers used. Czeslaw always had a smile on his face; his demeanor was uncharacteristically (for Poles) open and friendly. Though his responsibilities did not require that he work with this group at their table, Czeslaw spent a great deal of time joking with "the girls" as he called the group (it did not seem to matter to him that there were two men in the group). Maciej (employed 8 years with the company) and Helena (19 years with the company) were the last two members of the group. Both, though generally quiet and shy, enjoy the banter by laughing and occasionally adding "one-liners" to the conversation.

The work that these workers perform is a self-coordinated assembly process. To complete the assembly of one locking device requires from six to fifteen different tasks. The first line supervisor tells them the number of locks they must make on a given shift, and they coordinate the tasks among themselves. The blue group likes to rotate the individual tasks required on a daily basis; each day the workers take on a different task than the day before. Other groups, the red group for example, tend to change jobs continuously throughout the day.

On this particular day I was observing Joanna as she lubricated a metal part of a door-knob assembly. This process of lubrication makes it easier to slip this part into the main door knob casing. The group had been discussing the impact of machines on their jobs. This was a very serious topic for them, because a new machine had recently been purchased that signaled the end of their positions. As the conversation lulled, I asked Joanna what she was doing. She described to me the process of lubricating the part and placing it into the casing. I commented, "Oh I see, so you must spread this lubricant on or it will not work." Before Joanna could respond, Maciej said "Yes, you must always spread it on or it will not work." The group burst into hearty laughter. I asked them to explain what was so funny about this. They told me that "spread it on" (Jesli nie posmaruesz to nie pojedzie) was a phrase that they use to describe the process of bribing officials, managers, service people and others to get things accomplished.

This group invoked the same reference by using another phrase several months later. We were discussing the difficulties of their repetitive jobs and the low pay that was associated with it. This time Czeslaw, who is actually better paid than the rest of the group, said "we came here on a rabbit, this is why we have such a bad job." Again, the laughter rang out in the large assembly hall. They told me that the Polish expression for an employee who bribes a potential employer is, "He came here on a calf," the reference being that the calf is the bribe to the new employer. Several comments followed that took on a more serious tone related to their lack of right connections or enough money to place themselves properly within this factory.

There is tremendous disagreement about the prevalence of bribery in post-communist Poland. It is clear that side payments are still necessary to receive adequate medical services, and even entrance into universities. A disagreement about the prevalence of bribery occurs primarily because of differences in classifying what should be considered "bribery." For example, to get into a university you must pass a particular exam. To pass these exams one must obtain special tutoring from the university professors, since the content of the exams are a closely guarded secret. Some Poles call this a bribe to the university professors, others call it simply payment for services. Bribery is just one manifestation of a system of privileges, power dispersal and political access that is called "kumoterstwo" in the Polish language. Kumoterstwo comes from the word "kumo" for friend, chum or crony. Kumoterstwo is translated into English as favoritism, but it tends to encompass a great deal more in the Polish experience. The Polish system of networks, or action-sets, supports a heavy (to almost exclusionary) reliance on social contacts for a number of official or unofficial services or products. These connected power trails, as with all action-sets, extend outside organizations to the community and then back into the organizations as the human relationships naturally occur. These networks tend to generate resentment and suspicion among those that do not have them. Often the networks that are associated with power are accompanied by these monetary payments for favors, or bribes. These relationships are not accepted as right or good but only as necessary or a fact of life. Their specific existence is kept very hidden under layers of denial, but they are fair game for general discussion, ridicule, and jokes.

Kumoterstwo results, in part, from attempts by the Polish people to deal with the ironic disconnect between theoretical and "real" socialism, or communism. Theoretical socialism promises egalitarianism of opportunity, meritocracy, and social justice. The manifestation of strong egalitarian attitudes generates a belief in "the same for everybody," promoting unity and social homogeneity (Bojar, 1992).

Poles, though preferring to be free from the power of a central state, particularly one that was highly influenced by the Soviet government, were willing to accept theoretical socialism as they had envisioned it for the 50 years of communism (Marody, 1987). Socialism in practice, however, promoted the interests of the ruling class, primarily party members, at the expense of the rest of the society (Reykowski, 1994). Several authors describe the disconnect between theoretical and "real" socialism as a social accord or collective sense that involves a trade-off of freedom for security (Kolarska-Bobinska, 1989; Marody, 1987). Kolarska-Bobinska, a Polish pollster and sociologist, writes:

Those seeking to explain the stability of the social and political system in Poland often ask why it survives despite its relatively low measure of social acceptance and lack of political legitimacy. One of the answers describes a social accord established between rulers and ruled. This accord can most simply be presented as a trade-off: society lays aside its political aspirations and in return achieves its ideal of social justice and security, in short, the benefiters of a socialist welfare state. The planned economy is the field on which the trade-off is put into effect. The authorities are guaranteed control over social and economic processes while they secure for the people an admittedly low but sure standard of living and job security. . . . Thanks to this arrangement employees tend to achieve little but, on the other hand, neither do they have to work hard, show initiative, take risks or worry about their own future or that of their children (1989:126-127).

The ironic nature of this social accord is that the system for which the Poles traded their political aspirations, in fact, generated significant divisions between groups and produced social injustice. "Real" socialism utilized a system of perks and rewards for those who espoused the central ideology. Privilege became an integral part of Polish society in all areas of social life (Mokrzycki, 1992). This privilege took the form of special treatment for chosen social groups that were generally linked to the apparatus of power.

The essential fact is that privileges are distributed centrally (although not necessarily directly) in accordance with a certain principle of justice, which by its very nature is supposed to correct the 'injustices' of the market economy (Mokrzycki, 1992:272).

By correcting the "injustices of the market economy," the system set up it own set of criteria by which social injustice was practiced. Action-sets were frequently used as the vehicle by which this system of privileges was enacted. Connection with decision-makers was the main criterion for allocation of resources (Reykowski, 1994). New members of the ruling elite became those who accepted, at least superficially, the values of the communist ideology. Those who did this were known as the "nomenklatura." Being part of the nomenklatura was essential to acquiring positions of power in any public institution. Kurczewski (1992) claims that this process generated a new middle class, particularly since 1980, of individuals who were educated and skilled but were unable to assume positions within the power structure because of the "nomenklatura barrier." Thus, individuals who held posiyions of power outwardly accepted values that rhetorically were consistent with socialist ideology, but they completely contradicted these values in practice.

Wesolowski and Wnuk-Lipinski (1992) identify two areas where the meritocratic ideas of the socialist state broke down: in the selection process and in the process of remuneration. Selection for employment and promotions were not made based on competence and expertise but rather on political affiliations. *Kumoterstwo* became the method for selection.

> The school system encourages obedience rather than talents; the promotional system, although formally based on credentials, ignores real competence in favor of political loyalty; and the remuneration structure does not encourage the individual to plan his or her occupational career strategically (Kennedy, 1992: 296-297).

Remuneration became increasingly tied to these same factors more than it did education and experience. An education-pay gap emerged. Two examples of this are doctors and university professors, who today are among the lowest paid professions in Poland. In the socialist system this was accepted because of the safety net generated by the welfare state and the high prestige associated with these professions.

This political aspect of organizational life became the predominant impetus for decision making. Kostera (1995) points out that the communist enterprise was based on a particular definition of success. Survival was granted if the organization was able to "accumulate political influence or profit to effectively control the environment (where the political sphere dominated) " (Kostera, 1995:681). Kostera goes on to describe the depth of the influence that this political influence had on the inner workings of the organizations:

> To achieve their ends in the communist context, managers had to engage in extensive political activity. Most of the communist manager's activity was of a clearly political nature, where both the means and the end were political. Through such activity, economic gains for their own company were, however, granted. Managers could also play vital games as party members and activist, participants of

informal networks, etc., stressing the 'social and political' importance of their companies and/or their networks and positions outside the enterprise (1995: 683).

Politics permeated organizational life and became a preoccupation of managers for the most basic of organizational objectives. My discussion thus far of the political influence on the Polish system of organizing has focused on the communist period, and particularly conditions generated by the political climate in the 1970s' and 1980s'. This has been intentional, since the impact of the dramatic shift in political system in 1989 has not yet been adequately measured. My data suggest that the political nature of Polish life remains of paramount importance; jokes continue, accusations of political networks persist (e.g., the "television sets" event), and bribery is still a common practice. In addition, the systems that were set in place during the communist period of kumoterstwo continue to exist, if not in reality, clearly in the minds and beliefs of the Polish people. One further example demonstrates these beliefs. Eza (22 years with the company) talked about the political connections in the factory today, she said:

> In the old days if the group of people that were connected by the communist ties did not do the work, they were moved to the office to do easy work. Now these same people are not being laid off. These people would eavesdrop in the old system and tell on the others. They were rewarded and protected for doing this . . . snitches existed in the past and they still exist. They were not liked before and they still aren't liked. It is like the "Kapo" during the war. They were the people that would tell the SS men about the activities of their neighbors and friends. It is the same problem now.

One particular concern for the people of Goria is the survival of the nomenklatura. They fear the opportunism which they attribute to this group of people. My informants tell me that the nomenklatura have simply adopted the new capitalistic value system as easily as they did the socialist one. They are now taking advantage of their positions of relative power and their new freedoms to buy and sell public property for their own gain. The disillusionment with the property ownership was demonstrated by the referendum vote that occurred in early 1996. The Walesa government suggested a distribution of ownership coupons to each Polish citizen as a means of privatizing state owned property. The referendum that was posed to the people asked them if they approved of this property distribution method. The result was that less than 30% of the voters turned out, and the referendum vote was declared invalid. When I asked a group of Goria residents why they thought there was such a low turn out for the vote, they told me they were confused about the whole issue. They voiced concern that the nomenklatura would get the property anyway, so they did not feel that the vote empowered them in any tangible way. Whether this is reality or only speculation, the people appear to be acting as if this were the case.

In the Goria region of Poland in 1996 the political mood is confused, and mixed signals abound. Kostera describes this situation, she writes:

> Today mixed rules apply, political and economic rationalities coexist, and success is defined according to 'communist' as well as 'capitalist' standards by different actors and stakeholder (1995: 674).

The past conflict between the theoretical and "real" socialism produced a set of norms that continue to predominate even after the demise of the socialist state. Polish life continues to be very political. Lewis predicted this would be the result of the transition to communism when he wrote in 1973:

> What is overlooked by Western commentators who argue for the relinquishing of power by the party is that the cement which holds together the social system is political: the institution of the party provides for State socialist society what private property supplies for capitalism, namely a value system which is codified into laws and which promotes social and political solidarity (1973: 326).

Therefore, the political influences have helped shape the means of social organization that the Goria people have come to rely on, and they continue to impact the behaviors and attitudes of the people at the Lockem factory.

Religious Influences

It is difficult to overstate the importance of the Catholic church in the public and private lives of the Polish people. Hann goes as far as to say "Polish has come to mean Catholic" (1985: 100). The universality of this statement signifies the importance of the Catholic church's influence. The breath and depth of the church's influence on Polish life extends deeply into the arena of social organization.

Virtually every major holiday is religious in post communist Poland. Public processions of clergy and lay people carrying religious banners and relics are the primary rituals in many of these celebrations. In these rituals, neighborhoods, the youth, and Easter baskets are blessed. This is coupled with full masses, sometimes lasting as long as three hours. Wnuk Lipinski captures the connection between the Church and Polish tradition. He writes:

> the foundations of Polish national culture have always been closely interwoven with Christianity. The baptism of Poland in 966 brought the country into European culture, and there it remains (1987: 163).

The church established its remarkable stronghold on the Polish psyche through the transmission of ideas, values and myths that were passed down through generations (Wnuk-Lipinski, 1987). In addition, the Catholic church has played a particularly important role for the rural citizens in modern Poland. These parishioners continue to be a particular focus for the church. During the period of peasant emancipation at the end of the nineteenth century the church played an active role in acquiring freedom and land for the peasants, even though the Polish state was not an independent entity. This championing of the peasant cause positioned the church perfectly to play an active role in the creation of national sentiment, and it bound the Poles even more closely to the church. The result was that the parish became the focus for a collective Polish peasant identity (Hann, 1985).

This peasant-church connection is further manifest in the almost spiritual link that the Polish people have with their land. This is best demonstrated by the All Saints Day commemoration that is celebrated every November 1st. An excerpt from my field notes describes the activities.

After being told how different the Polish version of All Saints Day was to the way we celebrate Halloween in the US, I was quite interested. Several people told me that I should go to the cemetery on Rawicka near the Krakow Academy of Economics, so we decided to do this if the weather cooperated.

The day before we had gone to the center of town for dinner. The atmosphere was quite different than usual. I remember stopping on the tram at the top of Karmelicka street and noticing the increased number of flower salespeople. Everyone seemed to be walking quickly and it felt so different that I can not be sure if there were more people or less than usual. It is probably that there were more people hustling and less people standing and walking casually.

The next day at 2 p.m. we left for the cemetery. We decided to take a tram from the tram station in our neighborhood. The #12 tram would take us directly to the cemetery. We were surprised when we saw that all three of the trams parked at the station were #12s. We got on one with several people that looked like they did not ride the tram often. Women were wearing fur coats and many people were carrying flowers and bags with candles in little jars in them; I could hear them clanging together in the bags. I also noticed that there were an unusually large number of people waiting to buy tickets from the driver. Most frequent tram riders, from my experience, have passes or books of tickets.

I noticed there were tram workers at every major intersection along the way. It was a very dark and cold day, and the streets were sparsely populated. As the tram went along, we picked up more and more people. Most of them carrying flowers. As we approached our final destination, instantly I knew where all the people had gone. Streams of people were walking up the street. Along the sidewalk was a series of areas which had zigzagged sections, like a Disneyland ride, to line the people up. Each section had a post which displayed a sign with a tram number on it. People were lined up in each area waiting for trams. Stands were set up everywhere. People behind the counters sold flowers, candles, and little bags of what I can only guess were candy and chocolates. It was very busy and we had to wait as several trams ahead of us let people out at the stop and then looped back to pick up the people waiting in line.

We followed the stream of people into the cemetery, and we saw a beautiful cemetery that seemed to use every available spot of land for a grave. Many of the graves were family plots with the family name at the top of the head stone, and deceased family members engraved below. In most cases room had been left for more names. I do not think that I saw a single grave that did not have at least one candle on it. In fact, almost all of them had five or more. They were also decorated with flowers. We saw several graves that had crosses formed in chestnuts, which could be found everywhere in Krakow at this time of year.

As we moved over to the older section of the cemetery, we saw many graves that were crumbling and several that appeared to be for very famous people. For example, Matejki's grave was surrounded by hundreds of candles. The small chapels in the cemetery were running Catholic services and people filled them and the surrounding areas to listen and pray. The general mood seemed to be more one of solemn remembrance than sorrow or grief.

Several graves had groups of nuns and priests praying, singing, and chanting at them. I felt propelled through the cemetery by the crowd. Children were everywhere, but they were very well behaved. I was struck by the number of elderly and clergy who seemed to make up a larger percentage of the crowd than I was used to seeing on the streets of Krakow (field notes November 1, 1995).

The annual All Saints Day observance is an amazing cultural demonstration of respect for the dead that has turned into an "event." Its religious meaning serves to symbolically and literally connect the Polish people to their roots and to the land. This point is made clearer when taking into account the many Poles who have moved to the cities within the last few generations. Most of them travel back to their villages, some of them to the villages of both sides of the family. City dwellers who have these agrarian roots usually choose to be buried in the village from which they came, further preserving the connection and the importance of family lineage and agrarian heritage. In addition, the family plots establish a permanent link of generations to generations in the village, a lineage that is literally "planted in the ground."

Thus the Catholic church, through this religious ritual, symbolically connects the Poles to the land. The workers in the factory articulate the importance of this connection. Teresa, who works part-time on her husband's family farm, said, "here in the mountains the land is like a 'saintly' thing." Other employees told me that the transfer of the farm to at least one child is crucial. However, if their children do leave the area for a different section of Poland or the cities, they know that the children will return to be buried in the mountains. Helena told me "there is comfort in knowing that the souls of my children will rest on this land."

In addition to linking the Poles to their traditions and their land, the Catholic church has acted to collectivize the Polish people. The church was been able to contrast espoused values with the realities of living under foreign power domination and communism. This generated a sense of community that transcended the local and became universal and transnational (Wnuk-Lipinski, 1987). Thus religion in Poland has functioned throughout the periods of foreign domination and through communism to draw the community together (Hann, 1985).

The collective influence has come attached with moral codes of conduct (Hann, 1985). Among these codes of conduct is the belief in equality and fair division of resources. This promotes the church's sense of social justice (Kloczowski, 1992). The church has instilled values and assumptions which place importance on collectivity over individuality, and suffering over satisfaction of personal needs. This espousal of values has led to general inactivity. Sacrifice is seen as the best means by which a Catholic can find salvation. This belief has spread beyond religious life in Poland and has permeated Polish views of national identity. It has given solace to a people who have suffered long periods of political and economic domination for centuries, and the horrors of World War II. The search for explanations for why they have had to suffer so terribly has generated a natural connection between Poles and the Catholic church.

This is supported by several literary figures of the 19th century, most notably Mickiewicz (Davies, 1982b). The 19th century was a period when Poland had been partitioned between Russia, Prussia, and Austria. Poland did not exist on the world map. Mickiewicz converted his Catholic beliefs into a national justification for Polish historical events. Davies (1982b) writes that the literary works of Mickiewicz, Brodzinski and others transformed Poland into an "idea" which lived in the beliefs and aspirations of the Polish people. This idea contained themes of self-sacrifice and suffering which drew heavily from religious doctrine. Mickiewicz wrote:

> In the beginning, there was belief in one God, and there was Freedom in the world. And there were no laws, only the will of God, and there were no lords and slaves, only patriarchs and their children. But later the people turned aside from the Lord their God, and made

themselves graven images, and bowed down . . . Thus God sent upon them the greatest punishment which is slavery . . . But the Polish nation alone did not bow down . . . And finally Poland said 'Whosoever will come to me shall be free and equal, for I am FREEDOM.' . . . And they crucified the Polish Nation, and laid it in its grave . . . For the Polish Nation did not die. Its body lieth in the grave; but its spirit has descended into the abyss, that is into the private lives of people who suffer slavery in their country . . . But on the third day the soul shall return again to the body, and the Nation shall arise, and free all the peoples of Europe from slavery (Davies, 1982: 8-9)

The Polish literature of this era struck a chord with the Polish people, and its impact is still felt in the Polish sense of identity. This heavy reliance on Catholic doctrine and a belief that an omnipresent being would bring salvation lead to a giving up of control and an acceptance that faith alone is enough to reach the Polish "ideal."

The values and moral codes of conduct that the Catholic church has espoused have often been in direct conflict with the socialist state. The church, in fact, used its influence on the faithful to mark opposition. Father Kazimierz Jancarz from Nowa Huta describes one such example.

In 1970, the year of the uprising, new apartment complexes were built. Father Jozef Kurzeja put up a makeshift building to be used as a church. There were problems—the regime persecuted him for this. He used the construction of this building as a rallying cause to organize people. He taught children religion and the need to build a church (1992: 205).

The Catholic resistance points to the clash between the church and the state that existed in communism. But the clash is even more profound when considering, as another Polish priest, Father Kloczowski, did, that the origins of both the Polish Catholic clergy and the Polish communist party leadership are peasant. Father Kloczowski noted in 1989 that

most clergy still come from the countryside. You have to remember that the paradox is that the power structure, both in the Party and in the Church, is of peasant origin. Both Party members and bishops are sons of peasants (1992: 215).

Workers of Lockem have viewed this stress between the church and state with frustration. The conflict goes against the church's espoused values of cooperation and unity, and this is confusing and disappointing for the workers. In a discussion about the 1995 presidential elections, Anna told me:

> Here in Poland there are the Catholics and the Party. They should all be Polish. The president should not separate the people. It was the same as in the US when the south split from the north. Here it is the left and the right wings that are separate. It is not normal. We have spent five years listening to Walesa who has been dividing people.

Anna's vacillation between the various manifestations of social division (church vs. party, left vs. right, US north vs. south) is indicative of the confusing nature with which the Goria people talk about this church-state conflict. The church, however, is a vital player in this division. For example, the church forbade party members to take communion and to give confession in certain villages during the communist times. This influence continues today. The church openly supported Walesa in the 1995 presidential election, but perhaps more importantly, the clergy openly denounced the candidacy of the communist, Kwasniewski, in their pulpits and in their church schools. Kwasniewski, however, went on to win the election.

Workers at Lockem claim that they were freely able to practice their religion during the communist period, though the discussion was often a sensitive one, as the three sections from my field notes below demonstrate.

> Teresa said that they were Catholics and that they did not feel that communism was a problem. She said in the past it was not forbidden for her to baptize her kids. Maybe people in higher positions were forbidden to do so and to go to church, people in high positions in the party, but she was not.

> Beata said that the "party" was not a problem for anyone. During communism they would baptize their kids and there was no problem.

> I then asked Beata if there was a problem with going to the church during the communist times. (*This question brought on a complete change in Beata's demeanor. She had been quite open, laughing and*

joking with her fellow employees. But when I asked her this, she became uncomfortable and nervous. She looked down at her work and even transferred some parts into a box.) She said there were no problems as far as she could remember. She said that here in this area everyone is connected strongly with the church.

Beata's discomfort with the question points to sensitivity of this issue. The church's hold on the Lockem workers, though strong and deeply rooted, is not beyond questioning. For example, Eza disagreed with the church's stand on the participation of party members in church rituals.

During the communist time they [party members] were told that they should not go to confession. There were mistakes made by the priests which forbade party members to go to mass. I do not think this was a good position to take since these people needed support from their religion as well.

This questioning of the church's stand on political matters came up with a different group after the Pope stated that he disapproved of the November 1995 election of Kwasniewski to the Polish presidency. The Pope had said that the Polish people had been too impatient with reforms. When I asked Teresa, Beata and Maria from the red group what they thought about this, at first I did not get an answer, just smiles. They all three shook their heads from side to side slowly, but did not speak. It was almost as if they were thinking of what to say, or that the question had brought up a whole grouping of things that they were mulling over in their heads. Finally, Beata said that Walesa could have won but that he was "not saying the right words." An animated discussion began with all three of the women speaking at once. They talked about the debate between the two leading candidates and how each had presented himself. As the conversation died down, Teresa looked up at me with a look of recollection, as if she had remembered what my question was. She turned her head back to her work and in almost a whisper said "Maybe the Pope understood the election differently than we did."

Disillusionment with the church in some circumstances is discussed openly now. As the new capitalistic values are assimilated into the Polish consciousness, the church is finding a new set of evils to battle, and the workers of this factory are beginning to feel comfortable openly questioning the values of the church. Anna, whose daughter was killed in a traffic accident several months before, openly discussed her frustration with the support of the church. She said:

> The priest did not come by to see me or to console me. In fact, he did not say anything to my family at all. No one from my church did either. It was only a woman that I do not know very well that came by to console me. This woman is from another religion and she only knew me from passing on the road. She came by and reached for my hands and cried with me about my daughter. This meant so much to me. The people from my religion just gossiped. No one came to say they were sorry.

In summary, the church has served as a collectivizing influence which provided a haven of refuge and resistance against the socialist state. The values of sacrifice and suffering have made sense to a people who had suffered so much, and it gave them a sense of greater identity and purpose. This is reflected in the works of Mickiewicz and others. Furthermore, the church's power was sufficiently strong during the communist era that the peasants in this region did not feel inhibited from practicing their religion. The changing nature of the political environment in Poland, however, has provided opportunity to question the role of the church in the minds of the workers in this factory. This may produce a change in the way that the church encourages the Poles to act as social players on the Polish stage, but to change dramatically would go against the greater Catholic doctrine, which is unlikely. Therefore, the Polish people will need to decide whether the church will continue to play such an important role in their lives, and whether they will continue to believe that "to be Polish is to be Catholic."

Summary—Influences on Social Organization

Exhibit 10 summarizes the influences on social organization that I have just presented. The traditions, responses to changing political systems, and the Catholic church have each exerted influence that has shaped norms and behaviors in this region of Poland. These influences do not act in three separate vacuums. Throughout this discussion, I have identified how these influences have worked together or in opposition to each other. One example is the way the church utilized the action-sets, which are generated, in part, as a way to preserve long-standing regional traditions. Through obtaining needed church building material, the clergy acknowledged that bribery was a necessary response to the political system the church opposed. Therefore, in this example the church parishioners are acting in a way that takes into consideration each of these three influences, and their attempts to work within these systems shape their approach and their behavior. These influences not only impact the norms and behaviors of this society, they also touch a deeper level—the values and assumptions of the people of Goria. The next section of this chapter will look at these values and assumptions.

Exhibit 10. Summary of Influences on Social Organization in Goria

1. Traditional Influences
   a. Inheritance traditions forced farmers to work off the farm.
   b. Farming interests were sacrificed for industrial interests by the communist state.
   c. Action-sets (networks of dyadic relationships) connect individuals to power and resources, and promote peasant identity.
   d. Semi-legal activities are socially accepted because they are considered "necessary."
2. Political Influences
   a. Theoretical socialism promised egalitarianism, meritocracy and social justice.
   b. "Real" socialism promoted the interests of the ruling class (nomenklatura).
   c. Bribery and kumoterstwo emerged.
   d. Politics dominate in "public" social relationships.
3. Religious Influences
   a. A strong historical church-peasant community connection. exists
   b. The Catholic church promoted a collective identity for the Polish people.
   c. Church and literary figures promote sacrifice and suffering.
   d. Catholic church-Communist party conflict produces frustration and confusion in post-communist Poland.

CULTURAL VALUES AND ASSUMPTIONS

The values and assumptions that the people of Goria hold are significant to understanding how they view change and how they will assign meaning to the events of their lives. As a point of comparison between the TQM philosophy which will be discussed in Chapter 7 and the cultural environment of this region of Poland, this section will provide support for the presence of certain cultural values and assumptions that are pertinent to social organization in this context. I will not present them as absolute in this environment, but simply as forces that tend to be present as Poles are making sense of their world. I do not assume that a predominance of, for example, "fatalism" in this context excludes the presence of determinism, because in fact there is a great deal of determinism in certain aspects of their lives. Nor, do I assume they are unchanging. I present these values and assumptions as indicators of a general approach to dealing with life in Goria, and a basis of comparison with the TQM philosophy. Where appropriate, I will present examples of opposing tendencies. Four values and/or assumptions are discussed: fatalism, ascription, high-context, and individualism.

Fatalism

The Goria people are generally fatalistic about their lives. This tendency was identified in the more general Polish society by Kolarska-Bobinska. She said:

> One can hardly expect a spirit of initiative and active support for the changes to come from people who are convinced that they are not masters of their own fate (1989: 137).

Fatalism is viewed in opposition to determinism. They both reflect the individual's relationship with nature and the perception of free will within the world context. Some cultures view man as the master over his environment and value harnessing and exploiting such things as time, space, and change (Schneider, 1992). People in these societies, which are classified as deterministic, have a belief that they are responsible as individuals or as a group for their actions and can affect the future. In addition, individuals in these societies find themselves unconstrained by environmental factors and capable of self-improvement (Boyacigiller & Adler, 1991).

    In fatalistic societies individuals perceive a lack of personal control over events, what Rotter (1966) called an external locus of control. In these cultures dominion over events lies ultimately with a greater power such as God, fate, luck, government, one's social class, or history

(Boyacigiller & Adler, 1991). They believe that the individual is subservient to, or in harmony with, nature, and that action taken by people will be overcome by the powers that control their destiny. Thus, responsibility for events lies not with the individual but with nature or fate (Schneider, 1992).

The tendency toward fatalism was seen in all levels of the society in this study. The perceived external force that controls their fate, however, was different for men versus women and for people at various levels of authority within the organization.[11] The women in the organization tend to look to some ambiguous "other" that is controlling their destinies. They use phrases like "we have to take it like it is" or "it is all planned, we have no control over it." They also focus on the changing economic predicament as being inevitable and uncontrollable. When I asked one group of women if they saw a greater disparity of wealth now compared to communist times, Maria told me "people who have it are going to have it." Beata from the same group told me that the people in the mountains blame the "western countries" for drugs, sex and everything bad that is coming to their communities.

The men, including those in higher positions of authority also assume very fatalistic attitudes. They, however, tend to focus on more specific targets for their subjugation. Due to the specific nature of these targets, they are changing with time. The men in lower levels of authority blame management and politicians for their state of affairs. They claim that they have little control in a world where these powerful men rule their lives. The men in management, however, have changed their focus from the communist party, or the government, to the "market." They claim that market conditions now dictate their destiny, and thus they have little, if any, control over this situation. In a discussion I had with the production manager, Mr. Jozef Kwit, he told me about the centralized system that existed under communism. He said that they were directed by this government on all issues of capital investment, product line, and the quantity of products to manufacture. Now he says:

> The market dictates the machines and the number of people that we have in the factory . . . times are better and we are making investments. We are making lots of changes and it is very stressful. C'est la vie. It is getting better and better day by day. The salaries and wages . . . well, it is not like we can do everything. It is up to the market.

About their specific jobs, however, the men even in the lower levels of the organization, tended to be more deterministic. For example, while talking about the series of layoffs that the employees were expecting, I asked Janusz if he thought that he might get laid off. He first answered "Yes," but then he said "Well, I am an optimist. Everyone is afraid of the layoffs, but I am not modest. Someone has to stay here and I think one of them will be me."

These fatalistic attitudes and responses to current conditions, however, are contradicted by a study done by Reykowski (1992). His study of normative beliefs found the greatest amount of the variance (16 percent) was explained by a factor which he described as showing a general belief that

> an individual should play an active role in society: he/she should take an enterprising attitude in life and strive for a role of an actor (an independent subject) in the family, in the work place, in society at large (Reykowski, 1992: 220).

This contradiction might be explained by the period in which this study was performed, in the early 1990s. During this time the new government led by the Solidarity Union dispensed a tremendous amount of propaganda designed to change the mindset of the Polish people and to eliminate the anomie that existed in Polish society. A wholesale acceptance of this approach as "good" or "right" may account for the difference in findings. In addition, Poles may generally feel that this is a desirable way to think, but may be conflicted by the weight of years of societal experience of domination by foreign and unwelcome powers and little ability to control the "official" system. Finally, determinism may be on the rise, but my data reflect that the optimism and deterministic belief that accompanied the initial stages of the transition to a free market economy have experienced a decline. Impatience and a realization of the negative implications of this transition have brought this on.

Ascription

The ascription/achievement orientation addresses the means by which a given culture assigns status within the society. Trompenaars (1994) states that achievement status refers to "doing" and ascriptive status refers to "being." Ascription, as opposed to achievement, assigns status and power based on some type of characteristic of the individual, for example age, gender, social connections, education or profession (Trompennars, 1994). In ascriptive societies status requires no justification, and status necessarily implies "power." In addition, these societies associate status and power with position, and they attribute obligation to one's standing in society (Hofstede, 1984; Stewart, 1991). Achievement oriented societies place a high emphasis on skill and knowledge, and authority is assigned on this basis. Power comes with position only if the job is performed effectively.

The highly political nature of Polish society, and the utilization of kumoterstwo as discussed earlier in this chapter, points to the ascriptive nature of status assignment, which occurs through "political" affiliation. Networks that link individuals to the ruling class are the only means by which real power and status was attainable. Thus, managers in the communist period had to play a political "game" to elevate their own status, and to make life as easy as possible for the organization. Kostera describes this process:

> Managers tried to protect their own and their companies' integrity, seeking to buy a certain amount of independence by making the 'right' declarations at 'right' moments, and developing an informal old-boy network preferably with high party-officials as powerful mentors. . . . They would thus ensure that 'the planned quotas for their companies would be minimal, thereby making it easy to accomplish and even exceed them. This was the prerequisite for gaining extra financial and material means for social programmes, bonuses for employees (which were often more attractive than standard pay), foreign travel, etc. and achievement recognized by colleagues as 'good management' (1995: 677).

Through this process managers were able to improve their status and increase their potential for further advancement. This reliance on ascription and management connections with "power" centers continues in post communist Poland. Kostera tells of a manager who had to rely on the old methods of status attainment and political networks to obtain success in the transition period

> In order to save his company, he performed the old organizational role of a communist manger; engaging in political games, lobbying, and party politics, developing a network of political support. 'He's

gonna run for Parliament', one of the other directors commented. . . .
The rumor goes that Mr. Gorecki is the perfect director, because 'he
knows people'. Some of the important political posts are now
occupied by his friends and colleagues (Kostera, 1995: 685).

This mentality and method of operation exist at Lockem as well. The
"television sets" example once again provides evidence of this. The
management staff implemented Mr. Sroka's decision to reward
employees for perfect attendance. When given the responsibility to
decide whom among the group to give the limited number of television
sets, they relied on the only method they knew—to give them based on
who was connected in the political network—thus perpetuating the
belief in all the workers that "nothing had changed." The old system of
preference based on affiliation and not achievement was still at work.

It is important to note that the process of favoritism based on
criteria other than pure achievement is found in all societies. What is
interesting to observe in this Polish context is the role that this process
plays on the psyche of the Polish workers who are not part of the power
structure. It serves to send a signal that achievement is actually
devalued in the system and thus it is counterproductive to attaining
personal objectives. This is true only in the public sphere of life. There
is a disconnect between the "public" and "private" Pole. The Polish
people still highly value accomplishments when it comes to objectives
that are not influenced by the "public" sphere, for example, working on
the farm. Thus, they find frustration because of their desire to play by
the same set of rules in the factory as they use at home. They have been
taught, however, through years of experience that this is not a good
idea.

Therefore, as with determinism, signs of achievement orientation
may be on the rise. The Lockem employees, at all levels, claim that
achievement "should" be the means for status assignment in their
society. Fatalism, however, or potentially self-serving interests in the
case of the managers, gets in the way of expecting this to actually
happen.

High-Context

Hall (1959) views culture as communication. He proposes that one of
the ways that culture can be differentiated is through its "context."
Context is the amount of information that surrounds every event and

which is connected to the meaning of the event. It is found in different proportions in different cultures.

A high context communication or message is one in which most of the information is already in the person, while very little is in the coded, explicit, transmitted part of the message. A low context communication is just the opposite; i.e., the mass of the information is vested in the explicit code (Hall & Hall, 1990: 6).

Hall argues that the information networks among family, friends, colleagues and clients in some cultures eliminates the need for transmitting extensive amounts and depth of information in each communication. The information is exchanged through the network and is constantly updated through repeated contacts through these networks. Low-context cultures compartmentalize their relationships, and each time they interact they must provide detailed background information.

Polish culture in this region can be viewed as a high-context culture in the sense that important and real daily communication does not require much background information. Polish life is filled with an abundance of detailed information. The legacy of the socialist state and centralized economy has left an abundance of official forms, documents, procedures and processes. These official forms of communication do not, however, form the true basis of relationships either public or private. The existing high-context orientation of the Polish people may be in part a response to the government's attempts to generate a centralized system of control. Thus, the high-context orientation may be even stronger because of the socialist state than it would have been without it.

In my discussion of the influences of social organization in this chapter, I discussed the action-sets that form one of the primary and most salient means of communication and social organization in this society. Despite the extensive amount of bureaucracy in the communist state, the operating mechanisms for social organization existed outside this system, within the informal action-sets. These networks form the basis for the information that is transmitted through the structure, and eliminate the need for in-depth information in each communication.

There is another potential reason for the high-context nature of society. It is also a response to the socialist system, and the dominating governments before it. Through informal networks and high degrees of information within the structure, a community is more easily able to resist the external power and to function well almost outside the system. This generates a strong underground resistance force which the Poles utilized very effectively during World War II (Davies, 1982b). Therefore, official channels act as interference to the means by which things get done. The growing complexity of Polish society points to a need for interactions with a greater number of people than ever before. In addition, improvements in communication modes have made connections even easier. It is too early to tell whether these changes will perpetuate the informal action-sets that already permeate Polish society, or whether the shift will be toward a need for greater information to pass in each exchange, thus moving Polish society toward more of a low-context orientation.

Individualism

Finally, both the individualistic and the collectivistic orientations of the Goria people are salient to the understanding of social organization in this context. This topic was introduced in Chapter 2, with a review of the literature on the Individualism-Collectivism dimension of culture. Briefly, the individualism-collectivism orientations describe the importance of individuals in the society as compared to the group (Schneider, 1992). Individualism represents societies that prioritize individual accomplishments, while collectivism values group accomplishments.

Here, I would like to introduce the notion that individualistic and collectivistic tendencies coexist in a high degree in this environment. This dual tendency is reflected in Czarniawska's (1986) discussion of the Polish "national character." She writes:

> All these experiences are summarized in a picture of a 'national character', which is additionally embellished by the influences of the Catholic religion, and by literature and art, especially from the Romantic period. The resulting images that of a nation capable of the most heroic collective efforts in times of emergency, and incapable of living prosperously in quieter times, due to extreme individualism and a fatal tendency to anarchy. Looking at other countries, Poles tend to attribute their successes to what is lacking in the 'Polish character': order, efficiency, method. Therefore the system myth (Czarniawska, 1986: 327).

Therefore, I must describe the Goria region as being highly individualistic and highly collectivistic at the same time. The implications for this are discussed further in the next chapter.

Summary—Communist Culture

In this chapter I discussed the three primary influences on social organization in this region of Poland. These influences have worked together to shape the culture of the Goria region of Poland. Communism, through it political systems, was one of those influences, but it is important to note that this chapter examined "Polish" communism. It is clear from this discussion that the influences of tradition and religion worked extensively to sculpt the way in which communism would influence the Polish people. Therefore, the influences of communism in the Polish context were necessarily different from those in a Hungarian, Czech, or Russian context. The norms and behaviors that result may be similar within each of these environments while the pressure of an autocratic leadership, influenced by the Soviet Union, remained. The true impact on the values and assumptions, however, are seen only after that pressure is lifted. It is for this reason that I will incorporate my further discussion of communist culture into the regional culture which has been influenced by the political systems and ideologies.

The discussion in this chapter provides a background upon which we can examine the actions of the participants in the "television sets" event. The accusations of "spying" made by Joanna and others seem understandable in an environment where power and privilege have been applied through informal networks that have often involved bribery. Promises of change are meaningless when the outward signs "confirm" to the employees of Lockem that "nothing has changed." In addition, the managers' actions, which were driven by their past experience, are now couched in rhetoric of change. For example, the vice presidents claim that the awards were based on achievement-oriented measures, such as new ideas and innovation. Chapter 6 will explore these issues further, as we take a closer look at the perceptions the people of the Goria region have about social relationships, and how this is impacting their behaviors and attitudes at Lockem.

Exhibit 11 depicts Corpus Christi Day celebration in Poland.

Exhibit 11. Corpus Christi Day celebration.

Patterns of Shared Mindsets

If men define situations as real, they are real in their consequences
(Sztompka, 1995b: 21, quoting W.I. Thomas).

The social influences described in Chapter 5 have shaped the way the
Goria residents view the world. The data collected for this study
produced emergent themes which support the existence of perceptions
about social relationships. These shared mindsets produce resistance to
change at Lockem (see Chapter 7). This chapter will address what the
Goria residents perceive their relationships to mean: who they can trust,
how secure these relationships are, how connected they feel to the
greater whole, and how responsible they feel for themselves and each
other. It is important to note the domain of this discussion. I will be
addressing here the social perception of certain phenomenon and not
the actual existence or nonexistence of these phenomenon. Even though
the reality of the social condition is important, particularly as it
conflicts with perceptions, it is not the focus of this discussion.

INSECURITY AND INSTABILITY

Given the conflicting value systems and ill-conceived practices of
communism it is difficult to understand how this system was able to
maintain control in Poland for 50 years (Kolarska-Bobinska, 1989).
Many explanations are given for this phenomenon, and I propose one
here that takes into account the social perceptions that are the focus of
this chapter. One hundred and fifty years of foreign power domination,
with only a brief inter-war period of freedom, followed by the
devastation of World War II, left the Polish people above all else

looking for stability and security (Lewenstein & Melchior, 1992). Forty years after the inception of communism in Poland, Marody wrote that real socialism

> for all its inefficiency still retains the advantage in social consciousness over capitalism that it is seen as assuring work and, by the same token, the future. This sense of greater security, even if it has largely been constructed through propaganda, is reinforced by the habits and attitudes which are formed in the course of the individual's daily experience (1987: 146).

Rather than instilling a general sense of well-being, however, stability and security under communism were achieved through a combination of coercion, or the fear of it, instrumental motive, and institutional habits resulting from negative comparison and a sense of no alternative (Rychard, 1987). The joint forces of traditional and religious influences acted to fill the void. They worked in tandem with the political influences to generate a sense of security and a stability of the system. This left the Polish people with something they could count on, even if they did not like it.

One middle-aged farmer in Mokarszy told me "during communism we were all equal, equally poor, but at least we knew we would be that way." This drive for security and stability did begin to change in the mid-1970s' (Koralewicz, 1987). The need for security, a quiet existence, and an escape from the realities of life was replaced by a desire for greater personal control. This change was coupled with the uncloaking of the communist myth, and the increasing inability of the state to provide for the people as it had promised. The result was that the Polish people were willing to risk some of their security and stability for social freedoms, which they desperately missed and highly prized. The net result was an expanding base of support for the Solidarity movement and the eventual dismantling of the communist state.

Seven years later, the greatest difficulty for the people of the Goria region, and arguably for all of Poland, is that a free market economy and democracy have wiped away this sense of security and stability. They now perceive an ambiguous world of change and uncertainty, which generates stress and insecurity. Kolarska-Bobinska predicted this in 1989, when she argued that a market oriented reform would "disturb the existing balance" and that the people of Poland would lose the "equality and feeling of social security which it values highly" (1989: 127). Thus, the people in Goria perceive their lives to be unstable and ambiguous and the future to be very frightening. Janusz told me the he was not optimistic about the future of the company. He said, "It is not good here. It should be better by now, if it was going to get better. But, in fact, it is worse. There is more uncertainty."

Three additional patterns of social perception emerge from the data: distrust, reluctance to assume responsibility, and a struggle between individualism and collectivism. In the first part of this chapter I will discuss the first two. This discussion will explore how the inhabitants of Goria and the surrounding region perceive trust and responsibility. The majority of this chapter is dedicated exclusively to the struggle that is taking place between individualism and collectivism. This topic is the primary focus of this chapter for two reasons. First, the struggle between tendencies to base action on strong self-interests is coupled with an equally strong drive to maintain a collective unity. The two forces are in daily conflict at Lockem, and the result of this conflict is generating the greatest resistance to the changes that are taking place. Second, the very high level of both of these opposing orientations calls into question the prevailing national culture literature (c.f. Hofstede, 1980; Trompenaars, 1994; Stewart & Bennett, 1991). This example provides a basis for challenging the notion that cultures can be classified upon a scale anchored by collectivism on one side and individualism on the other.

TRUST

Trust has been defined as

> the willingness of a party to be vulnerable to the actions of another party based on the expectation that the other will perform a particular action important to the trustor (Mayer, Davis, & Schoorman, 1995:712).

I would add to Mayer, Davis and Schoorman's definition the willingness to be vulnerable to "parties," implying collections of people and even institutions, for the purpose of the discussion of trust here. Lewis and Weigert assert that trust is a social construction that answers both individual and societal needs for security by "seeming to be a fact when it is always a projected assumption" (1985: 982). Trust implies a willingness to take risks and to reduce complexity (Luhmann, 1973; Lewis & Weigert, 1985; Mayer, Davis, & Schoorman, 1995). Distrust also reduces complexity by signaling to social participants a course of action based on controls and safeguards from potential detrimental actions of the referent other (Lewis & Weigert, 1985).

This conceptualization of trust as a social reality helps frame our understanding of the "culture of distrust" which Sztompka (1995b) describes. Sztompka argues that a culture of distrust exists when distrust becomes contagious, and social sanctions are applied to those who do not act upon the basis of the general assumption that the risks are higher than the potential gains in trusting. Sztompka further describes trust as a "cultural resource, indispensable for viable agency, and thus for self-transforming [the] potential of society" (1995b: 5). A "pervasive deficiency of trust" (Sztompka, 1995b) exists in every level of Polish society. This study has identified a strong distrust that stems from a general sense of social injustice. I will use two theories within the distributive justice literature, relative deprivation theory and equity theory, to assist in my exploration of three facets of distrust in Polish society: distrust of government, distrust within the community, and distrust within the organization.

Distrust of Government

There is widespread distrust of government in Poland (Hanss, 1992). Three reasons can be found for distrust of both pre-1989 communist and post-communist governments: illegitimacy, corruption, and lack of control. Kennedy (1992), Marody (1987), and Rychard (1987) each present evidence that the Polish state was illegitimate in the eyes of the Polish people. Rychard defines legitimacy as "the credibility of the authorities" (1987: 52). The evidence of a disconnect between theoretical and "real" socialism (see Chapter 5) provides support for a lack of credibility in the communist era, and this sentiment continues through the present period. The theory of legitimization assumes a fit between societal values and the action of the authorities (Marody, 1987). Absence of this correspondence between values and action promotes system instability, problems of control, and significant activity outside the "public" sphere. In addition, illegitimacy of the government breeds distrust of institutions and of the individuals who run them.

The citizens of Goria generally do not view their government as legitimate. One example of perceived illegitimacy was expressed during the November 1995 presidential election. The overwhelming majority of the workers that I spoke to at Lockem chose to vote for Kwasniewski, the leader of the social democratic party and a prior communist. Most said that their vote was an anti-Walesa vote. In their eyes, Walesa had not kept his promises, was not an appropriate representative of the Polish people, and had been corrupted by the power of his office. They said that he had promised to provide housing for everyone who needed it, and to give a cash payments to every Polish citizen, representing his or her share in the state-owned property.[12] They felt betrayed that he had not kept his promises.

Much of the criticism about Walesa's suitability for office centered on his lack of education and his unpolished demeanor. For example, during a 1994 visit to Warsaw by President Bill Clinton, Walesa gave Clinton a saxophone as a gift. After Clinton had accepted the gift, Walesa asked him to play it for the news reporters and others present. Clinton laughed and graciously declined. The Goria residents told me that they saw this as an incredible breach of appropriate diplomatic etiquette. They told me that the president of the United States should never be put in the embarrassing position of playing a saxophone in public.[13] Finally, the employees at Lockem cited indiscretions of power, including a ballet scholarship for Walesa's daughter and tax evasion.

A perception of corruption, the second basis for government distrust, is reflected in a statement given by a young unemployed construction worker who lives in Goria with his parents. Wojciech said:

> The mentality of the Polish people is that generally we are free, our matters are in our hands. But the government . . . the people are always quarreling amongst themselves. Some people even say that what we need is a strong leader, like a dictator. They think that this would be good for now, just to put everything in order. There is too much of a problem with corruption. The government is full of simply ordinary thieves. They need to change the law, they need to change the constitution.

Wojciech's phrasing of this suggestion "they need to change . . . " reflects the abdication of responsibility for the solution to their societal problems, which I heard often. He later said "Polish people do not trust in general. They can't just trust the changes because they haven't learned how to trust. They have had so many years of learning how not to trust." His earlier statement also points to the perception of widespread corruption in government.

Politicians were among the most distrusted of all social groups in my study. I asked both Goria high school students and the workers at Lockem to, "rate these groups of people upon a scale of '1' to '5,' with 5 being highly trust and 1 being highly distrust." The answers to this question produced the results in Appendix E, reflecting high distrust for politicians, school headmasters, and police, with trust for doctors, nuns and farmers. When I asked the respondents why they distrust politicians, the most frequently cited reason was that the officials were all corrupt. They complained that the frequent changes in government simply gave the politicians an opportunity to "steal whatever they can" from the people since they know they will not be there for long. Foreign investors were partially blamed for this situation as well. The Poles with whom I spoke generally believed that the foreign investors were given very good deals on state property if they paid personal bribes to the officials responsible for negotiating the deals. Whether this practice actually occurs or not, and there is some prima-facie evidence that it does, the citizens of Goria believe that these officials gave good deals in exchange for bribes, effectively giving away the country's wealth for their own gain. They choose in part not to trust because of this.

Relative deprivation theory (Crosby, 1984; Homans, 1961; Martin, 1981; Martin & Murray, 1983) provides some insight into this perception. Relative deprivation "stems from a comparison between the rewards received by one's self and one's membership group and the reward received by some other person or group" (Stouffer, Suchman, DeVinney, Starr & Williams, 1949). The level of satisfaction or dissatisfaction is relative to some psychological standard which the individuals has and is not an absolute across comparers (Crosby, 1984).

Davis (1959) specified the conditions under which relative deprivation occurs. His model makes distinctions between (a) ingroups and outgroups, and (b) those who are objectively nondeprived (the 'haves') and those who are objectively deprived (the 'have-nots'). The comparer experiences social distance when the outcomes of a referent other's group are different from her or his own group. If the referent other is a member of the comparer's own group and the referent's outcomes are superior to the comparer's, then relative deprivation occurs. The basis on which the comparer determines the referent other to be a member of the same group varies among individuals, resulting in one person experiencing social distance and another person experiencing relative deprivation under the same comparison situation (Crosby, 1984).

The 50 years of socialist rhetoric that claimed equality among all Poles has impacted the assessment of who is a suitable "referent other" for the people of this region. An acceptance of this ideology necessitates that all Polish citizens, even the political elite, are considered appropriate "referent others." The disconnect with the privileges that the political elite have has produced a sense of relative deprivation, which generates resentment and distrust of the "government" and those who have power in the system. This condition exists in Goria under the new political system as well. The prosperity that was promised by the leaders of the Solidarity Union has reached only a small number of individuals, those in positions of power. The appearance of broken promises and the inability of the "ordinary" man to assess how to effectively maneuver in this "new" system compound the sense of deprivation.

This brings us to the final basis of government distrust, a lack of control over the system of government and power (Kolarska-Bobinska, 1989). The citizens of Goria, despite the vote, seem to continue to feel a lack of control. Interestingly, the lack of control is often blamed on "the people" and their interaction with the government. When a middle-aged farmer in Mokarszy proposed that it was possible that Walesa would return to office at a further date, his daughter exclaimed "Oh no, never that." Her father responded with "You shouldn't be so quick, Irena; you never know what the people will do." Another example came from a young college student, who was frustrated with the first round of election voting. She told me that she did not understand how all "those people" voted for Kwasniewski, the post-communist candidate. She said "I have no more control over my government now than I had during communism."

Distrust Within the Community

Trust is relatively rare within the Goria community, but it varies depending on the type of relationship. Specifically, differences can be seen along dimensions of proximity and control (see Exhibit 12). The feeling of genuine *trust* is felt only for close family and good friends which includes a very small number of people. Neighbors, however, are highly distrusted, and this distrust is amplified for community members in positions of authority. The higher the authority, the lower the level of trust, among those individuals that are seen to be in the same "group" or community. The reason often given for this distrust is a sense of social injustice. Butler (1991) found that trust is associated with a sense of fairness. Goria residents, when I asked questions about trust, frequently told me "I don't trust him because it is unfair that he. . . . " They filled in the blank with things like "takes bribes," "holds a position in the power stratum," and "shows off with his new money."

Distrust is so pervasive, and it is so linked to feelings of social injustice, that individuals who are not viewed as referents are given more trust, in general, than neighbors, and particularly neighbors in positions of authority. These neighbors are viewed as relevant, and their activities are well known by the Goria citizens. Both of these issues may contribute to the relatively lower sense of distrust expressed for Poles who live in other regions than for Poles who live in Goria. One important caveat to this analysis is that Poles who have moved out of Poland for financial reasons are highly distrusted. This will be discussed in further detail in reference to Mr. Sroka (see Chapter 7).

Similar to Goria, Hann (1985) found in Wislok that relations between neighbors there were not particularly good. "In fact" Hann observes, "the only close ties maintained by any of these families, inside or outside the cluster, are between families closely related to each other" (1985: 141). In addition, Hann documents cases in which individuals were not able to maintain good relations with extended family within the village because of prosperity or social differentiation by some other means.

Two women convey this reality in the Goria region. The first is Anna, who is in her mid-thirties Anna works at Lockem in the assembly area. Her daughter died recently, and the response of neighbors demonstrated, she said, how she could not trust them. She said that no one had come by the home to give his or her condolences after it happened. It was only after several months had passed that the neighbors came by to visit her. Anna told me "All my neighbors wanted was to see what I had bought with the money we got from our daughter's death." It is a custom in this region of Poland to give money after the loss of an immediate family member. Extended family and organizations to which the family belongs give the money.[14] When I spoke to Anna's fellow workers about the death of her daughter, they told me that they had not gone by to see Anna because they thought that she would want time to grieve. Anna rejected this explanation, when I posed it to her hypothetically, and preferred to accuse her neighbors and co-workers of more sinister motives. She said, "I simply don't trust them."

Exhibit 12. Levels of Trust by Referent's Proximity and Authority in Relation to "Self"

Distance in actual experience and control lowers the level of distrust. Residents of Goria are willing to place at least a general trust in strangers because they are not viewed as "referent others" (Adams, 1963; Festinger, 1954; Kulik & Ambrose, 1992) and thus justice comparisons do not apply. This is particularly true with foreigners from Western countries. Kulik and Ambrose (1992) found that individuals select person (s) or group (s) for comparison based on (a) the perception that the referent is relevant, and (b) whether there is access to information about the referent. The determination of relevance of comparison generally follows the principle that individuals select referents that are similar to themselves (Adams, 1963; Festinger, 1954). Therefore, in this case foreigners are not viewed as relevant referents nor is there adequate information about them.

Referents Position of External Authority		Near (Family)	Semi -Near (Neighbors)	Semi- Distant (Poles)	Distant (Foreigners)
High	1		6	5	2
Med	1		6	4	2
Low	1	4		3	2

Referent's Proximity to Self

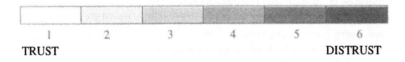

1	2	3	4	5	6
TRUST					DISTRUST

A second example, is Irena, a 21-year-old unemployed agriculture technician graduate. When I asked her whom she trusted, she said "No one. You cannot afford to trust anyone around here." She then hesitated and said, " well I trust my family." I asked her who she meant by "family" and she said "my mother, father, sister and brother." It is curious to note that Irena did not include in this her grandparents, who live in her home, and with whom she appears on the surface to have a good relationship. When I asked her about this omission, she said that some people can trust their grandparents and some people cannot. She did not identify where she fell within those two categories.

Distrust Within the Organization

One significant example of distrust at Lockem is the pervasive, reciprocal distrust between managers and their employees. The general problem was articulated by a participant in a manager's club meeting in Krakow which I attended. He was the managing partner of a Krakow consulting firm which specialized in Human Resource Management. He said:

> In the communist system, the very nature of it was based on a lack of trust. The general managers of these state owned factories must be party members. They were often brought in from outside the area where the factory was located. In order to develop a sense of safety, the manager would hire and promote members of his family and his friends. Often these people were incompetent for the jobs that they took on. The distrust by the competent employees of this set of events was natural. The communists repressed the good workers that were not party members. The managers did not have much history with the factory, and they were strangers to quite often an otherwise tight-knit group of people. They did not need to communicate.

His depiction of the relationship between managers and their employees is an extremely accurate representation of the situation at Lockem. None of the managers at Lockem, neither the old nor the new guard, were born in the region. Some of them have married women from this region, and all of them attempt, in discussions about their backgrounds, to establish some form of link to the area. One of the two vice-presidents, for example, said that he was from the mountains so he understood the people here. He neglected to point out, in this representation, that he is not from this region, but from a different mountain area in a different part of Poland. This fact, however, was very important to the other employees of the factory. The lower level workers say "He is not from here," about all of the management staff at Lockem. This sense of distrust operates in the organization similarly to the way it functions in the general community. Only very close co-workers are trusted, and all other employees are distrusted. Employees say that they have to be very careful about what they say or it may get back to management. They talk of spies, and they even profess a fear of gossip, since the gossip may spread to management. Unfair distribution of pay, benefits, work, power, and opportunity are mentioned as reasons for the distrust of these individuals. Equity theory identifies that distress will occur if individuals perceive their relative inputs (contributions and attributes) to outcomes (rewards) does not favorably compare with the inputs to outcomes ratio of a referent other (Walster, Walster & Berscheid, 1978; Adams, 1965; Martin & Murray, 1983). In addition, Walster et al. (1978) argue that individuals will attempt to restore equity by requesting an increase in their outcomes, or by decreasing their inputs. It is the second approach that is most common in Lockem. The result of the inequity, however, is a distrust of the system and the managers who promote it and resentment for the employees who receive the rewards.

In addition to unfair distribution of resources, a history of poor and inaccurate communication has also created this climate of distrust. The *means* used in the distribution of rewards and power, through the system of *kumoterstwo*, is also a source of distrust and resentment. Power is not distributed based on achievement of members, but on ascription through social networks (see Chapter 5).

Sztompka maintains that the most important reason for the high level of distrust in Polish society is "uncertainty, insecurity, ambiguity, [and] opaqueness in the 'life-world' of post-communist people" (1995b: 26). My data suggest that social injustice is also a significant factor in generating a "culture of distrust" in Goria. It appears that the communist system generated a climate of distrust, but that the sense of social injustice continues and that the current environment of insecurity and instability actually enhances this climate of distrust.

RESPONSIBILITY

Experience soon showed clearly enough that it was better to sit off in a corner than to show initiative (Kurczewski, 1992: 158 quoting from Kazimierz Wyka in 1945).

The experience of the Polish people that prompted Wyka's observations was expanded in the years that followed the war. The result of the political alienation and the widespread practice of kumoterstwo was a general abdication of responsibility that can be seen at all levels of society. Kurczewski indicates that the source of what he calls the "Polish anomie" is not rising aspirations or rapid changes but the social structure that enables "individuals not to answer for their behavior, and that rids groups and communities of responsibility for the state of affairs that touches them directly" (1992: 165). The acceptance of "social peace" and "welfare security" as it was espoused by the political elite was tantamount to relinquishing the role society plays in unifying its people, in effect, giving up this role to the political system (Marody, 1987). One example of this mentality is the up-keep of public property. In the socialist state theoretically public property was the responsibility of everyone, but in practice it was badly neglected. The quality manager at Lockem, Mr. Litwa, told me, "In the old system responsibility simply disappeared." This attitude is seen in "face" or external appearances that Poles present. The churches described in Chapter 3 represent one example of this. Public buildings and exteriors to all buildings tend to be bleak and plain. Only the interiors of these buildings and the private spaces of Polish life are adorned. This represents a further example of differentiation between public and private spaces.

One explanation for this reluctance to assume responsibility is that rights in the socialist system were given to those who dutifully fulfilled obligations to the government, and not for assuming duties and obligations to oneself, others, or even to God (Kurczewski, 1992). This practice, coupled with the Polish history of oppressive political systems whose objectives run counter to the needs of the Polish people, has given rise to a general condition of learned helplessness (Marody, 1987; Kolarska-Bobinska, 1989).

Learned helplessness is a generally lowered state of functioning that results from experiences of uncontrollable events (Zimmerman, 1990) and a faulty connection between behaviors and results (Seybolt

& Roney, 1994b). The state of learned helplessness is characterized by a "giving up" response. This response results in the generalization from the original activity to later activities, and Seligman suggests (1975, 1981) that motivational and behavioral deficits and emotional withdrawal can occur when individuals experience learned helplessness.

Abramson, Seligman, and Teasdale (1978) extend Weiner's work (1974) on learned helplessness as an attributional phenomenon by differentiating between internal and external causes of helplessness. Internal causality relates to issues of inability, lack of effort, task difficulty, or bad luck resulting from failure experiences. External causality relates to issues of environmental control. The importance of the distinction between internal and external causality lies in the potential to identify distinguishable effects and interventions. Why people give up, or engage in decremental responding, can be viewed as the outcome of logical thinking which is based on calculations about the individual's own abilities or about the degree of insurmountability of the environment (Seybolt & Roney, 1994b).

This sense of learned helplessness has been reinforced by the reluctance to accept responsibility (Marody, 1987). Marody describes the values that arise from these conditions.

> In a situation where one suspects the existence of learned helplessness among a considerable section of society, the absence of unemployment and the lack of responsibility for one's own fate become important values (1987: 147).

These values are pervasive at Lockem. Fear of unemployment is coupled with the futility of assuming responsibility. Maria captured the general sentiment of the workers with whom I spoke. She said, "They will lay-off who they want; it doesn't matter how hard we work or what we do."

This reluctance to assume responsibility has turned the place of employment into an extension of the domestic workplace. "One's salary may come to be regarded as a benefit payment which is due merely for turning up at work; the latter is associated with a transfer of energy to areas of activity outside employment" (Marody, 1987: 151). This sentiment is expressed at Lockem. Iranusz, a quality inspector, said during a discussion about what was needed at the factory, "There has to be discipline. Where is it? There is such a problem in Poland with discipline." Anna responded, "The work is like the salary." Anna was reflecting a common view that the salary was so low that there could be no expectation of "discipline." Teresa, in a separate conversation, was talking to me about the television sets that were awarded for employee perfect attendance. She said, "We must pay 40% of our salaries to the government for ZUS (the Polish Social Security system). This should give me the right to be ill." Finally, Agnieska told me:

> I do not think that the new owner wants to make salaries higher. Everyone says he pays for coming here, but not for work. He does not give us enough money for the work we do, only enough to get us to show up to work. There is only discipline here. I don't like working here; there is not satisfaction. I work here only because there is nowhere else to go. I used to like working here.

A second explanation for the low acceptance of responsibility may be found in the discussion of equity and relative deprivation theories (Adams, 1965; Crosby, 1984; Homans, 1961; Martin & Murray, 1983; Walster, Berscheid, & Walster, 1976) from the previous section of this chapter. These theories describe social distancing and reduction of inputs as potential consequences of a sense of injustice. Assuming responsibility could be one of the methods used to restore equity. Therefore, the sense of injustice can prompt the employees at Lockem to refuse to invest more in the context, and thus refuse to assume further positions of authority.

A final explanation for the relinquishing of responsibility is a strong pressure to conform, coupled with the practice of kumoterstwo. One effect of this pressure is to mute the desires of employees to accept responsibility, particularly when it is accompanied with an elevation in title. Though individuals would like to take on increased responsibility and the pay that is assumed to follow it, they fear formalization of this process. An elevated title, for example, would alter the social status which the person holds, because various assumptions are made by the group about how this promotion was obtained. Kennedy (1992) observed a general reluctance to assume positions of authority in Polish society. He found that the individual mobility process has been

> gradually deprived of substantive meaning both for the individual and society in Poland . . . with the consequence that qualificational

mobility ceased to become a desirable goal of action. Instead, a good family life or interesting private life rather than getting ahead became a central life goal" (Kennedy, 1992: 296).

Kostera (1995) notes that organizational "borders" within the socialist system were extended to include the political networks necessary to accomplish even basic company business. Despite the maneuvering of managers in the world outside the organization, however, these managers did not wish promotions outside their organizations (Kostera, 1995). Employees must therefore weigh the potential benefits of the increased responsibility with the problems that will be associated with it. Without a marginal benefit that exceeds the costs, the individuals will strongly object to taking on more responsibility, even when it will mean more interesting work and better pay. The impetus for this conflict is the topic of the rest of this chapter.

INDIVIDUALISM AND COLLECTIVISM: THE STRUGGLE BETWEEN OPPOSING CULTURAL TENDENCIES

Double Standards

The perceptions and behaviors of one worker at Lockem sets the stage for our discussion of the struggle between individualism and collectivism. Janusz stands out among his co-workers. He is nice-looking with blond hair, and he looks more like a German than a Pole. At 30 years of age he does not have the "lived a hard life" look that so many of the workers in the factory have. His confidence and ingenuity set him apart as well. He works outside of Poland on a temporary basis in the summer doing construction work in Germany and Austria. This practice of working outside of Poland was common during communism. Mostly, the people in this region worked in Czechoslovakia or Hungary doing a variety of jobs, including construction, truck driving, auto mechanics, baby-sitting, and even engineering work. New restrictions of movement have made it more difficult for Poles from this region to go to work in these countries. Jobs in Western Europe are rare also, because of newly imposed work restrictions implemented to curb the flow of East Europeans who have contributed to the already high unemployment of Western Europe after the fall of communism. Janusz says that he knows he is fortunate to have this work.

Janusz is very inquisitive about the world outside of his own. Questions he would ask me ranged from what was the pay in American factories (a very frequent question from other workers in the factory), to whether it was true that American Indians lived in Utah, to what languages were spoken in Northern America. His approach to asking these questions was as if they were part of a stream of consciousness. He would often interrupt conversations I was having with his co-workers to ask these questions, even though they were unrelated to the topic I were discussing with others.

Janusz is well liked by his co-workers. Teresa, Beata and Maria, who are all in their forties, speak of him fondly, like a favorite son. They voice a respect for Janusz, noting his education (he has a technical school degree in auto mechanics) and his competency in the work that he does. Janusz was born and has lived all his life within 5 kilometers of the factory. He lived with his in-laws for several years after his marriage, but has since bought his own home in the same village. His wife works as a librarian and had recently gone to Krakow to get further education in her chosen field. Both the house and the education in Krakow require money that was not plentiful in this region during these times. His work in Austria and Germany made a tremendous difference in his ability to afford these things.

Janusz's longevity in the area has not promoted the strong commitment to the land that I heard from many of the other workers. A union announcement had been posted in a display case on the wall near the front door early one day. Teresa had run into the union representative as she was picking up some boxes in another side of the hall, and he had told her that the announcement stated that the union had agreed to a shutdown of the factory during several days before and after Christmas. These days would be unpaid for those who did not have vacation time to use. The information that Teresa had, however, was incomplete as to the number of days and which days they would be. Speculation within the group was rampant. Several of them thought that the factory would be closed for entire two weeks of the holiday period. The incident provoked a discussion around the worktable that spilled over to the surrounding groups. The weight of this shutdown loomed heavy, and the workers' conversations led to their anticipation of another round of layoffs.

It is in this atmosphere that I asked Janusz if he would consider leaving the area to get a job. He said:

> This is a good option for people with no family or house. I would be
> willing to leave this region if I could sell my house. I am not very
> connected to this region.

I asked him if he thought it was common for people in this region to not
be connected to the area. He said, "I think my response is unusual." He
then reflected for a moment and said, " It would be easier for the
younger people." I then asked if his wife shared his willingness to leave
the area. He said with a chuckle "It would be worse for my wife, but I
could work on her."

Janusz is more confident in his abilities than many of the other
workers to whom I spoke. At one point I asked him if he thought things
would be better in the future.[15] He said:

> I think many will be lost. I cannot say that things will be better. There
> have been many bad things happening before Christmas. But, I am an
> optimist. Everyone will be afraid of the layoffs. But, I am not modest.
> Someone has to stay here and I think one of them will be me.

His education, though it is not directly related to the work he does (he
says that he only uses it a bit), provides him a certain degree of
confidence. Janusz's co-workers view education as an asset that
enhances status, but it does not necessarily imply greater skill. This is
common throughout the factory. Education is assumed to be something
that elevates a person in status.[16] There is, however, no assumed
correlation between the education and the skills of an individual. This,
therefore, is the meaning that is expressed in the numerous statements
made in the factory that "only a person with education" can do this or
that job, and "only a person of education" for example should hold the
presidency of the country or the company. It is status that they are
applying to this meaning, not the skills that education provides.

A connection of education with pay is not assumed by most of the
employees either. The Lockem factory recently initiated a new
employee pay scheme that would pay workers with more education a
higher wage even when they are performing the same job. Most of the
employees I spoke to strongly objected to this plan, but Janusz saw it
differently. When I asked him if he thought it was fair for people doing
the same job to get different pay when one person has a higher
education, he told me "I do not think it is fair that a more educated
person make the *same* amount of money as everyone else. I heard that

they were going to change the pay policy here, and I think this is a good idea."

Janusz has been able to maneuver effectively within the constraints of the world in which he lives. He is able to gain favor with the management of the factory, while maintaining membership in the group. Those who know him make allowances for the means by which he sets himself apart from the others because he has compromised his individual goals for the group when it impacted them. Those that do not know this side of Janusz do not make allowances for him, and others within the factory had difficulty with his recent promotion.

The purchase of a new assembly machine was a major concern for the assembly workers of the blue and yellow groups. The new machine signaled the potential end of their positions, and certainly an end to work as they have known it for so long. It was brought to the factory to replace their jobs and for many months it sat in a corner of the assembly hall in which they worked. Long before an official announcement was made about the machine, the workers knew that it would replace the work of ten employees. Two employees would be required to operate the machine, but the workers in the blue and yellow groups assumed that it would not be one of them. They said that it would require someone with more education.

It was an understandable assumption. The machine is modern looking, especially compared to the machines that these workers have worked on for so long. It is square in shape with glass covering the top half of the machine so that a monitor could see many work processes that are performed by the machine. The machine was covered with parts of the packing material, plastic and tape, for many of the months that it sat there. It looked as though it was partially exposed to inspect and then left for the final unpacking at a later time. The instructions on the machine are in Italian, and it has a computer panel on the outside for programming and monitoring the machine. Everything about it seemed out of place in the assembly hall, the intricacy of the machine, the glass, the modernness, the language on the instruction panel.

When the machine was finally assembled, management selected two employees from a separate production hall to operate the machine. One of them, Grzegorz, had held a technical job, fixing and adjusting the assembly and other production machines. The other was Janusz. Janusz told me that the supervisor of his department simply asked him if he wanted the job and he said "yes." He assumed that an increase in pay would come with it, but he was disappointed to learn later that it did not. The transition to the new machine was difficult for Janusz. Grzegorz had long been considered a "favorite" of management. He was a former communist party member, and would later be one of the employees selected for the television sets. For Janusz, however, the visible change in his "rank" generated tremendous stress for him and resentment among many of the co-workers. Members of the blue and yellow groups openly objected to Janusz's promotion. They told me that they had employees who worked in their production hall with equal education. They felt it was unfair to bring someone from a different production department when employees were being laid-off in their group.[17] In addition, Janusz had to deal with constant machine failures, what amounted to lower pay than he had previously received, and an inflexible work schedule, making it difficult for him to take time off in the summer to work in Germany and Austria.

One day I watched Janusz operate the machine. He was by himself that day, and I asked him if he was able to run the machine on his own. He told me that he was not able to do it all by himself; it required two people at all times. So I watched as he would shut the machine off and move the parts around and then turn the machine back on again. While I was there, Janusz was constantly pushing the buttons on the control panels, changing the flow of the machine and frequently stopping it. He told me that working on it alone slowed the process down a lot. He had just told the manager about this, but the manager had said that he should just go back and do the best he could.

In addition to moving completed parts out of full bins, Janusz was dealing with a serious quality problem with the machine. The machine rejects parts that it is not able to assemble properly. The machine in what was seemingly a random pattern, was rejecting the parts, but the rate was quite high. Every time a part would fall off the rejection side of the belt, it would crash to the floor; we would hear it and turn. Janusz frequently went over to pick up the rejected part and inspect it. This went on constantly throughout the time that I was talking to Janusz. I asked him what he would do with all the parts that were being rejected by the machine. He said that a person was supposed to fix them. It required putting glue on the area where the grooves were and then screwing the mate to it. He said "I will fix the parts, but I need time to do it."

Several hours later I saw that Janusz had moved over to a tool that was attached to a table against the far wall, under the windows. The table was next to the new area where the manual assembly work was being done since the machine was set up. Janusz was fixing the parts that the machine had rejected earlier. He put glue on the rivets and then screwed the two parts together. After this, he affixed one side into the tool, clamped down the bar onto the other side and turned a very large metal bar that effectively screwed the two parts together very tightly.

Janusz was clearly frustrated with the difficulties of his new job, and he became nostalgic for the "old" way. He told me that it used to be that he could make a pretty good wage here. When he worked on his own, he could produce a high volume of parts. Since he was paid by the part, he was able to bring home pretty good money. I asked him about the norms, production targets set by the engineers. The norm was set as a rate that a person should make for a given part in an eight-hour shift. When the parts are assembled in groups, they generally work to the total of the individual norms for each person. This is the way they are evaluated by management, as well. Janusz had in fact told me in the past that they do not work over the norm that is set for the part because it causes the norm to go up. Many times I witnessed groups that slowed down their work as they approached the norm. Some groups even stopped work as much as an hour before their quitting time when the norm was reached. Janusz told me that when he works in a group, he never exceeds the norm. It was a sort of agreement that they had among themselves. He confirmed that the reason they did this was to keep the norm from going up. If the norm goes up, they have to work harder "every" day. All of the assembly groups that I spoke to at Lockem had this same agreement. Janusz told me, however, when he works by himself he does not have this agreement, so he can work has hard as he can to make some more money. I asked him why the group did not work together to make more money as a whole. He looked puzzled at this question, and then he said, "It just isn't done that way. No one wants to work harder than they have to."

Individualism or Collectivism?

Janusz's confusion seems to stem from the different, and in actuality, conflicting assumptions under which he is working. When in a group, he works under the assumption that if one works harder, the norm is raised for everyone. Group norms necessitate a particular course of action when working in the group.[18] When Janusz works by himself, however, the rules are different. In this situation, his self-serving desire to increase his income dictates that he expend more effort for the immediate gain that it will produce: more money. One of the greatest forms of resistance to transformation at Lockem is rooted in this intense struggle that is waged at the heart of Polish society, and within each individual. Desires for individual success and fortune that are strong in the Polish spirit are constantly limited by a strong social norm rooted in collectivist mentality. This section will explore the prevalence of both individualism and collectivism in the Goria region. I will detail what happens in numerous cases, like Janusz's, when the employees at Lockem struggle with these opposing tendencies. I will then discuss how this context sheds a new light on the current organizational literature on the individualism-collectivism continuum. Finally, I will examine deviance from group norms and social adjustments that are made in toleration of socially deviant behavior generated by this conflict.

Individualism—Looking out for number one. Frustration with the individualistic mentality of the peasants in the Goria region was voiced one day at Lockem in a Solidarity union meeting. The union representatives were talking about the low pay and reductions in social benefits that the employees were experiencing. These representatives were frustrated with their inability to negotiate effectively with the new owner, and they were considering their options for the future. One of the members mentioned that they might have to go on strike, but another acknowledged that in the present climate that option was very unlikely. I asked him why. He explained that:

> In my opinion Sroka would have no chance if this factory was in any one of the many Polish cities. Here 70% of the workers are *just* peasants. Peasants are farmers that work in the factory to supplement their income. If we had more "pure" workers we would have gone on strike by now.

I asked what was the difference between peasant and "pure" workers. He said:

> It is a problem with the source of income. The peasants have income from the farm *and* the factory. The pure workers have only the factory. In my personal case, I am a pure worker, and I have only my salary to support my family. It is not enough. The peasants have divided loyalties. They are not educated, and they don't care for

doing a good job. This is bad for the other workers. They are not involved with what is going on in the factory.

He felt that they would be able to get the votes for a strike if the peasants did not have their farm income, and they had to rely solely on the factory income for survival. This segregation between public (the factory) and private (the farm) life permeates Polish mentality and is a manifestation of the conflict between the socialist system and the traditions of the indigenous Goria residents. Each individual exists simultaneously in both worlds and must take into consideration the needs and benefits from both in his/her actions. The private side of peasant farming has generated a strong individualistic mentality. Marody (1987) has identified a trend toward placing more importance on the private sphere of life. Individualistic rather than communal activities are increasingly viewed as the best means for meeting both physical and existential needs. Turning inward utilizes the individualistic side of Polish society, at the expense of the collective side, which is expressed by the union representative.

The system of action-sets for power and information access provides a vehicle for acting on individualistic tendencies. These networks are dyadic relationships, established to benefit the individuals who participate and other individuals along a direct line of connected dyads. The purpose of these relationships is for individual gain rather than collective advantage. The system of kumoterstwo, which frequently uses action-sets to dispense favoritism and privileges, is a good example of how action-sets manifest individual interests. If collective concerns are impacted by these relationships, it is of a secondary importance. Wnuk-Lipinski claims that individualism is a tenet of a long-standing tradition.

> In the traditional system individuals exercised their freewill within the limits of Christian ethics which provided the axiological standards of self-realization. If traced far enough back, this value system would probably be found to stem from the ethos of the nobility (1987: 164).

This strong sense of individualism is seen outside of the farm community as well. At the Krakow meeting of business managers we were discussing examples of "unofficial" methods available to get things accomplished. What emerged from the discussion was an unspoken knowledge, a sort of "everyone knows that," that all the meeting participants seemed to share. One participant gave a good illustrative example of this shared "fact." He knew a museum manager who needed some renovation done on a livery stable which was part of the museum complex. The manager calculated that using the maintenance staff that he employed, at their current rate of work, it would take four years to renovate the stable. He did not have four years to do this task. So he called the group of maintenance workers together and asked them what to do. They asked whether this job should be done on company time or on their own time. He said whichever they preferred. They said that if they could do it on their own time, it would take four months to do it. The manager would pay the workers the set amount that he had budgeted for the renovation. They agreed, and it was done in four months.

Working for individual gain is a very common practice in Poland. This individualistic approach to life is frequently not appreciated by others, however. In a conversation I had with Jerzy about the changes in Poland, he told me that the behavior of government officials was not in the interests of the "collective."

> I am not against the changes, but the factories have all been sold to foreigners for basically nothing. For instance, they are only selling the best factories in Poland to the foreigners for very little money and they are leaving the rest for the Poles. The politicians are getting rich from every transaction. Recently they sold the very profitable cigarette factory in Krakow to a foreign firm. This is how it is done, there is a new government every 2 to 3 months. They are just there to try to get as rich as possible from the foreign investment, the money paid to make the sale of the factories etc. work, and then they leave. We have new governments all the time. They are only interested in making as much as they can, and then getting out. They are not interested in the future of Poland.

The residents of Goria also tend to prefer decentralized government. This is partially a factor of trust, local government is easier to "keep an eye on" than a centralized government, but given the Polish history of kingdoms with localized control (see Chapter 2), it seems to extend further. In a conversation with a group of young people from the Goria community, Wojciech had given me a number of reasons why a centralized government was a problem. When I attempted to confirm his position by asking him if he thought local control would be better than central government, he said with great conviction "Oczywiscie" ("Certainly it would").

Collectivism—All for one and one for all. Jokes are an important vehicle for Poles to address the confusions, frustrations, and inconsistencies of their lives with a good long laugh. Polish jokes are often political in nature, and typically they contain very dark, almost morbid humor. One Polish joke captures an important aspect of the Polish mentality. During my repeated visits to Poland I have been told this joke on several occasions. Each time the Pole who told me the joke, and the other Poles who were present to hear it, roared with laughter. This joke clearly hits a chord in the Polish experience.

A reporter visits the devil in hell to get an in-depth view of the conditions there. The devil shows the reporter around. The reporter notices that there are a series of large pits with guards posted around each of them. He asks the devil what they are used for. The devil says that inside each pit are the people from a different nation that have joined him here in Hell. The reporter then asked what the guards were for. The devil said that they were posted to make sure that the people in the pits did not get out and escape to the surface and out of hell. The reporter walked along the rows of pits and noticed one that had no guards posted. He asked the devil why. The devil said that this was the pit for the Polish people, but he did not need to post guards outside this pit because every time someone tries to escape the other Poles in the pit pull him back down again.

This joke captures a prevalent theme of Polish reality, that Poles are their own worst enemies. It also identifies a predominant and important aspect of the Polish society, a collectivist orientation. The belief is that no one individual should rise above the others, "We all should be equal, even if it is equal in hell." This is an important indication of a collectivistic value system which is widespread in Goria and throughout Poland.

Mr. Sroka expressed one example of a collectivist orientation. He had told me that he knew there was widespread unhappiness about some of his policies. His explanation for this discontent was that

Poles are always rebellious. You can go back in history and see that they have continuously rebelled. When there is a common enemy, they unite and fight.

In opposition to the authors cited in my discussion of individualism (i.e., Wnuk-Lipinski, 1987; Hann, 1985; Marody, 1987), Arsenberg (1963) identified a highly collective nature of the peasants of north eastern Europe. Arsenberg describes this area as "a countryside of endlessly repeated villages, without nomads" (1963: 96) that are typical of this part of the world. In part, Arsenberg equates the homogeneity of villages with the interdependence of the church and the village government. This interdependence and the associated value systems that reinforced each other, generated a climate of cooperation, conformity, and "congregational management of one's fellows" (Arsenberg, 1963: 69).

Both Gorlach (1995) and Kurczewski (1982) also indicate that religious and traditional influences promote collectivism within Polish society. Kurczewski's discussion of Polish resistance to foreign oppression points to the same Polish characteristic that Mr. Sroka was expressing in his justification for employee resistance

> The fundamentals of the doctrine upheld for home use were in agreement with the basic features of the popular social teachings of the Church which were in favour of social solidaritism, and with the Polish national tradition which as a result of the struggle for independence in the 19th and 20th centuries developed a culture of national unity in face of an external enemy (1982: 22).

The strong belief in egalitarianism (see Chapter 5) has also helped sustain collectivism in Goria. This egalitarianism leads to an opposition to all forms of social differentiation, leading to the sentiment implied in the joke, "We are in this together, equally" (Kolarska-Bobinska, 1989; Bojar, 1992). Teresa expressed one example of egalitarianism, as an indictment of Walesa's presidency. She told the story of Lech Walesa's daughter.

> She is 16 years old, and just last week she was awarded a grant to dance in the ballet. It is for the best school for ballet in the country. She was not the only young girl who was awarded this grant, but she was one. It was supposed to be a grant for the most capable kids. I do not think this is fair. There are many clever children who could have received these grants. Walesa can afford to educate his daughter. There are so many clever kids who can not afford it. I think they should only give the money to families who could not send their kids

to school otherwise. As it is, they give the money only to those who already have enough.

Teresa is not expressing a belief in egalitarianism based on equality of "things," rather she, as with many others in Goria, expresses a belief in equality of "opportunity." A second example of this mentality arose when I met with a group of village people. They were expressing the view that everyone should be guaranteed a job and a decent wage. They phrased it as "Everyone should be equal." I asked them what they would do in their "ideal world" if someone chose not to work hard. Irena answered, "That is different." Her father, Miroslaw, added, "That is up to them. They can go on the street and live in slums if they don't want to work; it is up to them. When we say equal, we mean equal opportunity."

Finally, the political ideology of the communist state espoused values of egalitarianism and fulfillment in life through the "collective." The ideology of this regime emphasized usefulness to the broader community and subordination to the group (Wnuk-Lipinski, 1987). To the extent that this "communist culture" penetrated the psyche of the Gorians, it has also contributed to creating the ethos of collectivity. One of the participants of the Krakow managers' meeting saw a connection between the political influences for conformity and the reluctance to assume responsibility, which was introduced earlier in this chapter.

> It really comes down to self motivation. The communist system did not want people to stick out. Thus they have been trained to not take on responsibility because this may cause them to stick out above the other people.

The evidence (see Chapter 5) points to "real" socialism having an opposite effect than its ideology envisioned. The circumvention of the system used by the common people, the church, and even the party, highlights the ever-present influence of the individualistic spirit of the Polish people.

Individualism and collectivism. So, the question remains, are the employees at Lockem all in this together, or are they each looking out only for themselves? The answer seems to be, both. Hann suggested that the resistance to the "external enemy" in Wislok came from both a sense of collective identity emphasized by the church and through "the persistence of private ownership which has made resistance practicable, as well as serving as its symbolic fulcrum" (1985: 12). The private ownership, a manifestation of individualism, was coupled, therefore, with collectivism encouraged by the church.

Referring back to the example of Janusz that began this chapter, individualistic and collectivistic orientations are expressed by the same person, performing the same job in two different contexts. He had learned to skillfully adjust his behavior so that he can address his desire to achieve personal gain, in instances where this is possible, without putting him in conflict with the collective. Janusz just as easily shifts, while working within the group, to lower productivity so as not to exceed the norm. He is able to justify this behavior because it is for the benefit of the "whole." From my repeated discussions with Janusz about this, he did not appear to see any contradiction in his behavior. It is simply expedient and wise to be looking out for his own interests in one situation, and looking out for the interests of the group in another. The coexistence of these two tendencies is clearly found in all the Lockem employees, to one extent or the other, although not everyone was able to as skillfully adjust his or her behavior to accommodate these conflicting tendencies as Janusz had done.

A New Conceptualization of Individualism-Collectivism

The juxtaposition of individualistic and collectivistic orientations in post-communist Poland generates a difficulty with applying the prevailing conceptualization put forth by Hofstede (1984), and others (i.e., Trompenaars, 1985; Stewart & Bennett, 1991). These authors seek to classify cultures along a linear continuum anchored by the opposing orientations; individualism and collectivism. Reykowski describes the forces acting in Poland in the present period.

> The processes that take place in post-communist countries are not unidirectional . . . there is an increase in the occurrence of individualist attitudes and opinions. People tend to take individualist positions in various spheres of life. But, there is also an opposite tendency to search for new opportunities for identification with a greater whole. The large increase in nationalism and religiosity seems to be the effect of this process. In cases of national and religious identification there is a high degree of militancy, intolerance of outgroups, strong ingroup bias and outgroup discrimination. This militancy is an indicator of an early stage in group development

suggesting that collectivist sentiments are on the rise. In addition, recent research data from Poland indicate that collectivist attitudes tend to recur. (1994: 247).

So how do we explain the coexistence, and even the growth, of individualistic and collectivistic orientations in light of the conceptualization presented by Hofstede and others? It appears that this representation of cultural orientations is simply not accurate in this context. As Reykowski (1994) implies, application of this linear conceptualization may be inappropriate in at least the post-communist countries and potentially in many others as well. The problem with assigning a country along this continuum—as in the case of Poland, for exampl—is where do you put it? A wealth of data exists on individualism-collectivism for many cultures, but very little research exists for Poland. Trompenaars (1994) is the exception. He classifies Poland as having relatively high individualistic tendencies, as it relates to "preferring individual decisions" (5th out of 38 countries) and "taking individual responsibility" (2nd out of 39 countries). My data support the high level of individualism as this classification indicates, but how then do I explain the highly collectivist tendencies that are also present in my data?

I propose a different way of looking at country orientation, one that allows for the coexistence of two seemingly contradictory tendencies in the same society, and even within the same individual, as was demonstrated in the case of Janusz at the beginning of this section. This representation takes into account that both of these orientations are extremely influential in dictating responses to external stimuli and daily routine. Exhibit 13 represents pictorially the traditional conceptualization of individualism-collectivism and the one that my data suggests.

Cultures are not easily classified, though we as researchers attempt to do so for purposes of scientific inquiry. Cultures are difficult to classify because people have an incredible capacity to maintain values that represent contingencies. The proposed conceptualization makes it possible to deal with the contingent nature of various cultural environments which may promote individualism and collectivism in the same environment.

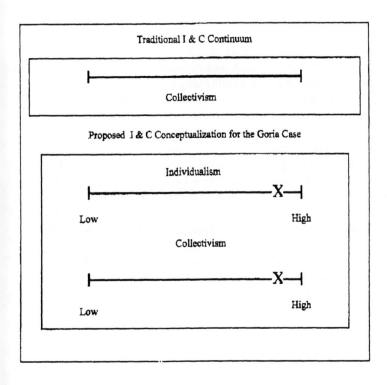

Exhibit 13. Individualism—Collectivism (I & C) Conceptualizations

Value systems adapt to accommodate contingencies, though one culture may adapt differently than another. The classic example is the value found in most all societies that murder is forbidden. Contingencies under which this becomes an acceptable, and even a desirable, behavior, however, differ between cultures. Many Western societies, for example, accept killing another person in self-defense, in times of war, and even to protect a much larger group. In contrast, some Asian societies accept infanticide of female babies. They do this to preserve traditions that have sustained the society, or to deal with new contingencies. One such new contingency is the "one child" rule in China. To accommodate this government directive and the traditional value that prefers male to female babies, the response has been an increase in infanticide of female babies. This practice is considered unthinkable, however, in many Western cultures.

The human capacity to shape its value systems to fit circumstances is great. The people of the Goria region have developed a system to deal with their external contingencies that promotes individualism and collectivism under different circumstances. What happens, however, when the environment goes through dramatic and pervasive change like that at Lockem and the Goria region in general? In the next section I will address what is happening in this factory when individualistic and collectivistic values collide. I will address how this society is sanctioning its members for behavior that is viewed as inappropriate in certain situations. I will also examine the relaxing of sanctions for behavior generally considered deviant, but acceptable based on the circumstances.

When Individualism Meets Collectivism, What Happens?

Political, economic, and social changes in Poland have been accompanied by changes in the way individualism and collectivism interact. In the communist era, individualism and collectivism seemed to form an unstable equilibrium. The two orientations found compatibility within the background of the political climate and clearly defined routes of opportunity. The action-sets, a manifestation of the strongly held individual values, and all activities aimed at furthering self-interests, found a balance with the forces to maintain collective identity and egalitarianism. The balance was an uneasy one, filled with resentment and difficulties. Within the existing external constraints, however, the balance was maintained.

This unstable equilibrium can be seen in a variety of social patterns of behavior. One example is reflected in the brief periods of strong collective behavior, particularly as a collective resistance against a powerful "other." The most recent examples of this were the Solidarity Union strikes of the early 1970s. The years that followed saw a growing unity of various social groups in Polish society bound by a common enemy, "the communist state." This unity culminated in the 1989 round table accords and the destruction of the communist state in Poland. Since then, however, the Polish people have been unable to maintain this collective identity. Growing divisions between groups and frequently changing governments contributed to the defeat of Walesa in 1995. Ironically, the forces of real socialism and Solidarity repressed the interests of individual groups, yet the resulting logic of reforms pressed for individual differentiation within these groups (Boyar, 1992).

The incredible power with which the Polish people are able to collectivize has historically been a short lived phenomenon. History has shown that Poles lose this sense of common purpose quickly after the common objective is attained. This may be explained by the strong individualistic orientation that lies temporarily dormant during these times of collective activity. Thus, one consequence of "individualism meets collectivism" is that collective activities of resistance are possible for only limited periods of time, and then they break down.

Wolf (1966) identified this characteristic among peasant groups. He said:

> In our discussion of peasantry two characteristics of social organization stand out: First, the strong tendency towards autonomy on the part of the peasant households; second, the equally strong tendency to form coalitions on a more or less unstable basis for short-range ends. In entering a coalition, the household cannot over commit itself. In operating within a coalition, it will show a tendency to subordinate larger, long-term interests to narrower, short-term ones. This combination of features has been understood clearly by those modern political figures who realize the potential power of a peasantry when aroused to common action, but are equally aware of its inability to remain organized both in action and afterwards, when the fruits of action are to be harvested (1966: 91-92).

Wolf also argues that political figures like Marx and his Russian practitioners, Lenin, Trotsky and Stalin, identified this potential of the peasantry. These leaders realized the peasants' capacity to form a powerful collective force toward the overthrow of the social order, but they also knew that what the peasantry really wanted was land. Once land was obtained, the peasants would no longer act as a unified force. These leaders acknowledged that the peasants would need to be controlled by the other classes, once their collective power was dispersed.

Czarniawska (1986) has identified the impact that this equilibrium has had on the psyche of the Polish people. She discusses what she calls a "system myth." The myth involves an image of collective character. The Polish history of "dramatic events" and resistance to much stronger enemies, coupled with the inability to survive autonomously for any length of time, has generated pride and disappointment. Czarniawska points to failed attempts at democracy, for example the period between 1652 and 1764 before the partitions of Poland, as a defining period in Polish history. During this period the parliament, comprised of wealthy land owners, was paralyzed by the "liberum veto" which allowed individual members of parliament to veto virtually everything at the expense of the rest of collective. Czarniawska ties these events into the "system myth" by saying:

> All these experiences are summarized in a picture of a 'national' character,' which is additionally embellished by the influences of the Catholic religion, and by literature and art, especially from the Romantic period. The resulting image is that of a nation capable of the most heroic collective efforts in times of emergency, and incapable of living prosperously in quieter times, due to extreme individualism and a fatal tendency to anarchy. Looking at other countries, Poles tend to attribute their successes to what is lacking in the 'Polish character:' order, efficiency, method. Therefore the system myth (1986: 327).

Therefore, the first legacy of the dual-orientations of individualism and collectivism is a difficulty with collectivizing over long periods of time. The implications of this at Lockem will be discussed in Chapter 7.

Another popular Polish joke reflects another consequence of the co-existence of individualism and collectivism in this context, jealousy.

While fishing one day a Polish man caught a very special fish. It was a golden fish and it spoke to him. The fish offered the man three wishes. He would receive whatever he asked for in his wishes, but his neighbor will receive twice what he gets. The man agrees to this and asks for a house. The fish grants him his wish and he receives a nice house. But as he was walking home to his new house for the evening he noticed that his neighbor had a house twice as big. The next day the man asked the fish to grant his second wish. He asked for a Mercedes Benz. The fish granted him his wish. This day, as he was driving home in his new Mercedes he noticed that his neighbor had two new Mercedes parked in his front drive. The third day the man went back to the fish to request his last wish to be granted. He said, "for my third wish I want you to chop off my hand. . . .

This joke (told in the typical dark and morbid Polish humor) is representative of the extreme jealousy that Poles have of each other, and the lengths to which they will go to be certain that their members do not gain status (financial, social, political) or prosperity without paying a serious price. The man in the joke wants wealth for himself, but is willing to pay a horrible price to assure that his neighbor does not do better. The opposing internal signals that come from these very strong dual orientations generate what would appear to the outsider to be inconsistencies, paralysis, and even self-destructive behavior. This system, however, has maintained a balance between individualism and collectivism. The joke, as most jokes, exaggerates the phenomenon. In Goria, however, the consequences are similar, though not as extreme. An example of this process of working toward individual gain while sanctioning others for doing the same was observed at Lockem in a series of events that was prompted by a simple invitation to tea.

Tea and Jealousy

One day in early fall, I was speaking to several of the workers about their emotional commitment to the land and the region in which they all have lived their entire lives. Teresa's passion for this subject was strong; she called the land a "saintly thing," and said that it was deep in the souls of the people that live here. As she spoke I watched Beata and Maria nod their heads in agreement. All of the members of the group were listening intently to Teresa as they continued to assemble the small parts of a locking device.

The mood was peaceful and calm this day. Teresa remarked that the discussion of her commitment to the land reminded her of a song and then suddenly, without hesitation, she began to sing. I sat in amazement, and a bit of shock, as I listened to her beautiful voice, as she sang from her heart the sweet and melancholy melody. The amazement came less, however, from the beauty of the song than the inharmonious surroundings in which she was singing. As she sang, I could hear the sounds of the electric screwdriver, the forklifts, the movement of metal boxes, and the pouring of metal parts from one box to another, if I chose to hear it. But all I could hear was her song. It began:

> Highlander don't you miss. . . . . . .
> Highlander don't you regret leaving your home
> . . . . the wonderful forests
> . . . . the meadows
> Don't you miss the silver springs?
> Highlander don't you miss. . . . .
> Highlander come back to the mountains
> . . . . . come back to the green forests
> Highlander looks at the mountains and forests
> He wipes a tear with his sleeve
> Highlander has to leave because of the need for bread
> Highlander don't you miss. . . . .
> Highlander come back to the mountains and the green forests.

The rest of the group did not skip a beat as Teresa sang. They simply listened respectfully as she sang. I got the impression that this was nothing unusual.

Teresa is the self-designated spokesperson for her group of six workers, but she is not the leader of the group. That role is held by Beata, a beautiful woman, who is married to Grzegorz, who was the second person selected to operate the new assembly machine. Beata is the individual in the group who attends union meetings, and management also selects her when a representative of the group is required. Both Teresa and Beata are the same age, just over 40 years old. Beata is quiet and guarded, but Teresa is almost reckless in her willingness to "tell it like it is." Beata often warns her friend to watch what she says. Teresa is full of fables, tales and legends about just about everything. The first time I spoke to her she told me that the length of the summer meant that there would be winter after winter after winter (her prophecy was remarkably true this year). Another time she told me that her second name (Wanda) came from a tragic figure in Polish history who had committed suicide by jumping into the Wisla (the river that runs through the heart of much of Poland) rather than marry a German. She told me that her dedication was as strong as that of her namesake, but she was not as courageous. "I am too afraid of the water," she said. "I can't swim."

Teresa's husband, Miroslaw, owns the farm that he works, about 10 hectares. Miroslaw is an only son, so he took over the farm upon his marriage to Teresa. His parents live in the house with them, and they continue to work the farm with their son. They grow potatoes and other vegetables, as well as some types of beets, and hay for the livestock. They grow only for their family consumption, not for sale.

Teresa's stories and opinions and her penchant for talk is a source of amusement, discussion, and friendly ridicule among her co-workers in the factory. She is generally liked in the factory, but co-workers like to say with a laugh "Teresa likes to talk . . . " Joanna told me that she had gone to school with Teresa's sister. She laughed at how Teresa's sister talked almost as much as Teresa did.

After I had been visiting the factory for several months Teresa asked me to visit her at her home for tea. I eagerly accepted her invitation, and over the course of several conversations we finally settled on a date for this meeting. Earlier, she had mentioned that it would nice for the entire group to meet me away from work some time, so I did not know what Teresa had planned for this tea. When I arrived at her home I learned that she had simply invited me to visit with her and her family. She provided a full meal with soup, meat and potatoes, and cake for dessert. We talked for several hours, and she offered to take my family and me into the forest that they own to cut down a Christmas tree when the time came. The next time I saw Teresa at Lockem I thanked her for her hospitality.

Soon after my first visit to Teresa's home, she asked me not to tell anyone I had gone there, or about any future visits. She said that she did not want the rest of the group to think that she was trying to gain favor with "the American." The consequence that Teresa was trying to avoid, however, was already in motion. Soon after she asked me not to tell anyone about my visit, the rest of her group chose to stop answering more than basic questions, and some were even unwilling to talk to me

Exhibit 14. Conflicting Orientations in the "Tea and Jealousy" Example.

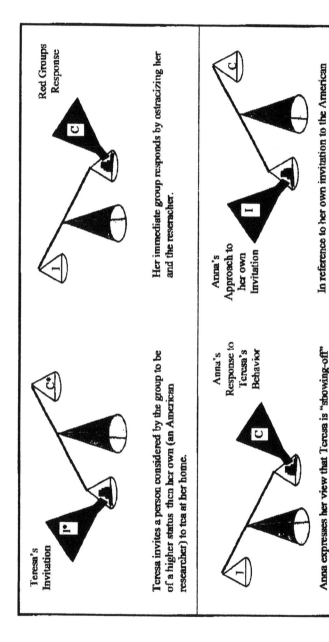

Teresa's Invitation

Teresa invites a person considered by the group to be of a higher status then her own (an American researcher) to tea at her home.

Red Groups Response

Her immediate group responds by ostracizing her and the researcher.

Anna's Response to Teresa's Behavior

Anna expresses her view that Teresa is "showing-off" and talking too much about having the American to her house. Anna says that Teresa deserves the ostracism.

Anna's Approach to her own Invitation

In reference to her own invitation to the American researcher, Anna says that she "welcomes the gossip" that she expects from her neighbors.

* I = Individualism, C = Collectivism

at all. Teresa reiterated several times, during subsequent conversations at the factory, that she did not want "anyone" to know I was coming to her house. I could tell there was extreme tension in the group, and Teresa became very quiet when I approached. She looked to be almost in pain, and when she could get my interpreter aside, Teresa would tell her a time that I could talk with her when the group was not around. So we arranged the Christmas tree excursion clandestinely. Teresa was comfortable and friendly away from work, but not when her co-workers were present. When I asked Teresa what the problem was, she simply told me again that she did not want anyone to know that I was meeting her away from work. I was unable to get her to give me a more detailed explanation.

Several weeks after my tea with Teresa, I asked Anna, who works in a different production hall from Teresa, if I could take her up on a previous offer to visit her home. I told her that I was particularly interested in meeting her without my interpreter because I found it quite easy to understand Anna's Polish and I was trying to improve my language proficiency. She said that this would be fine, but she did not want to go to a big deal like Teresa had done, just some cakes and some coffee at her house. I knew from the way that Anna phrased this that I was getting at the heart of the problem with Teresa's group, so I asked her about it.

She said that she had heard that my visit to Teresa's house was a big deal. It was evident from the conversation that she knew only about the first visit, and not the second visit. I asked Anna if she could think of a reason it was a problem for me to visit a person's home. I told her that I had sensed that there was a problem from Teresa's co-workers. Anna said that she thought that Teresa had been talking about my visit a lot and showing off about it. "Teresa likes to show off," she said:

> By Teresa's showing off, she may have appeared to think that she was a chosen one. Others don't like this. It is not a good thing for people to make themselves more important by appearing to associate with important people. This was not accepted by Poles. Poles are jealous about other's fortunes and they laugh at other's misfortunes.

I asked her if this is always true. Anna responded:

> We will help each other out a great deal, but when one person assumes a position of arrogance we quickly put them back in their

place by ostracizing them. This might be the problem with Teresa. Teresa talks too much, and if it is, she has brought it on herself.

I asked Anna if this would be a problem for her if I went to her house. She laughed and said, in a way that made me feel that she wanted the provocation that this would bring, "I would welcome any gossip from my neighbors." She told me that she would not talk about it like Teresa does, but she would welcome the "whispers."

Shifting Orientations

Jealousy is a manifestation of the collision that occurs when the actions of one member, in this case Teresa, conflict with the pressures of conformity to the group. Teresa chose to deviate from the accepted norms of behavior by inviting someone of a higher status (an American) to her house. To make things worse, she told people about it. The group's response was to sanction her for this. In addition, they sanctioned me and avoided any similar ostracism by retreating from lengthy conversation. An even more interesting contradiction is found in Anna's reaction to this set of events. Anna sets herself apart from Teresa by saying that "It will not be a big deal like at Teresa's." In addition, she supports the group sanctions by criticizing Teresa for "showing off" and "talking too much." She draws on cultural values to explain the group's response to Teresa's behavior. However, when I asked Anna if these values would compromise her, to the extent that she might not want me to visit her home, she turned quite defiant, apparently rejecting these values and challenging her neighbors "to talk." Exhibit 14 shows how the unspoken conflict between orientations is occurring in this example.

In a second example of shifting orientations I refer back to "Double Standards" that opened this section. Janusz had found a way to balance both of the opposing orientations by changing his behavior to accommodate the situation. As things began to change in the Lockem factory, the easy boundaries that defined the appropriate segregation of individualistic behavior from collectivistic behavior became blurred. Janusz found himself in a confusing and uncomfortable position as he accepted the promotion to work on the new assembly machine (see Exhibit 15). This action placed him in a conflict between his desire to accept the promotion and the reaction that doing this would bring from his co-workers, particularly the workers in his new work area.

Exhibit 15. Conflicting Orientations in the "Double Standards" Example.

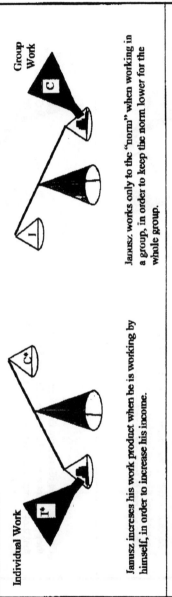

Individual Work

Janusz increses his work product when he is working by himself, in order to increase his income.

Group Work

Janusz works only to the "norm" when working in a group, in order to keep the norm lower for the whole group.

Janusz Accepts New Job

Janusz accepts a job with more responsibility, expecting more pay to accompany it.

Group Response

Other employees respond to Janusz's promotion by questioning why he was selected, resenting a person from a different hall taking the job, and by not accepting him into the social system of his new work

* I = Individualism,   C = Collectivism

Exhibit 16. Conflicting Orientations in the "Spies with Television Sets" Example.

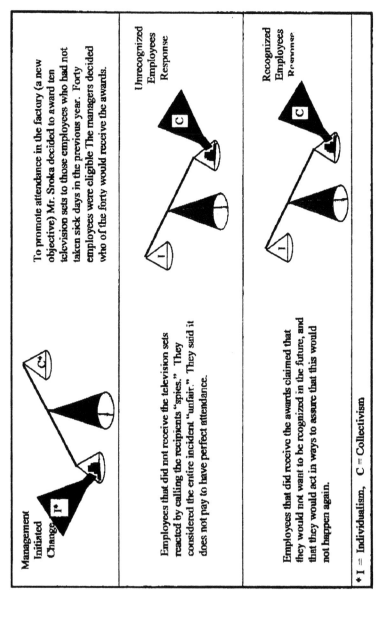

Management
Initiated
Change   I*

To promote attendance in the factory (a new objective) Mr. Sroka decided to award ten television sets to those employees who had not taken sick days in the previous year. Forty employees were eligible The managers decided who of the forty would receive the awards.

Unrecognized
Employees
Response

Employees that did not receive the television sets reacted by calling the recipients "spies." They considered the entire incident "unfair." They said it does not pay to have perfect attendance.

Recognized
Employees
Response

Employees that did receive the awards claimed that they would not want to be recognized in the future, and that they would act in ways to assure that this would not happen again.

* I = Individualism, C = Collectivism

Finally, if we look back at the "Spies with Television Sets" example (see Chapter 5), we can follow the same progression of changing influences and conflicting results. Exhibit 16 shows the conflicting orientations. In this case, management is attempting to instill individualistic behavior and a sense of personal responsibility. Yet the immediate response is collectively motivated backlash with counter-productive results.

The consequences of the juxtaposition of individualistic and collectivistic orientations present a conflict in the values of the regional traditions, the church, and the political ideology. This conflict of values generates a code of behavior that is separate from the espoused value system. Behaviors that are not considered in the espoused value system to be deviant are sanctioned as such because of this conflict. Things such as improving one's status, financial situation, or position, become unacceptable behavior and risk sanction from members of the community. The conflict also has the reverse effect. Behaviors that might be viewed as "deviant" by the members of the culture (for example stealing public property, refusing to work hard, or making "arrangements" through semi-legal means) is not subject to community censure. Both the sanctioning of behavior that is consistent with espoused values and the tolerance of deviant behavior serve to maintain social control, given the external control systems. Despite the replacement of the communist government in 1989, much of the political nature of Goria life remains (see Chapter 5). With it, kumoterstwo persists, and confusion over what the "new rules" are has made the perpetuation of these norms of social control even more important to societal functioning. Both forms of social control are seen at Lockem. I will conclude this section by examining each in more detail.

Socially unacceptable behavior. As two of the examples discussed above, "Tea and Jealousy" and "Spies with Television Sets" clearly demonstrate, deviance from generally accepted behavior will be sanctioned by members of the social group at Lockem. Behaviors such as increasing financial wealth or setting up connections with important people are not considered wrong. They are, in fact, considered viable and important goals for individuals. However, their enactment, in certain contexts, is seen to deviate too significantly from the norm established by the group. For the purpose of my discussion, a norm is "a belief shared to some extent by members of a social unit as to what conduct *ought to be* in particular situations or circumstances" (Gibbs,

1981: 7). Behavior, or the "appearance" of behavior, that does not conform to the norms is sanctioned through a variety of means, including derision, severing of action-set ties, and exclusion from social activities. In addition, individuals who are ostracized in the manner described become "fair targets" for gossip regarding a full range of their behaviors that extend far beyond the incident that prompted the sanction to begin with.

The sanctioning that is dispensed is a powerful tool for obtaining conformity in that it generally serves to force a change in behavior (Bacharach & Lawler, 1980). Its coercive nature, however, produces only short-term conformance. Sanctioned individuals tend to reject the power of the group to administer punishment for their behavior, and they will either hide their behavior, or in some other way circumvent the scrutiny of the group. Behaviors that warrant social censure include fraternizing with people with higher status, increasing education, increasing wealth, or assuming a position of authority. Individuals who choose to disregard the social norms may be relegated to a classification of "them" that gives rise to the distrust discussed earlier in this chapter. The distrust is reciprocal. Those people in Goria who have undergone censure cite the lack of authority by the sanctioning group, and a confirmation that they cannot be trusted.

Hann (1985) found that in the Wislok community censure occurred for acts of social differentiation as well. Several farmers chose to make significant advances in their farming techniques and thus improve their financial status in the community. Neighbors saw this as a reproach of traditional peasant egalitarianism. The farmers, therefore, were put continually on the defensive and were embarrassed about their accomplishments, but their wives paid a higher price in the community. Even family members within the community ostracized these women.

> I often heard them described as "chytre," meaning crafty and keen on material gain. It is they who are more isolated, who must pay the penalty for breaking with traditional values, while their husbands may gain from prestige." (Hann, 1985: 155).

A similar process was occurring in the Goria community. Genowefa and Witold present one example. Genowefa worked at Lockem. When I was looking for a room to rent, Maria told me that Genowefa had an extra room in her house. I rented a room from her and her husband, Witold, one night a week in the cold winter months. The room I rented was kept extremely cold; Genowefa and her husband turned the heat entirely off at night. After a particularly cold night, several workers from the red group, Teresa, Beata, Maria and Ewa, asked me about my sleeping accommodations. I told them it was very nice but a little cold at night. This comment prompted a lengthy discussion about Genowefa, and particularly her husband's socially unacceptable behavior. They told me that Witold had worked at Lockem for several years while he and Genowefa lived in his parent's home and helped farm, as many of the employees at Lockem do. He had quit the company seven years before and joined a small construction firm. Soon after this, they began construction on the beautiful new home in which I was renting a room. Teresa told me of several disagreements that ensued between family members on both sides, but the focus of the disputes seemed to be Genowefa and Witold's rejection of the old way of living, farming and the acquisition of the new home and all its contents. The new house had prompted curiosity within the community. As stories emerged about the family squabbles, community expectations about Genowefa and Witold's greed and disposal of "traditional values" were confirmed. Beata told me that Genowefa used to be a very nice person when she was younger, and she would never have suspected that she would do some of the things that she had done. They blamed Genowefa's state of affairs on her greedy husband, who, by way of confirmation, was now cutting costs at my expense by conserving on the heat, even though I was paying "good" money to rent a room in their home. Teresa told me that she felt sorry for Genowefa because she thought that she did not have many friends and was very lonely now.

Genowefa and Witold experienced the same social alienation that Hann (1985) described in Wislok. Their behavior was not considered "deviant" by common social standards, but their "implied" motives gave rise to social condemnation. Teresa in the "Tea and Jealousy" event, and the recipients of the television sets (Chapter 5), experienced the same social ostracism. In the next section I will explore behavior that is considered "deviant" but is highly tolerated within the social system of Goria.

Socially acceptable deviant behavior. Wnuk-Lipinski (1987) identified a dimorphism of values between the state espoused values and the individual's true values in Poland. He wrote, prior to the change in the political system in Poland:

this inconsistency could explain why, for example, chronic drunkenness, bribery or theft of public property are perceived as 'evil' and at the same time meet with considerable emotional and instrumental tolerance—they are treated as signs of individual or collective resourcefulness or of innovativeness (Wnuk-Lipinski, 1987) : 165.

Wnuk-Lipinski is addressing the paradox found in Polish life, the tolerance of behaviors that are considered deviant. Examples of this in practice are plentiful. The "arrangements" discussed in Chapter 5 by the Catholic priest Father Jancarz is one example of a semi-legal activity that is not sanctioned, not even by a Catholic priest, because of the particular circumstances. The bribery that is assumed to be part of these "arrangements" is a prevalent activity, even today. When I asked the students at the Goria high school (see Appendix E) about the relatively low trust scores given to politicians and police, they told me that one of the reasons they do not trust these groups is that politicians and police accept and expect bribes as a normal course in their daily work lives. I then asked the students about the relatively high scores they gave to doctors. I had heard from numerous sources that it was necessary to pay bribes to doctors in order to be seen in both private practice and in hospitals. When I asked them whether they did not pay bribes to the doctors, the question was met with uncomfortable laughter. Yes, they agreed, they did pay bribes to the doctors. They laughed because they had made the connection to my next question, which was, why they trusted the doctors and not the police and politicians when they pay bribes to all of them. The answer that I got in every case was related to a sense that they "must" trust the doctors because they have their lives in their hands. They simply do not view the payments to doctors as outside of acceptable behavior. The police and the politicians were viewed as having less "important" jobs. Bribery in their case was considered deviant.

Another example occurred one day at Lockem. I was standing in the middle of the assembly section of hall #4 talking to Anna, when Czeslaw walked up beside us. He handed Anna what looked like a brass plate. She made a remark of appreciation and quickly placed it in the pocket of the smock she was wearing. Czeslaw, whom I had gotten to know very well at this point, explained with no apparent attempt at justification, that he had made the metal plate out of the material that they use for the production of the door-knobs. He told me that Anna would use it for cooking. Czeslaw then walked away with a smile. At this point Anna seemed a bit embarrassed by taking the plate, and she seemed to feel that this behavior required an explanation. She said very simply, "They steal much more from us than a simple metal plate."

The openness with which this transaction occurred led me to believe that it was a relatively common practice. Yet, it was apparent that Anna saw this as behavior that was not appropriate, or required an explanation. She was quick to explain her actions as "justified" given the environment in which she saw herself.

Wnuk-Lipinski notes:

> The law sometimes designates human behavior as incompatible with the generally accepted norms of social co-existence. These are the norms which the center introduces into the controlled public domain and which it itself designates as accepted. Deviations from these norms are then apt to be regarded as forms of social or psychological deviance (1987: 165).

The climate at Lockem seems to support Wnuk-Lipinski's (1987) observations. The effect of the simultaneous functioning in the consciousness of various kinds of norms and values which may be mutually inconsistent provides a point of cognitive dissonance (Kwasniewski, 1984), which is resolved through the social acceptance of deviant behavior. In addition, it serves to maintain social control in an environment where rules are changing, opportunities and risks are increasing, and external controls over behavior seem nonexistent.

SUMMARY—PATTERNS OF SHARED MINDSETS

This chapter has explored several means by which social actors in the Goria region of Poland perceive their relationships and their environment. Exhibit 17 summarizes the shared mindsets discussed in this chapter. The patterns which these shared mindsets form provide a window into the meaning in this context. A climate of distrust, reluctance to assume responsibility, and a struggle between individualism and collectivism have been amplified by the instability and insecurity of post-communist Poland. For the employees of Lockem, the greatest change came with the privatization of their company. Attempts to modernize, westernize, and mechanize the factory have caused the Lockem employees to fear for their jobs and to rely heavily on the patterns that were established in the communist era for controlling their members. Individuals who choose to embrace the "new" way of working are met with a plethora of obstacles set by co-workers and management alike. The message that these innovators receive is that accepting the values of the new system, without finding a way to incorporate the social control systems that operate in this environment, is personally risky at best, and generally counterproductive. In the next chapter, I will analyze, specifically, how this web of resistance impacts the decentralized control structure of TQM. Exhibit 18 through 20 depict interior scenes in the Lockem factory.

Exhibit 17. Summary of Shared Mindsets in Goria

1. Security and Stability
   a. Security and stability were achieved by the communist regime through coercion, instrumental motive, and a sense of no alternative.
   b. Pressures for personal freedoms exceeded the need for security and stability at the same time that the government began to lose its ability to provide.
   c. Personal freedoms brought instability and insecurity which is generating tremendous stress in the Goria region.
2. Distrust
   a. Distrust is pervasive in Polish society.
   b. Distrust of government comes from a sense of government illegitimacy, corruption, and the citizen's lack of control over government.
   c. Distrust within the community differs along dimensions of proximity and control.
   d. Distrust within the organization stems from unfair distribution of resources, the kumoterstwo system for resource distribution, and poor communication.
3. Reluctance to Assume Responsibility
   a. The socialist ideology of communal responsibility translated into abdication of personal responsibility in Poland
   b. The general societal sense of learned helplessness (Seligman, 1975), which resulted from the oppressive communist government and rights assignment for dutiful service to the state, contributes to the reluctance to assume responsibility.
   c. Strong pressures to conform to social standards and unfair distribution of rewards have also contributed to the reluctance to assume responsibility.
4. A Struggle between Individualism and Collectivism
   a. Social orientations of both individualism and collectivism exist in the Goria region of Poland at a very high level.
   b. In the communist period these opposing orientations found an unstable equilibrium.
   c. In the post communist period these orientations are out of balance and they struggle, daily, for dominance in social interactions.
   d. This struggle allows for only temporary periods of unity and collective behavior.
   e. This struggle produces a contradiction between some behaviors that are sanctioned and behaviors that are considered deviant by the general society.
   f. The high level of both orientations in Goria society contradicts the traditional conceptualization of individualism-collectivism in organizational literature.

Exhibit 18. Production Hall # 4.

Exhibit 19. The old assembly process.

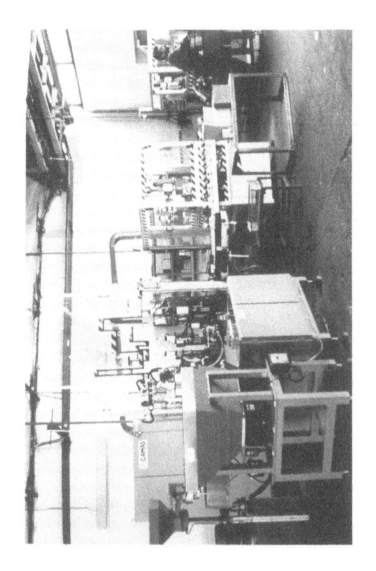

Exhibit 20. The new assembly machine.

CHAPTER 7

Resistance to Change

THE QUALITY DIRECTOR AND THE DIRECTION OF QUALITY

Mr. Litwa, the quality director, is a man caught in the middle, like so many of the managers at Lockem. He is caught between his manager's directives and the direction of change in the company, and his intuitive understanding of the people and the climate of the company. He is struggling with the changes, trying to make them work within the context, while all the while believing that they truly will not work. Mr. Litwa was hired immediately after Lockem was privatized to head the quality department and to lead the TQM implementation program. He was one of the first employees hired directly by the new owner. He is one of the "new guard," but he, as is true of most of the new guard, is not necessarily a strong supporter of Mr. Sroka's changes in the factory.

I have chosen to focus on Mr. Litwa among the many managers in the factory because, as is the case with all of the managers, Mr. Litwa is struggling to learn how to "manage" in this new world, although he is a bit more reflective about the obstacles than most. In addition, his job is at the heart of the quality changes that are occurring. Mr. Litwa is in his mid-forties. He lives in a small village about 10 kilometers from the Lockem factory. He has lived in the area since his marriage to a local "girl" 20 years earlier. He received an engineering degree from a university in Krakow, and then accepted a job in another factory in the area, which had recently closed.

During the course of this study I held three in-depth interviews with Mr. Litwa. What follows is a portion of the third interview. These excerpts are taken from the responses to four questions: 1) What is the status of the quality program and the application for the ISO 9000 certification? (2) What efforts are being made to empower the employees at Lockem? (3) What types of teams are currently functioning at Lockem? (4) How is the purchase of new technology being impacted by the quality of the parts that are produced from the old machines? "J" indicates my own voice as researcher in the excerpts that follow.

I entered Mr. Litwa's office through an entry office where his secretary has a desk. His office is quite small, but nicely furnished with a modern black table and desk, and new upholstered chairs. He motioned for me to sit down at the long table that was set against the far wall from his desk. He chose to sit at his desk, which was rather far away.

1) What is the status of the quality program and the application for the ISO 9000 certification?

> Litwa: We have worked on the system of certificates, and beginning in April we will apply to the board that would certify our quality and whether we should be awarded the ISO 9000.

> J: What changes have you made recently in the factory, as a response to the ISO 9000 application?

> Litwa: We have been making a lot of changes. The quality is not going to come from heaven. We have done a lot of work on the system, we have to get people to know that they have to work on quality. First, we have two training programs; the first is easier and the second one much harder.

> The second thing is that we have been working on improving the quality technologically. Many people have been laid off lately and this has made them more concerned. It is difficult to change the mentality of the workers to get them to think toward better quality in the things that they make. I think that he need some time, at least one year. When a person is 40 or 45 they may need 10 years to change. In the old system, someone else did all the thinking for you, the employees did not need to think. But now they must learn how to think. The ordinary worker should feel his responsibility for the quality of the product.

He then went to the front room to get a form.

Litwa: This is one of our new forms and the employees like it very much. You can find it everywhere in the factory. It is a quality problem form,that describes the problem and the manager's response to the problem and it has a place for signatures. Everyone can get one when he sees a problem. If they want to, they can come to me with the form, and they can be sure that everything will be checked very thoroughly. The employees are very happy with this, because now they have a word.[19]

J: How many forms have you received, and who are they coming from (what level in the organization are the workers that are submitting the forms) ?

Litwa: In the three months since I implemented this program there have been 17 responses. Sixty percent are from supervisors and 40% are ordinary workers.

2) What efforts are being made to empower the employees at Lockem?

Litwa: Every employee knows his/her responsibilities. They have a manual attached to their machines that tells them what they are expected to do. We are planning to give the employees more responsibility in the future. The managers, however, have not come to the decision yet. They do realize that they must broaden the responsibility of the employees.

J: Do you think the managers will have any difficulty with actually empowering the employees?

Litwa: This is a difficult question to answer, because I am supposed to only say good things about the company. This is a great problem for us. It is very hard to change the customs of the people. The supervisors and the managers are generally more educated people, and you would think that they would be more open to changes. But they are not open to the changes. They are trying to protect themselves.

J: How do you plan to address this issue?

Litwa: It is very difficult, and I am trying the best that I can to convince them that it is good to change.

He pulled out a quality wheel. It was hand drawn, first in English (Litwa does not speak English) and then in Polish in separate pen (see Appendix F).

Litwa: I have ordered 12 of these, to put them around the factory. I want to have one up wherever there is any kind of decision being made.

He then pulled out the book that he had showed me at our last meeting. It is an introduction to ISO 9000 and the quality approach to management. The book is written in very basic Polish language with cartoon illustrations to support the text.

Litwa: This book is very good. I have made copies available to the supervisors to give to any employee that would like one. The ordinary workers should be able to read these. I have found that people do not want to read the detailed quality manuals but they like to read this book. The supervisors are responsible to supply this to the employees. The book says that everyone is responsible for quality. Even the cleaning lady can get one and read it.

Generally the employees do not understand yet. They want to have more responsibility, ISO 9000 has created this desire. Whenever there is anything wrong they search for the worker that is responsible. They must change their approach. The workers have to be more responsible.

J: Are the employees being rewarded for taking more responsibility?

Litwa: There is a problem with the pay system. It is a natural thing, to want the pay system to give more money to those workers that do very good work and not to those that are not doing good work. So far we are forced to do quality work, but there is no pay incentive to do so. There is a plan, as far as I know, to reward creativity and responsibility in the future.

We need to be checking the quality of the work. If it is pretty good, then that is good; if it is not, something is wrong. They need to decide if it is the machine or the worker. Now the workers that are responsible are punished.

3) What types of teams are currently functioning at Lockem?

Litwa: We have started it, to organize the process of production in a different way. Now we look for teams to be responsible for a given product. Before the responsibility was spread all over the whole department, and it was hard to know where to go if there was a problem. In the old system the responsibly disappeared. I want to organize nets of responsibility for central things. When people are working in a net, they are part of the whole net. They are then all responsible, and they will get upset with any one that is not doing a good job. They will put pressure on him or her to take their share of the responsibility. This will change the mentality of the workers, through the pressure of the workers in the net.

J: I asked him if he thought that the history of suspicion of your neighbor within the communist system would impact the success of teams?

Litwa: This is a very difficult problem. But I think the problem of suspicion is a problem all over the world with teams. One member of the team will force the others to do their share, and they will tell their colleagues when someone isn't doing their share.

J: In the US we have found that the Japanese approach and acceptance of teams has been quite different than in America. How do you think that the Polish culture might impact this?

Litwa: I have been reading about the Japanese, and it is very difficult for me to understand why the Japanese respond in the way that they do. They are working for the firm and have a commitment to the firm. That is unheard of in Poland.

He pulled out of his drawer a song that he had written (see Exhibit 21).

I have read that the Japanese have songs that they sing to bring them together. I wrote this song to see how it would come out, but I also wrote it to see what the reaction would be. I pinned it up in the display board outside and waited to see the reaction. The reaction was amazing and mixed. Some were surprised, and others thought that I was a nut, and still others were pleased with it.

I think that it is still in the hearts of people not to accept this type of approach to management. I don't think that the problem is so much with the workers but more with the supervisors, the ones that are not on the assembly line. If it were up to me, I would leave it up to the people to construct their own groups. Now it is up to the supervisors and the manager to decide who works together. The people have worked in a group before, and they know who they like to work with. I see a problem, maybe not the biggest, but maybe it is. Only the best teams will appear and the rest of the employees will not belong to a team at all. It is hard to say if this will happen or not, but I can see that this might be a problem.

J: Are there other types of teams that are planned in the quality program?

Litwa: They have appeared already. They are connected with changing the machine and everything. It was Mr. Sroka's idea. It is what he wants to achieve in the future, but there are problems with money. We do not have enough money to buy all the technical machines and new machines.

It is not a good idea to form the teams until the new machines are bought. Then the teams can organize naturally around the machines. The two new machines that we have reorganized everything in the area where they are operating. We need a team to operate the machines.

Exhibit 21. Quality Director's "Japanese-style" Song.

> *In English: Lockem's Hymn*
> Let's unite our strengths and minds
> Let's do everything for production development
> So that our goods find their way to the nations of the whole world
> Let them be sold there again and again, and always
> As the water from an eternal fountain
> Grow, company, grow
> Long live harmony and honesty
> Long live Lockem.
>
> *In Polish: Hymn Lockem*
> Zjednoczmy nasze sily i rozum
> Zrobmy wszystko dla rozwoju produkcji
> Niech nasze wyroby trafiaja do narodow calego swiata
> Niech tam idz wciza i zawsze
> Jak woda z wiecznej fontanny
> Rosnij Fabryko rosnij
> Niech zyje harmonia and uchciwosc
> Niech zyje Lockem.

J: Have their been any teams established for engineering or design purposes?

Litwa: They have appeared recently. We formed them as circles of people from quality, production, and technology. They are responsible for quality checking, and they meet every Wednesday for 1 1/2 hours. They are analyzing all the problems that the factory is having, and they are usually solving the problems. They tackle the serious problems, the ones that are written down on a second form. It is the same with Marketing and Production, these type of meetings, but they are meeting on different days.

We are doing these teams in a similar way to Japanese quality circles. The statistics for these teams are that they have addressed 21 problems in 9 meetings, and only 3 of these problems have not been solved, because these problems need more time and money.

The teams are small and can solve the serious things. But it is all up to the president. I decide if it is a problem that should be solved or not, and then I sign and stamp the form. If there is a problem and I think it is serious then the solution will go to the president.

There was a third form that is used for this and he showed me this form.

J: How many of the problems actually went to the president when the team came up with a solution?

Litwa: One hundred percent went to the president. Even an ordinary worker can go directly to the president or to me if there is a problem.

J: Can the employees do this with immunity from punishment by their managers if the managers are unhappy that they did this?

Litwa: There may be a problem. You can't help it. Practice will show this. I have spent a lot of time informing the employees that there is nothing to be afraid of. It is not like spying.

They are all working on improving quality. If, for example, a manager is drunk and the employee tells them that this is the case, then the employees will be protected. This is obvious. The workers are sure to have problems, however.

4) How is the purchase of new technology being impacted by the quality of the parts that are produced from the old machines?

Litwa: It is up to the production director to make sure that the machine is running properly. The new assembly machine was a real problem. It was the first time that we had this kind of problem. It is not usually the fault of the machine. The machine requires parts that are made thoroughly, but the parts that are going into the machine from other places in the factory are not being made thoroughly enough, and they can't be, because the machines that are making them are too old. This new machine is very sophisticated. The parts that are made by the old machines are not a problem for the workers. Getting the quality to the needed level is above the workers that are making the parts. The solution, so far, has been to get some new tools from Germany to fix the problems they are having with the machine and the bad parts going into it.

J: Tell me a bit about the process you go through when you have a problem like this.

Litwa: It is very complicated. A lot of money goes into buying these machines, and then you expect the "net" to work. It can be a real financial problem. The changes to accommodate the machine can not happen in one night. The machines are the enemies of the workers. This should be taken into consideration.

J: Why didn't you buy new machines to replace the ones that were producing the input parts first, to avoid this problem that you are now having?

Litwa: When we started we did not realize that this was going to be an issue. We brought parts that were made here down to Italy. The Italians tested the machine, and it worked just fine. Everything was positive. But they have had different conditions when they moved the machine to Poland, and we have had the problems.

J: Do you think it was a wrong decision to buy this machine at this time?

Litwa: It is hard to say for me. Maybe it was the wrong decision. They should have noticed that it would be a problem.

J: Who was involved in the decision to buy the machine?

Litwa: The purchasing VP, production, and the engineers.

J: Then, you were not involved in any of the decisions that went into buying the machine?

Litwa: That is correct. I think that I could have made a big difference if I had been involved in the selection process.

As I was getting up to leave the interview Mr. Litwa added,

Litwa: I am seeing a real change in the people in Poland. I am a local official in my town. The mentality of the people is changing regarding paying taxes. In the past no one wanted to pay their taxes.

They would try to avoid it. But now they are willing to pay because they know now that the roads, for example, are their roads. They realize that when they pay the taxes that it is to improve their lives. On the side roads, there used to be no signs because the kids would destroy them. But now they know that the roads are theirs and they have respect for them. Now they have a different approach.

The first thing, though, is money. Taking money and giving it. It is the most important thing to people in Poland.

Litwa is struggling with the directives of Mr. Sroka to implement TQM in the Lockem factory. He struggles because he understands the resistance that exists to many of the elements of TQM in the Goria region. In this interview, he identified resistance from both management and employees to empowerment, resistance to developing a personal commitment to the company, and supervisor interference in establishing teams. These areas of resistance will be explored further in a later section of this chapter. First, I will examine the cultural influences and the values and assumptions embedded in the TQM philosophy.

INFLUENCES ON THE TQM PHILOSOPHY

In Chapter 5, I outlined the three major influences on social organization patterns in Goria regional culture. The traditional, political and religious influences have helped shape the ways that this society has chosen to organize so as to maintain social control and order. Very little has been written in organizational literature on the cultural influences that shape management approaches and philosophies (see Chapter 2). Much, however, has been written about the differences identified in the way managers view their organizations and the way these organizations process information, view time, and deal with power and status, to name just a few, across cultures (c.f. Hall & Hall, 1990; Hofstede, 1983b; Trompennars, 1994). Organizational philosophies do not exist independent of the people who create and mold them in practice. These philosophies are imprinted with the values and assumptions that are held by the individuals who shape them. I propose that TQM represents a philosophy that has been imprinted in this way. When organizations choose to embrace the basic tenets of TQM, or even if they choose only to adopt certain techniques commonly associated with TQM, they are introducing management approaches that are culturally embedded. These approaches are based on certain assumptions about what is valued, appropriate, and meaningful in the same way that individuals make these same assumptions in their behavior as members of cultures. One brief example is the long-term customer focus advocated in the TQM philosophy. This element of TQM assumes that there is value in maintaining long-term relationships. Additionally, if the objective is to continue doing business with these customers, then acquisition of wealth is implicitly valued through this TQM tenet.

TQM's history, which was briefly discussed in Chapter 1 and 2 of this book, provides the best clues to the cultural values and assumptions that this philosophy holds. This philosophy was introduced to the Japanese through American assistance in the rebuilding process after World War II (1945-1955). It was a time when America's influence was particularly significant in Japan. It included

> the break up of the great *zaibatsus* (large, highly diversified organizational conglomerates) in order to decentralize the economy, anti-monopoly regulation, encouragement of the formation of labor unions to counterbalance the power of management, land reform, and educational reforms. Again, during this wave of technology influx from abroad, Japan adapted the new organizational forms successfully. Of particular notability is Japan's nation-wide adaptation of the quality control philosophy and techniques introduced by W. Edwards Deming in the 1950's which launched a national campaign to improve quality and productivity in Japan (Brannen, 1994: 111).

TQM's origins were American, embedded with capitalistic ideology. Its tenets were readily embraced by the Japanese as part of the necessary transformation process. As Deming and others worked with the Japanese to mold this approach to management, it began to take on some elements of Japanese society, arguably those that were most important to the Japanese and were essential to making the philosophy their own. Westney (1987) argues that the Japanese propensity to successfully adopt western organizational forms comes from an ability to transform the environment. I propose that that is exactly what happened with TQM, from its introduction after the war through the early 1980s.

In the 1980s, the US business community looked to Japan, which had emerged as an economic world power, for clues to improving profitability. At this time the work culture that TQM represented was imported back to American shores. The reasons for the difficulties with the adoption of TQM in the US (Harari, 1993; Myers & Ashkenas, 1993; Papa, 1993) have been the source of great speculation. I propose that one of the problems rests in the way that TQM was now imprinted with Japanese culture, making it inconsistent with American values and assumptions. With the exception of Osland's (1995) study in Central America (see Chapter 2), virtually nothing has been written about the TQM philosophy as it relates to values and assumptions. It is against this backdrop that I will discuss these values and assumptions that are embedded in the TQM management approach.

TQM VALUES AND ASSUMPTIONS

In Chapter 5, I identified four values and assumptions that are relevant to a discussion of social organization in the Goria region. Exhibit 22 lists these four values and assumptions along side the corresponding values and assumptions of the TQM philosophy. In this section I will provide support for the TQM values and assumptions and discuss the similarities and differences that exist between them and those of the Goria regional culture. As with my examination of cultural orientations in Chapter 5, the basis of this discussion is to assess general assumptions.

Exhibit 22. Comparison of Values and Assumptions.

Goria Region	TQM Philosophy
Fatalism	Determinism
Ascription	Achievement
High-context	Low-context
Individualism and Collectivism	Individualism and Collectivism

Determinism

At the Lockem factory, the employees have tended to look outside of themselves to explain the causes of various events in their lives. Goria residents blame both religious and political forces for their fate, and recently they have attributed power to "the market." Total Quality Management assumes a very different perspective. Issues of empowerment, decentralized decisionmaking, and holistic process responsibility assume that individuals perceive control over events that impact them, and can act to change the circumstances and outcomes of those events. TQM assumes that individuals have an internal locus of control (Rotter, 1966), or what Paulhus (1983) calls control in both the personal efficacy and interpersonal efficacy spheres of control. Finally, it assumes that the individuals who work within a TQM organization will hold the belief that they are responsible for their actions, can affect the future, and are capable of self-improvement (Boyacigiller & Adler, 1991).

A major area of potential conflict between the deterministic TQM philosophy and the fatalistic Goria culture is seen in empowerment of employees. Empowerment requires the cognitive perception of an individual's ability to influence his or her environment and an acceptance of responsibility at the individual level (Thomas & Velthouse, 1990). Process diagnosis and improvement require that an individual believe that performing problem solving analysis and correction will have an impact.and that the risks are worth taking In addition, the drive to improve individual quality must be seen as having a tangible purpose. Attempts to establish reward systems to encourage individual decision making will be hampered by individuals who have an external locus of control. For example, if the Lockem employees feel that the "market" is directing their future, then it may be difficult to convince them that their hard work, attention to quality and restructuring of work processes will help them to influence the market in their favor.

Achievement

Status in Goria regional culture is assigned through the highly political network of action-sets and the practice of *kumoterstwo*. What an individual achieves, for example, in education or quality of work product, is secondary in promotion decisions to whom he/she knows and to what extent reciprocal obligations have been met. In the TQM philosophy, personal achievement through creativity and innovation are highly encouraged. TQM focuses on personal or group achievement, particularly as a means of improving the situation for the organization as a whole. The belief is that individuals can each prosper when the organization as a whole prospers. All rewards, whether they be intrinsic or extrinsic, are based on personal or group achievement, hard work, and acquisition of skills that will make an individual more beneficial to the organization.

The devaluation of achievement that is generated by the system of kumoterstwo in Poland stifles opportunities to channel individual efforts toward organizational objectives. Attempts to meet personal objectives necessitate that individuals spend energy on developing political alliances rather than on "hard work." Channeling personal efforts toward anything "public," as the organization is viewed, will be difficult in this environment. In addition, empowerment of the workforce would be seen as generally irrelevant if the true "power" distribution is assigned through ascriptive means.

Low-context

The network of action-sets that was described in detail in Chapter 5 generates less of a need for detailed coding in the transmission of information between parties and what Hall (1959) has called a high-context culture. Despite the plethora of data that accompanies many "official" transactions in Poland, the reliable information—that which the Goria residents rely on—transfers through these action-sets. TQM assumes a low-context cultural environment. It originated within large bureaucratic organizations. It was designed to help these organizations amass their vast workforces toward greater efficiencies and higher quality products. Many of the TQM practices and techniques require extensive documentation, measurement, and tracking to be effective. The process focus of TQM emphasizes identification and measurement of all steps, in all work processes. These measurements are coded in a consistent manner and then transmitted across the organization for various purposes. In addition, the individuals that create this information are expected to use it to personally improve the quality of their products and processes. The reliance on teams is also representative of the low-context assumption of TQM. Teams of various types (cross-functional, action, project) meet regularly to transmit information and to analyze and discuss relevant topics. Frequently these meetings are recorded and minutes are distributed to interested parties outside the team.

The high-context response to bureaucracy, which was the hallmark of communism, was to view documentation and measurement with suspicion. At the very least, it was viewed as ineffective, containing only "half-truths." TQM's heavy reliance on this information necessarily breaks down if employees do not view this information as "good" or "important." Bushe (1988) found this problem when the organizations that he studied displayed charts with data from each work process on the walls of all work areas. The use of these charts changed the method of communication in the organization, and in several cases was rejected for this reason.

Individualism and Collectivism

Though the TQM philosophy is strongly rooted in the foundations of US culture, the collectivism that is the cornerstone of Japanese society may have left its greatest impact here. Both individualistic and collectivistic values are seen in the TQM philosophy. Sitkin, Sutcliffe, and Schroeder (1994) identify two "orientations" of TQM, "control" and "learning." [20] These authors propose that environmental conditions, particularly the degree of uncertainty, nonroutineness, and/or instability in the environment dictate the focus most appropriate for a given organization. The learning focus addresses scanning for new customers, exploring new skills, and increasing learning, while the control focus utilizes monitoring, benchmarking, and increasing control and reliability. The incentives for implementation cited by these authors demarcate the more general cultural orientations that are inherent in TQM. The learning focus, for example, is associated with incentives for innovation, leadership support for independent thinking, learning-related feedback, and autonomy, what we could call individualism. The control focus is associated with rewarding teamwork, constructive conformity and evaluation through precise standards (Sitkin, Sutcliffe, & Schroeder, 1994) ; what we could call collectivism. The identification of these dual foci, learning and control, in TQM is by no means a widely accepted belief within the TQM community. It does, however, suggest that there may be two sets of assumptions working within the TQM framework. I propose that these represent the presence of both individualism and collectivism in the philosophical value system of TQM, and the capacity to deal with either depending on the context. Sitkin et al. evaluated the differences in market factors, but I propose that this discussion is also helpful in looking at differences in regional cultures.

The dual orientation, of individualism and collectivism, of the Goria people seems consistent with the dual orientations of the TQM philosophy. Difficulties arise, however, in channeling these competing orientations to capitalize on the power of each in the appropriate situation at Lockem. Promoting one orientation, by rewarding for individual behavior, for example, may impact the employees' willingness to work together in teams in another situation. The balance between the two, particularly in Goria, where it is coupled with distrust and reluctance to assume responsibility, would be a daunting task. However, the opportunity does seem to exist for finding the first area of compatibility between the Goria regional culture and the TQM philosophy.

TQM AT THE LOCKEM FACTORY

Exhibit 23 depicts the basic objectives of the quality control structure within the TQM management approach (see Chapter 2). Teamwork, empowerment, and visionary leadership combine to provide a hospitable environment for continuous improvement of quality. At Lockem, the social patterns of distrust, reluctance to assume responsibility, and the struggle between individualism and collectivism work together to resist change and, with it, the objectives of TQM. In this section I will address how these objectives are being received at the Lockem factory.

Exhibit 23. Comparison of TQM Objectives and Actual Outcomes at Lockem

TQM Decentralized Control Structure Objectives	Actual Outcomes at Lockem Factory
Empowered Workplace	Reduced Sense of Empowerment
Teamwork	Team Goals are Counterproductive to Organizational Goals
Visionary Leadership	Autocratic Leadership and Poor Communication
Continuous Improvement of Quality	Increased Focus on Quality

Teamwork

Several issues that we have discussed thus far, combine to produce an unfavorable environment for effective teamwork and, particularly, team decision making that is advocated by the TQM philosophy. First, the struggle between individualistic and collectivistic tendencies makes creation of long term "action" teams a problem. The inability of Poles to collectivize in general society over long periods of time can be expected to repeat itself in the organization, particularly when the objectives for collectivizing are seen as organizational "them" as opposed to employee "us." Additionally, the jealousy that accompanies the desire for uniformity in group status may make team creation a problem. Selection of team membership would be viewed suspiciously as either an unfair opportunity or a unwelcome burden, thus stimulating resentment either within the team members or among those that do not participate.

The second area of resistance to teams at Lockem comes from the tradition based "action-sets" and the politically-influenced practice of kumoterstwo that utilizes these means of access to power. The power, and thus decision making, in this community is intertwined in this system of networks. Allocation of appropriate authority to teams to tackle critical issues is difficult, because the power may remain inextricably linked to the outside system, and thus outside the team. Attempts to secure binding decisions within teams might easily be overridden by individuals external to the team, but strongly bound to one or more members of the team.

Finally, collaboration and cooperation require trust (Deutsch, 1985). The open exchange of ideas that makes team synergy so desirable for problem solving is virtually impossible when workers fear that fellow team members will tell management what was said, and reprisals will follow. Employees at Lockem are fearful of participating in any newly opened channels of communication, distrusting upper management's proclamations that the workers will not be punished by immediate managers for using these channels.

As I discussed in Chapter 6, trust is rare in Polish society. Elements of trust, however, do exist in the Lockem factory, particularly between members of some natural work groups. In this section, I will explore the signs of trust that are exhibited by these groups, and then evaluate how team solidarity is often mitigated by circumstances. Finally, I will discuss the management view of teams at Lockem.

The commitment that employees have to their natural work groups at Lockem raises an apparent contradiction. Under certain circumstances, the commitment of these groups is very strong, but under others these same groups break apart. Rituals and norms that signify cohesion have developed within all three of the work groups that I observed at Lockem. Members of the "red" group, for example, seem to perform their jobs as if they are interconnected parts of a single "well-oiled" machine. They work together, each performing the repetitive tasks with precision. As one task is completed, boxes are moved in and out of the assembly area to allow the workers to move on to the next process. Very little is spoken about what needs to be done, and workers change places as if the process were choreographed through years of performing the same dance. All of this happens seemingly with no discussion about the job. Individuals simply see what needs to be done and just get up to do it. I commented on this one day. Teresa said that they had been working together for so long that they do not need to communicate. "We know the job and each other so well, and we know how to do all the tasks required in the job, therefore, communication is not necessary."

Another day I observed four cups of coffee sitting inside a box that is used for packing completed parts. It is common to see these boxes on the table, but I had not noticed the coffee in any of them before. I first saw the coffee when Grzegorz, Beata's husband, came up to the table and took a cup of coffee out of the box. He quickly finished the coffee and then placed the empty cup back in the box. I asked Beata why they had the coffee in the box. She laughed uncomfortably as if she had suddenly realized that this ritual signified a deviant act. She told me that they were not allowed to drink coffee while they are working, so they make the coffee and put it in the box to cool. This way, the manager walking past the table cannot see it. When the coffee is cold enough to drink quickly, they look around to see if the manager is in sight, and then they drink the coffee. I asked her if they like cold coffee. Beata gave a very shy smile, cocked her head and said, "Well, it is better than no coffee at all."

Later, I learned two interesting pieces of information about the coffee ritual. First, workers throughout the factory knew the ritual. When members of the "blue" group asked me if I was talking to any other groups, I tried to describe to them the members of the "red" group. My interpreter interjected, "They are the ones with the cold coffee." There was instant recognition from the "blue" group members from this description. Second, I found out that the manager, who had forbidden the workers in this group to drink coffee while working, had moved on to another group and was no longer their manager. The ritual, however, had taken on a life of its own, and the participants did not question its necessity anymore.

A final example of the red group's cohesiveness was experienced one day when I walked up to the group. They were working in an area on the side of the production hall opposite from their normal location. The work pace was furious, and they did not greet me with the smiles to which I had become accustomed. I asked them if this was a bad time to talk, and Beata and Maria responded that it was. Then Janusz said that the work that they were doing was actually given to Teresa and Beata to do. The rest of them were helping Teresa and Beata because they were unable to do it on their own. Janusz said, "This is for your ears only, please. I don't want anyone else to know we are helping Teresa and Beata." He later told me that it was management that he did not want to know, since they would assume that Beata and Teresa were unable to perform the work that they were given.

A second work group that had developed a set of norms and rituals was the "blue" group, which was introduced in Chapter 5. This group's activities seemed to revolve around Iwona. Iwona is very straightforward in her conversations with others and me but she is also quite political in her approach to management. She insisted that the supervisor be included in a picture that I was taking of the group one day. In addition, she frequently offered the managers candies and smiles when they walked up to this work area. She is also the instigator of the entertainment of the group. She did not deliver the majority of the "one-liners" or funny quips, but she did seem to lead the rest of the group into them. Iwona rarely expressed negative emotions; she simply turned everything into a set-up for a joke. Her re-directions of negative conversations served to release tension and to stimulate cohesion in the group.

Helena was quiet and always cautious about management and their "watching eyes," but when Iwona whipped everyone up she was happy to join in with the banter. Alek, Maciej and Zygmunt were the men in this group, although they tended to be secondary players in the conversations. Czeslaw, the man responsible for repairing the machines in this area, spent a great deal of time around this table. Czeslaw was often a major participant in the banter. The jokes were generally political or sexual in nature. Sexual innuendoes were common, and groping and pinching were met with only feigned objections by the women.

The group loved to joke about the various practices that were common in communism. In Chapter 5 I talked about the "spread it on or it won't work" joke, and the "we came in on a rabbit" joke. These represent the nature of the humor. Current conditions in the factory or in the political environment were only discussed seriously. Iwona tried to avoid these conversations, but when they took hold, the men of the group would dominate the conversation, and the women would generally stay rather quiet.

Iwona became very ill over the Christmas holiday and did not return to work for over six months. Her absence created a huge void. The laughter and joking had disappeared, and a gloom seemed to descend over the group. The release that the joking provided was gone, and anger filled its place. Joanna's outburst at the worker that received that television set occurred after Iwona had gone. Alek also became very aggravated and vocal about his frustrations. One day he asked me what the average life span of an American worker was. I gave him the average life-span as I knew it of an American male. His question was rhetorical because he countered my answer with the statement, "At the rate we are working here, a man couldn't live another 10 years." He had stopped his work and was standing in the middle of the hall discussing the low pay and bad conditions at the factory. He did not seem to care if management heard him or not.

Over the course of the first quarter of 1996, Czeslaw was moved to another shift, and Alek, Maciej and Zygmunt were moved to other jobs in the factory. Joanna later said that it was tiring without her friend Iwona, with whom she enjoyed daily conversations. Several months later I asked Czeslaw if he had seen Iwona. He said that he had not seen her. I asked him if he missed the old group. He said, "Yes, especially Iwona and her speeches."

These signs of group cohesiveness reflect a potential for good teamwork, but when one looks at the ways in which these groups channeled their collective efforts, a different picture emerges. In reexamining the case of Janusz a member of the red group (see Chapter 6) who switched between increasing productivity when working as an individual and reducing productivity when working in a group, the way in which group pressure is directed begins to emerge. Additionally, the groups choose to help each other when it means hiding certain activities from the "common enemy," management.

The preference for working in groups was expressed by many of the workers. Group commitment, however, was easily mitigated by fatalism as conditions began to change in the factory. Each of the three groups that comprised my core informants were broken up over the course of this study. They seemed to be quite committed to each other, but when I asked about their feelings about being split up permanently, I received comments that initially surprised me. Below is a sampling of these comments.

> When I asked how they would feel if someone in their group was laid off. Eza said,"It would be a smaller group."

> When I asked what the rest of the group thought about Janusz and Grzegorz working in the other hall and breaking up the group. Beata said, "Everyone will be going somewhere else, or will lose their jobs. It is just the way it is."

> After the blue group *had broken up,* Maria from the red group had been moved to the blue area to work with Joanna and Helena. I asked Maria what she thought about moving to this new group and she said that it was what the manager told her to do. I asked her what she thought about her group breaking up. She said that "You get used to it. We knew that it was going to happen, and we are just happy to still have a job."

It may be that fatalism gives these workers a way of dealing with the disappointment of losing the support system that the groups provide. Or, it may be that the groups are not as strong as they appeared to be. I asked Teresa about this one day when we were not at the factory. It was during a discussion of political affiliation, and she had told me that two of the members of her group were communist party members before 1989. I asked her if political views were divisive to the group. She first said yes, they were, and there were tensions especially now that the election was fresh in their minds. However, when I told her that I was surprised because they seemed to work so well together, she said that they did work well together, and that these issues were simply not discussed a great deal so that there were no problems.

This cohesiveness may also be explained as a collective force against the joint enemy, "management," which dissolves as circumstances change and the need takes on a different form. One last point may shed light on the potential for teamwork at the Lockem factory. This is best demonstrated by several comments made regarding layoffs and morale in the factory. In one example, when I asked the production manager about the morale in his department he said, " You could divide them in their opinions. Some are for the changes, but the majority is against. Now everyone is afraid of losing his job, especially in the weaker teams." The supervisor of a different production area answered the same question by saying:

> Many of the employees are very unhappy with what is taking place now. Capitalism tends to weed out the weak and it is these that are unhappy now and will be the most likely to be laid off.

In a separate conversation that I had with Beata I asked her if there had been a large number of employees hired 20 years before, since I had seen a pattern that a large percentage of the workers I talked to had worked for the company for exactly 20 years. She said that she did not recall this, but many of them had stayed together. She added, "Only the people that are strong are still working. The others have gone." Both Beata and her manager referred to weak versus strong as opposed to "better" or "more productive" teams. This highlights the perspective of work that is held by workers and managers alike that it is a matter of *survival* as opposed to *productivity*.

The implication for teamwork at Lockem is that natural work groups that have existed for long periods of time seem to function in a manner consistent with cohesive teams. Their objectives, however, are generally counterproductive to the organization as a whole. The commitment to these groups is tempered by the strong fatalism that exists in the culture. Finally, the focus of groups has traditionally been to present a vehicle for "survival" as opposed to a unit for effective work. These existing work groups, therefore, provide a window into the way that these employees tend to function as small teams. Mr. Litwa's proposal to allow teams to form on their own may certainly be inefficient to the organizational objectives, but it may also be ineffective since traditional teams have channeled their efforts toward organizationally counterproductive activities.

Empowerment

The general climate of distrust, the reluctance to assume responsibility, and the struggle between individualism and collectivism have made successful empowerment at Lockem virtually impossible as it is currently viewed in the organizational literature (c.f. Spreitzer, 1993; Thomas & Velthouse, 1990). In fact, employees described a lessened sense of empowerment from the days of communist control of the organization. They have cited that their jobs are less meaningful than in the past, and they have less impact on the decisions that are made. In addition, they have a lowered sense of self-determination and competence since employees are being moved between jobs with virtually no choice and no training. In Chapter 2, I reviewed Speitzer's (1993) four constructs of empowerment: meaningfulness, impact, self-determination and competence. These will be the basis for the discussion of empowerment at Lockem.

One example is indicative of the climate that is generating this lowered sense of empowerment. Teresa told me of an incident that affected her greatly and shattered her faith that things were improving in the factory. Over the past several weeks the brother of the new owner had been working with several of the employees on producing a new part. This part would be shipped to the owner's factory in the United States. The brother, Tadeusz Sroka, was also now living in the United States, and Teresa and others had told me that they were very surprised by his management style. He was quite strict with the employees, expecting them to work long hours and to produce perfect parts, but they told me that he also seemed to expect the same of himself. He did not take long breaks or stand around telling the employees what to do; he worked hard himself. In addition, Tadeusz Sroka was very supportive of the employees, giving them praise when it was appropriate and detailed directions on how the work could be improved. Some of the employees disliked Mr. Sroka, but others admired his dedication and appreciated his support. Teresa had been put on a new job assignment associated with the parts that Tadeusz Sroka was supervising. She and Maria were required to polish the doorknobs that came out of the machines, inspecting them for flaws. Teresa said that when Mr. Sroka left the factory for several days she continued to perform this same task. Many questions arose during this time. She found many parts that she did not feel were of the quality that Mr. Sroka had expected. In addition, she thought that the parts that were coming out of the machines, while Mr. Sroka were gone, were of a different shape than they had been when he had instructed her on the process. Teresa said that she had asked several people if they were ok, and they were not able to give her an answer. These other employees told her just to keep doing her job and not to question anything that she was not specifically told to look at.

Teresa decided to follow her instincts and she put several of the parts aside. She was subsequently moved to another job. Teresa told me that she was very nervous, but when Mr. Sroka returned to the factory she went over to him and showed him the parts. She asked him if they were right. He said that they were not of a good quality, and he thanked her for pointing out the problems to him. Teresa told me that when she walked away she felt good about her job and herself. She said that she really believed, for a moment, that she was responsible for the quality of the parts. It gave her hope for the future.

Several hours later, however, when the first line supervisor found out what she had done, he yelled at her and told her to do her own work and mind her own business. He said that she was saying too much. Teresa told me that she cried in the factory that day for the first time in 20 years. She later reflected that the new system was very hard on her. "Before I could tell the truth, because they [she was referring to the managers] could not really do anything to us if we disagreed with them. Now," she said, "they can fire you."

Other workers echoed Teresa's sentiments about the past. I asked Anna if the employees were given more information about things that were going on in the factory during communism. She said:

> yes, before we could tell management about our problems. All the information was given to us and we were able to tell the managers everything. Now they don't care about the worker. The worker does his job and nothing else.

Another example occurred when I was discussing with some workers from the yellow group how their work was evaluated. Eza told me that there is a system of points. Management had recently implemented a point system to provide a basis for evaluation of individual performance. "But," she said,

> I know very little about the point system. All I know is what is most important, that is that you don't argue with the person above you.

That's the honest truth. This includes anyone in a position above you. This is how the point system works. We have nothing to say about what job we do. You do what you are ordered to do and nothing different. You can't have a say in what you will do.

Invariably a process of selective memory is occurring when these employees refer back to "the good old days," but the perception remains that they have less say in the work that they perform. Their jobs are simply "work." In addition, they have less opportunity to express problems and concerns than in the past. Together, these things lead to a lowered sense of empowerment.

The employees at Lockem also express a low sense of competence. All of the assembly workers expressed a competence in the jobs they had performed for many years, but all of the female, and several of the male, workers expressed reservations about learning any other jobs in the factory, even the most minimally skilled jobs. During the course of this study, the "brigadzista" position was eliminated. This position was held by minimally more qualified employees who would adjust and set the hand operated machines in the factory. I asked several of the employees if they would like to be trained to take on these responsibilities. Beata's comments are representative of the women who responded to the question.

A woman could not set the machines. It is not possible! The women have not been educated to set the machines. The men are taught over three years in the job school. The machines have engines in them and the men are taught mechanics and electrical. We would never be able to set the machines.

At a separate time, I spoke to another member of the group, Krzysztof, who had the job school education that Beata had been talking about. He gave this answer to my question.

The brigadzista job is very difficult to learn. I would have to be trained for a year or two. You could not learn this job quickly, during a day or a month. Of course, it depends on a person's abilities.

In contrast, Janusz answered "Anyone can do that job. It would take only a week or two to learn." Janusz is clearly an exception.

The feeling of incompetence intensified as the extensive restructuring began to break up groups and move individuals into multiple new jobs, sometimes three or four different "new" jobs in one week. The uncertainty of these changes was further compounded by the lack of training for the new tasks. Many of the employees expressed frustration and anger over not being trained as they were put in new positions. They were told to ask the other workers in the area how to perform the jobs. Teresa told me "I feel so afraid that I will make a mistake, a really big one!"

Workers in the offices also expressed a low sense of empowerment. They shared the sense of low impact and self-determination, but some felt more meaningfulness in broadened responsibilities that came with changes in the system of doing business. A purchasing officer, Dorota, who was hired after the privatization of the firm, told me that all decisions were made by the vice president who is also her director. She is told from whom to buy and how much. She does not communicate with the suppliers except to translate communications to foreign firms (she is fluent in English). Her manager's job is to communicate the directives from the vice president and to organize the work. He does not communicate often with suppliers either. I asked Dorota how the mood was in the department, and she chose to answer my question by speaking only for the other workers in her department. She said:

> They are not happy. It is very stressful. If they fail, the president will scream at them. They have meetings with the president and the manager of our department gets directives, but he doesn't know what to do first. There is no priority given, so he does not know what is important, and thus, they don't know either.

The marketing department is new to the Lockem factory. Engineers previously dealt with all marketing issues. The employees in this department feel that they are forging new territory, and this gives them a sense of purpose. I asked Dagmada, a marketing representative who had been with the company for 15 years, how she comes up with new marketing ideas. She said that "When there is a need, the idea will appear." It was a similar expression to the English "Necessity is the mother of invention." She said, "I come up with the ideas because I need to. Things have changed a great deal in the Polish market, and the needs for these innovative ideas is quite recent."

Once again, however, Dagmada has been put in a position of having little control over her work product. I asked her if she went to see clients. She said that "Only the manager goes to see the clients, I only correspond with them. I do go with the others to the commercial fairs where I meet with the clients." I asked her if she thought it would be a good idea if she spoke to the clients directly. She told me that it would make things easier and it would avoid some of the problems she now has.

After Jerzy, the quality inspector, had given me his version of being less empowered than before, similar to the others I have cited, I asked why he felt this was the case. He told me:

> It is a private company now. The owner decides everything. When the government owned the company, we worked together. Now the owner is the master; we have nothing to say. When it was a government factory the team worked together. The director represented all of us; it belonged to all of us.

Jerzy is clearly relying on the very egalitarian rhetoric of the socialist regime that claimed that all property was collective. This is the most common aspect of the socialist ideology expressed by the workers at Lockem. It represents the "attraction" of socialism.

It is interesting to contrast Jerzy's explanation with that of the mangers of the factory. Mr. Witowski, the manager of the largest production department told me:

> Now people feel they are working for themselves. I am not talking about the managers here. The workers realize they are working for themselves. They are very eager to work, and they are very hardworking. Now the approach to work is much different; it is much better.

Mr. Kwit the director of production told me that the workers " realize they own the factory, each of them. But it is not obvious, of course because their part of the factory is very small. They feel that they have nothing." When I asked the vice president of production, Mr. Psowka, if they were making attempts to empower the employees on the production floor, he said:

> Every employee knows his responsibilities. They have a manual attached to their machines that tells them what they are expected to do. They are planning to give the employees more responsibility in the future. The managers, however, have not come to the decision yet. They do realize that they must broaden the responsibility of the employees.

Mr. Psowka's initial answer to empowering his employees was to attach manuals to the machines. Though he said that more responsibilities were forthcoming, he also acknowledged the reluctance of the management of his department to accept this change.

These managers' reactions are not surprising given their insecurity about the changes that are taking place. I felt that in virtually all my repeated interviews with the management of Lockem that I was hearing a "mantra" from the mangers which came directly from Mr. Sroka's lips. Statements like "The employees are the owners now," were repeated almost word for word from manager to manager. This may represent a fear of my "spying" for Mr. Sroka, despite my assurance of impartiality. It may, in addition, depict a failure to understand and/or embrace these principles as their own. Finally, it may also represent a low sense of empowerment on the part of the middle managers.

In general, the managers claim very little knowledge about key issues such as pay and other personnel issues, and a low degree of impact on organizational issues. For example, when Janusz asked his manager why his pay was actually reduced when he was moved to a more complicated job, his manager told him that he had no control over pay; it was decided in the office building. In another example, a supervisor emphatically assured his employees that selection of workers for lay-offs were decided by a computer, and not by himself. In a third example, when an angry employee told his manager that he took home only 2.5 million zloty ($100) last month, the manager told him that he was unaware that anyone was paid so little in this factory. In each case the employees did not believe the proclamations by their management. It is hard to know how much of the managers' denials and abdications are genuine. Given the high degree of senior management decision making at Lockem, it may be that these managers do not make these decisions or have this information. It seems more likely, however, especially given the strong employee belief that the managers are more involved than they claim, that they may be suppressing their involvement as a means of exerting power and avoiding confrontation. Whichever is the case, and it may well be that it is a combination of the two, the managers do not present behavior consistent with empowered employees. Teresa expressed this too, as she was telling me about the lack of training that they had been given for their new jobs. She said:

> The management are like rats sitting in the corner with a horse whip. They just wait for you to make a mistake and then they crack the whip. The rats are afraid also, so they want to bite us, to get at something. So they just sit in the corner and cause problems for everyone else.

As a final commentary on management's views on empowerment, I would like to recall the discussion, outlined in Chapter 3, with the new owner, Mr. Sroka. I repeat it here for emphasis. Mr. Sroka had told me, when I asked about empowering the workforce, that he would empower the managers first. He said "I told them that they are apostles, but I am Jesus Christ. I will tell them how it should be." In actuality, it seems as though they are repeating his words, as if they were the gospel. With this view of empowerment coming from the top, however, it is easy to see why the level of empowerment is low and dropping in the factory. This leads this discussion directly into my examination of the visionary leadership at Lockem.

Visionary Leadership

Visionary leadership requires a break from the autocratic leadership that was prevalent in Poland throughout communism. The leader must have a clear vision for the company, be able to transform the needs and aspirations of the followers from self-interests to collective interests and open lines of communication throughout the organization (Dorfman, 1996). The extreme distrust of authority prevalent in Goria society makes the task of transforming individual goals into organizational goals quite difficult. The social system in the Goria region is designed to protect individual interests, and collective interests where they fall into the "private" sphere, against the "public" sphere controlled by the political elite. Organizations, such as Lockem, are considered a part of the "public" sphere in Poland. The pervasive distrust, therefore, provides resistance to visionary leadership.

The struggle between individualism and collectivism also complicates issues for the visionary leader. Dorfman (1996), who explores the issues of leadership in international and cross-cultural literature, highlights this issue. In examining the situational model of leadership proposed by Erez and Earley (1993), Dorfman considers the implications for individualistic versus collectivistic societies.

Consider how leadership processes might differ in individualist versus collectivistic cultures. According to this model, leadership in collectivistic cultures would be successful to the extent it influences a group toward valued goals as the leader must provide an opportunity for the followers to contribute to the group welfare. In contrast, in individualistic cultures, leaders should be effective to the extent they form an emotional bond with the follower and provide values outcomes and opportunities for personal growth and approval (1996: 311).

If we accept Dorfman's application of Erez and Earley's model, then what does it say for leadership in a culture that is at once individualistic and collectivistic?

The solution, cited by many informants for this study, is captured by the comments of a manager from the Krakow managers' meeting. An excerpt from my research notes defines the solution.

One participant said that when a group elects a leader, they usually pick someone with the least problems, not necessarily someone who is the most competent for the job. Everyone agreed that Polish groups do pick leaders this way. A second participant said that maybe they do this so that if they have problems, they have someone to blame, and they have an excuse to complain when it doesn't work out.

Therefore, the popular solution, according to my informants, is to select a non-leader who becomes a scapegoat if things go wrong. This solution effectively avoids addressing either the needs of the individualistic or the collectivistic nature of the society. When I asked my informants who would agree to be a leader in this case, they told me that no one with any legitimacy with the group will assume this role, but they will act as informal leaders for the group. This answer provides further explanation for the reluctance to assume responsibility in the society.

Given this set of circumstances, how possible is it for Mr. Sroka to represent a visionary leader in the organization? Several issues stand in the way at this time. The first relates to the personality of Mr. Sroka. He speaks of open communication, empowerment, and shared goals, but none of these issues was mentioned in his top six objectives (see Chapter 3). These objectives focus on personnel restructuring and reshaping in "Sroka's" image. One example was Mr. Sroka's objective to "inform supervisors that they could not be union members." His style is very autocratic, devoid of overt concern for the welfare of the employees. He does not appear to be able to present a vision for the company that can be embraced by the people he leads. The employees feel, as a consequence that they have actually gone backwards, and that things are worse in the privatized company than they were when it was state owned. They have lost the ideological rhetoric of the past leadership which pronounced egalitarian values and socialist protection. It has been replaced with what the employees see as Mr. Sroka's greed, self-serving interests, and lack of concern for the workers. One employee, Maria said:

> We do not have much faith in the suggestions of the owner. His suggestions take money, and we need to re-invest in the company. We actually don't know what the new owner will do with the money. We know he wants us to forgo salary increases. Our bosses tell us he even wants a decrease, but we don't trust what he will do with the money.

A Solidarity Union representative expressed his opinion about Mr. Sroka when he was talking about the television sets that were awarded (see Chapter 5).

> My supervisor said that there was a fax from Sroka that specifically said that the bonus money should not be paid out, even if a person deserved it, so that they would have money for the television sets. We think that this is all just Sroka's tactics. We do not think that this a system of motivation at all. You have to wait for three months to get the money that you should get per week as they do in western factories. Sroka is using the money. The single worker is losing because of inflation. Sroka is taking the money.

Managers also find it difficult to embrace the directives of the new owner, although their comments are less direct. As was demonstrated by Mr. Litwa at the beginning of this chapter, mangers act upon the directions that Mr. Sroka gives, but cautiously express their concerns to me about the wisdom of these directives. The marketing director simply said "Andrzej gets things confused sometimes." A supervisor in the production department said:

> They have been trying many new experiments, new ideas that the new owner has. The employees pay for these experiments with their health and their nerves. It also costs money. If it doesn't work, the experiments cost a lot. But most important is the heavy cost in non-monetary things, such as the stress.

Several managers signaled their dislike of Mr. Sroka and his changes by evading my questions on the subject. None of the production management would answer this question directly. Several refused to acknowledge that Mr. Sroka had implemented any changes. Others chose simply to change the subject. The body language in each case became very tense with this question. The topic is not an easy one. If the answer had been more supportive of Mr. Sroka's policies, I am certain that these managers would have been much more forthcoming in their answers.

Leadership is a complicated issue in Polish society. The leaders of the communist era still hold many positions of authority in the "new" Poland. Teresa told me how the mangers at Lockem were very quick to change their rhetoric after Mr. Sroka bought the company. When I asked her why she thought this was, she said:

> The managers of this company are opportunists and they were like trees that bend in the wind. As the political climate changed, they also changed. The old president was well connected in the communist party, and I think it is funny that he started going to church after the fall of communism. Now he has become a strong Catholic, and I see him at church.

The Lockem employees told me that they saw the old president, Mr. Gadomski, as a corrupt man who was well connected politically and thus able to make their lives relatively secure, painless, and uneventful. Several employees told me in effect, "He didn't bother me, and I didn't bother him." They cited Mother's Day gifts, annual bonuses equal to one month's salary, and candy for their children on Santa Claus Day, as the "nice" things that Mr. Gadomski did. They did not like the fact that many members of his family held "easy" positions in the company prior to his retirement, but for the most part they did not hear about the "bad" things that he did, and they preferred it that way.

The middle managers are the conduit for all communication from Mr. Sroka to the employees. Distrust and *kumoterstwo* that flow through all levels of the Lockem organization, distort this communication. The directives, therefore, are creating even greater fear, distrust, and suspicion. In addition, employees are scrambling to obtain favor with the management that they resent, while dealing with the condemnation of their peers. In many cases they see this as "survival." Confusion and frustration have been the result.

Leadership, therefore, is a very difficult issue at Lockem. Mr. Sroka complicates this by being an American-Pole. Throughout my interviews with employees, I heard tremendous distrust and contempt for Poles who have left Poland to live elsewhere. Employees told me that these individuals do not represent the Polish people well. Many of their comments can be explained by two things that I have already explored in this book. The first is jealousy, and the second is an emotional attachment to the land. Poles who leave this region, and particularly those that move to America, tend to prosper from this move. Several employees echo Eza's comment. She said that these individuals "go to America and get rich, and then they forget about us." The words of the song that Teresa sang for me at the factory describe the emotional issues that surround leaving the area. The attachments make it hard for some Goria residents to understand the motives of someone who leaves the area permanently.

The issue of Mr. Sroka's heritage may generate a problem from his perspective, as well. It may present an illusion of familiarity which in reality is exaggerated. Mr. Sroka frequently told me how he perceived the Poles to be. His assessment that Poles have continuously rebelled and that, when there is a common enemy, they unite and fight, is one example (see Chapter 6). His extrapolation of these assessments may be blurred by both his experiences during the 20 years he has spent in the United States and the changes that have taken place in the Goria region during that time. The familiarity may breed a misperception that impacts Mr. Sroka's assessment of the employees he now leads.

The future of Lockem includes a new president, Mr. Piotr Bylica, who was personally selected by Mr. Sroka. His presence mitigates the issues of an absentee "leader" that have persisted during Mr. Sroka's extensive periods away from the factory. This is the case however, only if he is able to assume a true leadership role and Mr. Sroka is able to step aside. It is too early to tell whether this will happen, and whether Mr. Bylica will be able to generate his own vision for Lockem.

Continuous Improvement of Quality

I have included the continuous improvement of quality in this discussion for two reasons. First, improvement of quality is the primary focus of the TQM philosophy. It is at the heart of the ultimate objectives of the organization for long-term survival and return on shareholder value. If applied properly, the focus on quality in the long run will work to improve competitiveness and help to meet these organizational goals. The second reason I have included continuous improvement of quality is because this is where I see the most significant positive step in the Lockem journey toward TQM. Potentially, it provides a glimmer of hope in the otherwise troubled picture I have painted thus far of the Lockem road to success. Quality improvement of Lockem products is one thing that everyone I spoke to, without exception, could agree on. I asked the assembly workers from the yellow group if they thought the quality was better than before privatization and they answered in unison, "yes." When I asked them why, they told me that they pay attention to the quality now. Iranusz, a quality inspector told me, " The quality in the factory has improved a lot. The privatization has been good for that. Now they have to be good or they will have to leave the market." I asked him why he thought the quality was so much better, and he said that he thought the increase in discipline and the efficiency improvements.

Supervisors give the same response. Marusz the supervisor for the red group told me when I asked him if the quality is better now than before privatization:

> Now it is *much* better than it had been in the past, oczywiscie (of course). . . . In the past they paid attention to mass production and now they pay attention to quality.

Quality of machines and processes do not, however, enjoy the same high quality rating from employees. A Solidarity Union representative told me:

> The whole factory needs to get new machines. They are not prepared to introduce ISO 9000. They can not get the high quality that ISO 9000 demands. It is hopeless. They are spending money and it is hopeless. They don't have any possibility to get ISO 9000 certification with these machines.

The poor quality of the old machines is causing a great deal of anxiety when combined with the new focus on quality, and the policy of assigning individual responsibility for the quality of parts. One example of this was demonstrated in an exchange I had with Teresa. I found her working on the last machine in the hall #4. I had seen her working on this same machine the week before. She told me that she was very upset because the machines have not been working. The day before she was required to work both of the machines that were run from the same elevated post, at the same time. She said that they were not working well, and she had to ask the man that works on the other machine to help her. She was really upset because she simply could not get the machines to work correctly. She said that she cannot sleep at night, and she cannot eat when she is so nervous, so she is losing weight. She lifted her pants up and down from outside her smock to demonstrate how she had been losing weight.

Quality is also the one thing that employees and managers alike say they are willing to assume responsibility for. A caveat to this proclamation is necessary, however. I have mentioned previously that the managers at Lockem assumed that what they said would probably get back to Mr. Sroka. As with many other issues, I repeatedly heard the same exclamations, that the employees and themselves had assumed full responsibility for the quality of the parts. In addition, even though I am certain that the majority of workers had relinquished their concerns about my questions on almost all issues, I did suspect a bit of posturing about this issue of responsibility for the quality of the parts. I feel confident that they believe that the quality of the parts has improved, but I am not entirely certain that they have embraced the *responsibility* in the manner which they profess they have. For example, when I asked Czeslaw if the quality of the parts was better now than before privatization, he said, "It is better compared to before. The market demands quality." But when I asked him if he was proud of the quality of the parts he produced he said, "Proud?" and then he made a sort of sarcastic laugh. "Maybe so, I don't really know." Anna who was standing next to him interjected, "Money would make us more happy." She pointed to a very large quality sign on the wall of the hall where they work. It was orange, blue and white and it spanned 3/4 of the width of the large wall. It read "Quality is the task for everyone." Anna laughed and then said, "It costs a lot of money to make signs. The money should have been spent on employees' salaries." In a second example, one of the managers of production told me with a smile what would happen if he did not keep the expected level of quality. He said:

> If I don't keep an eye on it, they would cut my extra bonuses or even lay me off. The quality control department verifies the quality of the products that my department produces. They do not check all of the parts, but if we sell poor quality, it is my responsibility and my managers.

Finally, referring back to Mr. Litwa's comments that opened this chapter, he acknowledged that the employees were "forced to do quality work." His explanation for this was that the pay system was not appropriate for instilling an appropriate sense of responsibility for the quality.

The focus on quality, as opposed to quantity, has reached every level of the workforce, but it is difficult to say whether employees have assumed responsibility for the quality, or whether they are simply focusing on it at the risk of losing their jobs if they do not. The dramatic improvements in quality that have been attained with relatively little effort point to two possible explanations. The first explanation is that the quality was of a very low standard before and that it was relatively easy to improve. The second explanation is that employees are able to harness a tremendous effort when they feel threatened. This theory is consistent with the tendency for Poles to collectivize for short periods of time (see Chapter 2 and 6). It is most plausible that the results at Lockem are a combination of these factors. The first will not help with subsequent attempts to improve quality of products, but the latter will, if the formula for rallying the troops can be repeated. Maintaining any collective focus, however, will be a problem. Clearly, acceptance of responsibility and further purchases of technology will be important factors in continuing the push toward quality at Lockem.

SUMMARY—CONFLICTING VALUES

> We must work on the changes step-by-step. It is a very long process, just like in the house when you clean up you tend to make a big mess (Mr. Kwit, production manager at Lockem).

Mr. Kwit's analogy may explain in part the observations and perceptions of the Lockem employees. The "big mess" that I have described in this book may be "transition pains." Success, however, will require finding a fit with the organizational policies and the greater culture of this area. Employees at Lockem repeatedly expressed that they had tremendous hope for their futures when the new owner first arrived. Their commitment to this area and the lack of alternative employment provides a powerful incentive for Lockem's survival. To date, however, Lockem's management has been unable to harness this motivation for the good of the organization.

Evaluating TQM as a culturally embedded management philosophy provides insight into its compatibility with this context. Major conflicts exist, but I do not propose that TQM necessarily be scrapped because of the conflicts. Several of the values and assumptions held by Goria residents, for example fatalism and high-context culture. may conflict with any approaches employed by management to modernize. As all modern developed countries have experienced through the period of transition, culture change occurs. In each case, however, that change is different in rate, and in kind, because of the unique qualities of the people that are changing. The Goria region's specific culture presents a web of resistance that is uniquely its own. Change will occur here, and it may resemble the values of TQM, but it will be in Goria's own image. Exhibits 24 and 25 depict two quality "reminders" in the Lockem factory.

Exhibit 24. Quality sign in production hall #2, "Working together—This new way of management ISO 9000."

Exhibit 25. Quality light fixture, "Our group—ISO 9000."

CHAPTER 8
Conclusion

On one particularly slow day, Zygmunt was standing around the assembly table talking to the women from the blue group. Zygmunt usually worked on one of the large machines that sits in the front section of this hall, but he told me that he didn't have any work this day. He was eager to tell me, as several others had on a previous visit, that Mr. Sroka had been in the department the week before. Zygmunt was frustrated. He said that Mr. Sroka did not treat the workers like human beings. "He treats us like a machine: we must just work." He told me that the workers did not care about privileges like the television sets that Mr. Sroka gave out the previous week. Zygmunt said:

> We just want a good salary. We don't care what's going on at the top, what agreements are made between the top people, we just want a fair wage for hard work. The people are so fearful here. We are so frustrated, and we are afraid every day that we will lose our jobs. We want to work, but we can be fired without an excuse. We do not know the criteria for firing a worker. We have a long way to go to be like other countries and to develop the culture of work that they have in these other countries.

I asked Zygmunt whether he thought that Mr. Sroka's experience in America wouldn't bring to the company this "culture of work." Zygmunt said, simply and succinctly, "Once a Polak, always a Polak." Everyone in the small group laughed in a way that seemed to applaud Zygmunt for the conciseness with which he put a commonly held "truth."

It is hard to overstate the extent to which our cultural backgrounds influence our way of viewing the world, and thus our approach to life. Zygmunt expresses a belief that these influences run very deep and that they are virtually unchangeable. He judges the actions of Mr. Sroka as the actions of a Pole, despite his American citizenship. Mr. Sroka himself identified this same attitude from the workers at Lockem. He told me, "They don't listen to me because I speak Polish." This study has examined what this "Polak-ness" means to the people of the Goria region of Poland. In addition, I have described the impact that the cultural context is having on the introduction of a TQM approach at Lockem.

Exhibit 26 represents a summary of the results of this study. It depicts the web of resistance that exists in Goria and the implications for decentralizing the control structure at the Lockem factory. The Goria regional values and assumptions: fatalism, ascription, high-context and the simultaneous orientations of individualism and collectivism, were discussed in Chapter 5. They are generated, in part, by the complex interaction of three primary influences: traditional, political, and religious. Over time, these influences have worked together in some situations, and against each other in others, to create the various means by which the people in this region choose to organize their lives, their relationships, and the way they view new stimuli from the environment.

Several patterns of shared mind-sets are discussed in Chapter 6. Distrust, reluctance to assume responsibility, and a struggle between opposing orientations of individualism and collectivism, are generating a force of resistance at Lockem that is working against the transformation process of TQM. In addition, these patterns interact in a world of tremendous ambiguity and instability, which has generated insecurity among the people of Goria.

Chapter 7 introduced the cultural influences on the TQM philosophy of management. For comparison, the values and assumptions discussed in Chapter 5 for the Goria people were contrasted with the values and assumptions embedded in the TQM philosophy. These deeply held beliefs of the Goria people were shown to differ in significant ways to the ones imprinted on the TQM approach to management. Finally, Exhibit 26 represents the desired objectives of the decentralized control structure of TQM and the actual

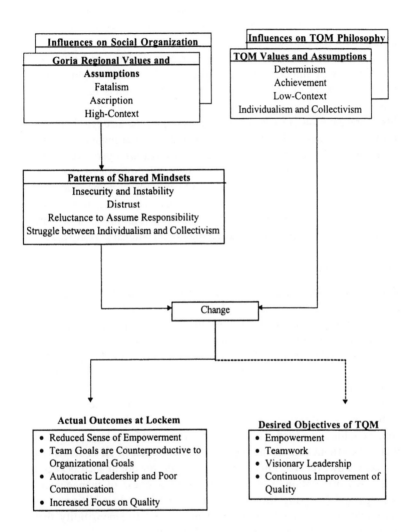

Exhibit 26. Responses to the Confluence of TQM and Goria Regional Culture

outcomes at the Lockem factory. The workers' responses to the changes can be traced to their culture in some significant ways, discussed in Chapter 7.

Exhibit 26 is not presented here to represent cause and effect or groupings with impermeable boundaries. This study explores the dynamic concept of "culture," and this exhibit depicts patterns and trends that are acting within this context. Many of the relationships in this representation are reciprocal. For example, the struggle between individualism and collectivism is depicted as a consequence of the traditional, political and religious influences that are operating in this context. However, it can just as easily be demonstrated that this struggle is influencing the political and religious systems, and thus molding the present into tomorrow's history. Therefore, this model should be viewed as representing just one possible direction of flow that is acting in this context and affecting organizational performance.

CONTRIBUTIONS

This study of the cultural resistance to the introduction of TQM at Lockem contributes to the field of organizational studies in four significant ways. First, I have presented a new conceptualization of the Individualism-Collectivism orientation. The work of Hofstede and others (Hofstede, 1983b, 1983a, 1984; Trompennars, 1994) represented a first step toward incorporating the vastly important influences of culture into the organizational debate. This study, however, has identified that both an individualism and a collectivism orientation are significantly impacting the behavior of the individuals in this same context at the same time. This is not an unreasonable finding, given that it is not difficult to imagine both orientations exist in all contexts. At Lockem, however, the impact of the struggle for dominance between these two orientations is limiting the effectiveness of management policies and lowering the morale of the workers. In addition, it is perpetuating the climate of distrust and social irresponsibility that generated the inefficiencies of the socialist system.

Second, this thesis has proposed that management philosophies, such as TQM, are imprinted with values and assumptions. The implications for this are widespread, not only for international management research but for all organizational research. Continuous change has become a consequence of the drive to maintain competitiveness in virtually all industries. In the rush to speed up this change, the transfer of management techniques and approaches is widespread. Understanding the embedded values and assumptions found in these management approaches will provide valuable information for assessing fit with organizational strategies and cultural climate. Uncovering this aspect of organizational phenomena may also help reduce the stress of change in organizations and assist managers who wish to tailor approaches to suit their specific contexts.

Third, this study casts aside the assumption that the wealth of organizational research that exists today necessarily represents a set of "global truths." To this end, I have performed an in-depth study in an area of the world that is going through massive and rapid transformation of its political, economic and social systems. Poland is strategically important as an economic participant in the global market, and represents a political buffer zone between East and West in Europe. This study of Polish culture, and particularly the impact of the 50 years of communism, provides a new and important area of study. This research has explored the complicated cultural web that has been, in part, the result of this communist influence, and has shown how this set of conditions impacts successful organizational operation in one factory.

Finally, this study represents a detailed ethnographic investigation into the meeting of two cultures by a relatively indirect but ever increasing means, transfer of management philosophy. This topic has had little attention in organizational studies with the notable exception of the work of Andre Laurent (c.f. 1992) and Michel Crozier (c.f. 1964). The ethnographic tale employed in this thesis generates thick description of the behaviors and attitudes of employees who are experiencing major change in their lives. The meaning they attribute to this change generates behaviors that impact organizational operations and success of the new management philosophy. My exploration of this topic using ethnographic techniques offers the beginning of a theoretical base upon which other studies can draw.

IMPLICATIONS: FATALISTIC INTERPRETATIONS?

After discussing the findings from this study with Professor Piotr Sztompka from Jagiellonian University in Krakow, he asked me, "So are you as fatalistic as we are?" His question was rooted in a separate question: "What are the implications of these findings for the attempts by Poland's people to stabilize her political systems and produce a functioning market economy?" The results of my study can be evaluated from four perspectives.

First, a holistic view of this study produces important issues of reciprocity between culture and organizational philosophy. One example provides the meaning here. Ford and Fottler state:

> Empowering a person to make both job content and context decisions that optimally respond to changing environmental conditions, technological innovations, and competitive challenges is the ultimate expression of trust (1995: 25).

Yet, in addition to generating trust, empowerment *requires* reciprocal trust on the part of management and employees. For employees to feel that they genuinely have autonomy in their jobs, they must trust that management will not continually reverse their decisions or punish them for taking risks. In addition, management must trust their employees to make good decisions and to perform in the best interests of the organization, to allow them to have direct impact in their jobs. A general climate of distrust makes trust on either side (employee or manager) more difficult. Therefore, the interrelationship and interdependence between culture (in this case a climate of trust) and management philosophy (in this case empowerment) become clear. Future research should explore the reciprocity of culture (regional and organizational) with changing management philosophies, to assess issues of fit and compatibility.

Second, at Lockem the culture represents a set of intricately woven webs of resistance to organizational change. Webs of meaning exist in every context and resistance to change is a natural and necessary protective mechanism for all life forms. What is important here is that the impetus of the resistance be identified and understood. This study has identified the *patterns* of shared mind-sets that are enacted in this environment, providing valuable information for purposes of making management decisions. Individuals and cultures can adapt to change if their basic values and assumptions are not violated. Many of the employees at Lockem identified a need and a willingness to change, as long as certain things are maintained. One of those things is a certain degree of security, particularly as it relates to the ability to continue living on their land. Another is the maintenance of individual freedoms. Future research should utilize the study of regional culture as a basis for understanding change, resistance to it, and ways to enhance organization effectiveness by capitalizing on unique cultural competencies. In addition, studies should compare the issues of resistance to change in other former Eastern Bloc countries to that of Poland. This period of rapid and dramatic change provides a unique opportunity to compare and contrast issues of culture as they relate to organizational change.

Third, issues of how to reward employees, how to motivate them to care about their work, and how to get them to think, present many difficulties for business practices in Poland. Though these issues are not unique to the Polish context, the intensity and prevalence with which they are encountered is extensive in this environment. Exhibit 27 depicts the advice one Polish business executive at Johnson and Johnson, Poland, provided to Western executives arriving in Poland for a foreign assignment. The issues raised in this book give background, focus, and dimension to the unique characteristics of Polish culture that have prompted these organizational challenges. Future research should evaluate a wide variety of management approaches in Poland and assess which of these approaches is able to balance the need for social egalitarianism while promoting the natural individualistic spirit of the Polish people. Additionally, both trust and responsibility should be studied in this environment to begin to formulate ways to adapt management's approaches to address these characteristics of Polish culture.

Finally, further study of manifestations of cultural orientations in organizational contexts is paramount and important to address in the classroom. Traditional approaches for examining this subject have generated a two dimensional picture of a much more complicated issue. This study shows that cultures possess a reserve of characteristics that may arise as contingencies change. Identification of cultural tendencies is important and helpful, but the danger is that theoretical relationships that are established that rely on these "classifications" may be misleading. Future research and teaching, therefore, must approach international management with the understanding that cultures may store opposing tendencies simultaneously and that organizations must find ways to accommodate or channel them.

Exhibit 27. Fifteen Commandments for a Western Executive Coming to Poland

1. By no means try to make your Polish office a xerox copy of your beloved home office.
2. Do no expect work to become the main purpose of your employee's life.
3. Make the authority areas as clear as possible.
4. Keep in mind that a group here is not a group (. . .) it is a collection of individuals.
5. Hire young people.
6. Don't waste time encouraging creativity.
7. Don't be mad if your people are trying to outsmart the system you have designed with such pride.
8. Don't count on Poles' loyalty as granted for all the good you've done for them.
9. Learn to live with a feeling not being trusted for a long time.
10. Do understand that as managers you are, by definition, a stupid, primitive thinking, short sighted, miserable and pathetic creature unless you clearly prove the opposite.
11. Know the informal structure of your personnel and its dynamics.
12. Wrap your logical argument in emotional package.
13. Remember that money does motivate Poles, but . . .
14. Don't try to play that "Friendly Johnny-the-Boss" game.
15. Don't attempt to treat women as so called "Persons"—the sex-less creatures of the Western office hemisphere.

Finally, further study of manifestations of cultural orientations in organizational contexts is paramount and important to address in the classroom. Traditional approaches for examining this subject have generated a two dimensional picture of a much more complicated issue. This study shows that cultures possess a reserve of characteristics that may arise as contingencies change. Identification of cultural tendencies is important and helpful, but the danger is that theoretical relationships that are established that rely on these "classifications" may be misleading. Future research and teaching, therefore, must approach international management with the understanding that cultures may store opposing tendencies simultaneously and that organizations must find ways to accommodate or channel them.

REFLECTIONS ON THE PROCESS—FIELD STUDY ABROAD

Fieldwork is messy. Themes that are so clear after prolonged immersion in the culture are difficult to express succinctly. No single example "tells the story." The examples work together, like the various tuning knobs on an old television set. To get a clear picture you must set the color, the brightness, the vertical and the horizontal tuning, laying one on top of the other. Every story has elements of exception. Thus, it takes a great deal of time to sift through the exceptions that are present in every case and to decipher the trend. This takes patience, a clear plan for the research approach in general, and a lot of flexibility to adjust the plan as circumstances arise.

Ethnographic research is time consuming, frustrating, and not just a little bit humbling. I found that in Goria, my extensive education and life experiences were quickly neutralized by my inadequacies brought on by my ignorance of life in this area. I didn't know, for example, how to hold a baby chick in my hands so that it doesn't get away and I don't squeeze the life out of it. Nor did I know when to address certain individuals using the formal "Pan" or "Pani," and when to use the more familiar form of the word. The Poles that I talked with were very gracious in allowing a whole range of "mistakes" in my Polish.

These difficulties, in some strange way, point to the greatest benefit for doing this type of research. The largest obstacles that I experienced often became the most illuminating. For example, it was not until after the red group, whom I had come to know very well, broke off communication with me, that I saw the power of group sanctioning and how an outsider could impact it. By accepting Teresa's invitation to tea, the impact of this social norm became very real. I learned more from my initial ignorance of the situation than would have been possible had I entered the situation inherently understanding that this would generate conflict.

Everything in Goria was new, a bit strange, and open to question. The experience necessitated a questioning of my own biases about how people think, what is acceptable behavior, and what is "struggle." Through my own questioning I was able to see more clearly the people that I was studying. This made it possible for me to tell their story of change, frustration, fear and hope. In conclusion, I would like to refer to Clifford Geertz's words about "good interpretation." Geertz has aptly described what I have sought to accomplish in interpreting the world of the workers at the Lockem factory in Goria, Poland. He writes:

A good interpretation of anything—a poem, a person, a history, a ritual, an institution, a society—takes us into the heart of that of which it is the interpretation (Geertz, 1973: 18).

Endnotes

1. For a detailed review see Chapter 3
2. Quoted from a lecture for Fulbright recipients given by Professor Lucjan Kocik from Jagiellonian University, September 1995, Krakow, Poland.
3. The theoretical debate about the definition of "peasantry" is prompted by the contradictory nature of peasant economy, and whether the peasantry should be classified as a social category given that they are dominated economically and politically by urban elites (Gorlach, 1995; Wolf, 1966). For the purpose of this book, the peasantry refers to those individuals who have farmed in rural Poland for generations.
4. Pseudonyms are used for all individuals in this and all succeeding chapters.
5. The process of participant observation employed here refers to immersion in the culture including observation of routine and unusual events of the target group, as well as participation, as an outsider, in the activities of the group (Jorgensen, 1989; Fetterman, 1989; Yin, 1994).
6. The snow ball approach involves a process of informant selection based on previous informant information, suggestion, or inference (Jorgensen, 1989). For example, I decided to talk to one particular employee after another employee told me about her reaction to a third employee's promotion. This strategy is used to uncover information that is not easily observable through other techniques.
7. These scholars include, but are not limited to: Professor Piotr Sztompka, Jagiellonian University, Krakow, Professor Stanislaw Walukiewicz, Polish Academy of Sciences, Warsaw, and Professor Lucjan Kocik, Jagiellonian University, Krakow.
8. All names are pseudonyms. Female names used in this thesis end in the traditional "a," common in Polish names, for example "Alicja."

9. Literature is employed in this and subsequent chapters to support the primary data, which use the "Polish" unit of analysis. The wealth of support for my findings from these sources leads me to present them here as relevant to this study. Throughout this study, however, I will refer to the regional, Goria, or Lockem people, values, behaviors, etc., and I will not attempt to generalize.

10. Core informant groups are given color codes for reference, and I will identify these groups by these colors for purposes of continuity. I must note, however, that over the course of this study all of the original groups that I reference by color were broken up.

11. No women are in authority positions at Lockem.

12. Walesa had, in fact, promised a share of all state owned property to each Polish citizen. The people in this community interpreted this as cash, since they have not known any other system of ownership. When a Walesa backed referendum was presented to the Polish people to address giving each person a coupon exchangeable for shares in the Polish stock market, there was a very low turnout (less than 35%). My informants told me that they were confused about the whole issue.

13. They were not aware of Clinton's Arsenio Hall appearance during the 1991 presidential campaign.

14. The Solidarity Union at the Lockem factory, for example, gives payments for death in the family, birth of a baby, etc. The amounts of these payments, however, are quite small, totaling less than $10.

15. Part of this quote was used for support in Chapter 5. I include it here in its entirety.

16. I am considering here only the status level that the person holds in the society at large, not how his/her opportunities for advancement may or may not be enhanced. Education is only a very small element in these decisions, and in some cases it is considered negatively.

17. During the course of this study none of the employees in either the blue or the yellow group was laid-off. Many of them were moved to other areas in the plant, two took ill and went on long-term disability, and two in each group remained in the assembly area to assemble locks that were too large for the new machine.

18. See the end of this chapter for a discussion of sanctions for deviance from group norms.

19. When I took the form to the employees that are in my core sample and asked them if they used this form, they told me that they had never seen it before. I received this response from all the employees who I asked about it. None of them had seen, or even heard about these forms.

20. To avoid confusion, I will refer to a TQM "focus" rather than use the Sitkin et al. term "orientation," for the purpose of this discussion.

21. Exchange rate in 1994 2.2 Polish Zlotys per US Dollar. 1995 Exchange rate 2.3 Polish Zlotys per US Dollars.

22. Increased cost in 1995 is the result of lease payment made to the Polish government, as part of the lease -buy agreement.

Company Data

Lockem Organization Chart

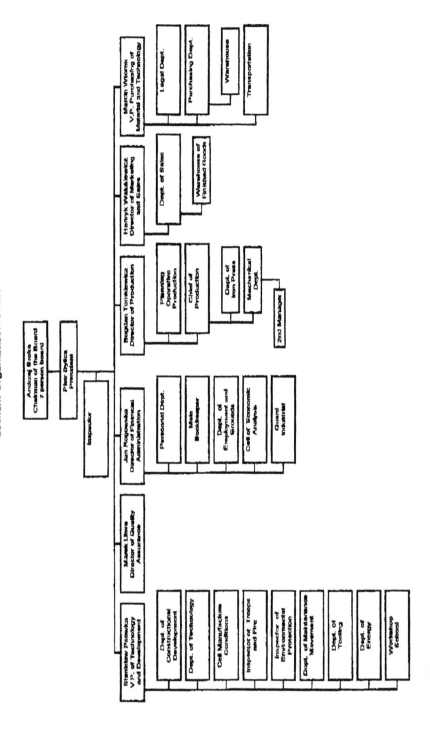

LOCKEM INCOME STATEMENT

Calendar Years 1994 and 1995 (000's -USD) [21]

		CY1994	CY1995	CHANGE (increase/ (decrease)
Revenue				
	Operations	11,805	13,097	1,292
	Sale of Material	1,460	2,964	1,504
	Other	174	328	154
	Total Revenue	**13,439**	**16,389**	**2,950**
Operational Expenses				
	Material	(1,145)	(2,810)	1,665
	Energy	(6,733)	(7,380)	647
	Salaries	(1,494)	(1,643)	149
	Bonuses	(762)	(818)	56
	Depreciation	(556)	(477)	(79)
	Other	(760)	(1,444)	684
	Operational Expenses	**(11,450)**	**(14,572)**	**3,122**
Profit from Operations		**1,989**	**1,817**	**(172)**
Other Operational Cost				
	Finance Cost	(554)	(441)	(113)
	Misc. other Cost[22]	(95)	(719)	624
	Total other Cost	(649)	(1,160)	511
Profit before Tax		**1,340**	**657**	**(683)**
Income Tax		(677)	(459)	(218)
Net Profit		**663**	**198**	**(465)**

Research Protocol

PREPARATION (SEPTEMBER 1993—JUNE 1995)

I. Extensive literature review
    a. review of Polish history
    b. cultural study of Poland, ethnographies
    c. communism and its impacts on culture
    d. study of key cultural dimensions
    e. TQM and its cultural implications
II. Language training
III. Three initial trips to Poland (one for 6 weeks)
    a. experience cultural change
    b. document the "surprises" and the "frustrations"
    c. discuss initial discoveries with colleagues (Poles and ex-
       pats)
    d. initial discussions with company owner
    e. initial tour of the factory
    f. ask a wide range of questions about the major changes and
       the problems with them
IV. Create initial theoretical model outlining initial domain of inquiry

STAGE 1- (JUNE 1995-JULY 1995)

1. Two month period of settling in
    a. experience cultural phenomenon
    b. document
2. Initial visits to the factory
    a. second tour of the factory
    b. interview with the owner
    c. explore, by walking around
    d. establish the best working location and employees of initial
       inquiries
    e. begin asking general questions about what is done
        1. about how employees feel about the changes in the country
           and the company
        2. about who the employees are
        3. about customs and behaviors
        4. establish trust
    f. talk to key managers about policies and changes.

    g. more detailed inquiries about specific people (the owner, president) and about who they trust, including the presidential elections upcoming.

    h. collect detailed demographic data on each employee in the target areas.

3. Collect secondary data from employees, managers and owner
   a. quality directives
   b. financial data
   c. personnel counts
   d. quality measurement charts
   e. training manuals
   f. strike vote announcements
   g. local songs
   h. organizational charts
4. Review initial results with Polish academics, business people, and American academics (peer reviews).
5. Begin teaching English in Goria—triangulate general data from the factory.
6. Collection of anecdotal evidence from other Polish organizations to support organizational data.
7. Detailed interview with owner.

PHASE 2— (AUGUST 1995—NOVEMBER 1995)

1. Step back and reestablish theoretical foundation for events and information.
2. Expand literature review.
3. Analysis of initial results.
4. Develop detailed model based on Phase 1 results, emergent themes.
5. Review with key academics re: methods and theory.
6. Field review (Dr. Janeen Costa)
7. Develop interview questionnaire for managers and executives.
8. Review of methodological literature.
9. Establish support group informants from support departments
   a. have initial meetings with these employees.
   b. gather biographical data on these employees.
   c. ask general questions about the changes and what they think of them in both the factory and the company.

10. Interview first line supervisors and technical personnel for all three of my core assembly groups.

PHASE 3— (DECEMBER 1995—JANUARY 1996)

1. Visits to employees homes and community activities.
2. Present topic of research and initial thoughts to Polish faculty, management group, students, and Fulbright students (American) and lecturers, and other American student group (peer reviews).
3. Interview top management personnel.
4. Rent a room one night a week with one of the employees to facilitate closer community contact.
5. Attend activities without interpreter.

PHASE 4— (FEBRUARY 1996—JULY 1996)

1. Code and analyze data.
2. Collect and analyze additional secondary data.
3. Review results with Jagiellonian professors (peer review).
4. Perform final member checking with Lockem employees and Goria residents.
5. Executive Review with Lockem management.
6. Write dissertation.

The Researcher as Instrument

The researcher's role as an instrument in all processes of research design and data collection, analysis, and presentation was particularly significant in this study. Therefore, it is important to briefly disclose my experiences, motivations and biases that have influenced this research.

Prior to embarking on this study I worked for an American defense contractor and was significantly involved in the company's attempts to implement Total Quality Management. The difficulty that this contractor had with implementing TQM was impacted by the incongruity of this management approach with the norms of the company. This experience with unsuccessful TQM implementation drove my interest in the values and assumptions that are embedded in this management philosophy.

I have ten years of management experience, with three large American corporations which provide a frame of comparison for evaluating the Polish organization that is the focus of this study. I have made numerous trips to Europe, but have never lived outside of the United States before moving to Poland to begin this project. I have extensive graduate level training in both quantitative and qualitative research methods. In addition, preparation for this research involved study of anthropological and sociological theories, methods, approaches and research. This produced a detailed understanding of the interpretivist approach that is employed in this study. It also helped shape the research design and provided project exemplars.

I have no connection with the Polish culture prior to my initial exploration into the topics that are addressed here. My heritage is Western European, but my family on both my mother's and my father's side have lived in the United States for at least five generations. I am married to another multi-generation American and we have a single daughter who was four years old during our stay in Poland.

In summary, my perspective is carved out in the American experience. My biases are shaped by the combined influences of interpretivist scholars from anthropology and sociology disciplines and management scholars and practitioners. Finally, my interest in the implementation of TQM in Poland comes from experience with an unsuccessful attempt to implement it in an American company. Wherever possible, the biases described here were evaluated in relation to emerging interpretations of the study data.

Informants

RED GROUP:

Teresa—20 years with the company (40 years old), lives on a farm.
Beata—20 years with the company (40 years old), married to Grzegorz, doesn't live on a farm.
Maria—23 years with the company (mid-40s), doesn't live on a farm.
Ewa—8 years with the company (mid-20s), fiancee owns a farm.
Janusz—8 years with the company (30 years old), doesn't live on a farm.
Krzysztof—12 years with the company (mid-30s), lives on a farm.

BLUE GROUP

Iwona—19 years with the company (40 years old), lives on a farm. Husband works at Lockem.
Joanna—6 years with the company (mid-20s), parents own a farm, which she will receive a piece of after her youngest brother (now 9 years old) assumes ownership.
Maciej—18 years with the company (40 years old), doesn't live on a farm.
Alek—13 years with the company (mid-30s), lives on a farm.
Helena—19 years with the company (early-50s), lives on a farm.
Czeslaw—7 years with the company (late-20s) (works in maintenance, fixing the machines). His wife works at Lockem, doesn't live on a farm.

YELLOW GROUP

Eza—22 years with the company (late-40s), lives on a farm.
Anna—8 years with the company (early-30s), does not live on farm.
Alicja—8 years with the company (late-20s), does not live on farm. Her husband works at Lockem.
Adela—20 years with the company (early-40s), does not live on farm.
Marcin—24 years with the company (mid-40s), lives on a farm.

OFFICE WORKERS

Marketing

Tomasz—1 year with the company (early-30s), owns farm 5 hours away.
Dagmada—15 years with the company (mid-30s), does not own farm.

Adam—24 years with the company (early-50s), does not own farm.
Elena—5 years with the company (late-20s), does not own farm.

Purchasing

Dorota—1 year with the company (mid-20s), does not own farm.
Margareta—25 years with the company (mid-50s), does not own farm.
Winusz—20 years with the company (late-40s), lives on brother's farm.
Henryk—10 years with the company (mid-30s), does not own farm.

OTHER EMPLOYEES

Iranusz—Quality inspector, 22 years with the company (50 years old), lives on farm, lived for several years in the US.
Tadeusz Sroka—Works for Andrzej Sroka's factory in the United States. He acted as a consultant for a new product that was to be shipped to the US. (mid-40s)
Genowefa—Quality inspector, 15 years with the company (mid-30s), does not live on farm. Married to Witold.
Zygmunt—Production department, 6 years with the company (late-30s), lives on a farm with his mother, he is not married.
Jerzy—Quality inspector, 12 years with the company (30 years old), lives on farm with his parents.
Grzegorz—Adjusts and repairs machines, moved to new job operating the new assembly machine. 23 years with the company (45 years old), does not live on farm. Married to Beata.

MANAGEMENT

Andrzej Sroka—Two years as CEO of the company. Fifty-six percent owner in the company (mid 40s).
Marek Litwa—Quality director, 2 years with the company (early 40s)
Marcin Wtorek—Purchasing V.P., 25 years with the company (mid-50s)
Tadeusz Gadomski—Old president, 25 years with the company (63 years old)
Piotr Bylica—New president, (early 50s), lives in Krakow.
Stanislaw Psowka—Engineering V.P., 25 years with the company (late 50s)
Witold Witowski—Production manager, 25 years with the company (late 40s)

Jozef Kwit—Production Director, 23 years with the company (early 50s)

VILLAGE PEOPLE

Miroslaw—Farmer (43 years old)
Bosia—Unemployed agriculture technician (21 years old)
Gloria—Retired farmer (65 years old)
Wojciech—Unemployed construction worker (30 years old)
Aleina—Cook (24 years old)

Trust Question

Question: Rate the following categories of people on the following scale:

Distrust A Lot 1	Distrust 2	Neither trust Nor distrust 3	Trust 4	Trust A Lot 5

Category	Mean Score	Category	Mean Score
Politicians	1.38	Priests	3.15
Headmasters	1.92	Factory Workers	3.38
Police	2.08	Americans	3.31
Russians	2.15	French	3.46
State workers	2.38	Univ. Professors	3.46
Germans	2.46	Farmers	3.53
Mayors	2.54	Nuns	3.54
Shopkeepers	2.54	Doctors	3.92

Sample: 110 high school students, and 25 workers at Lockem factory (management were not included).

Quality Wheel

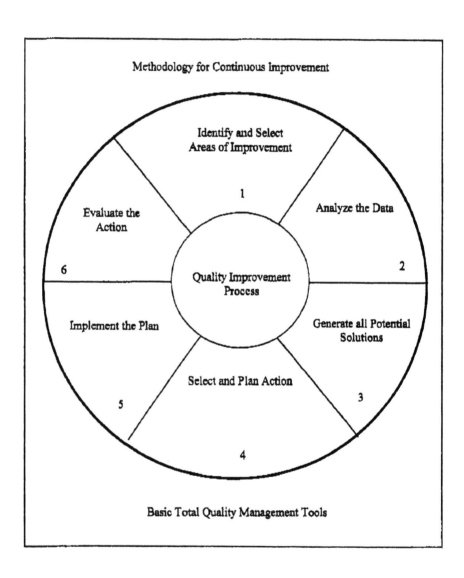

Methodology for Continuous Improvement

Identify and Select
Areas of Improvement

1

Analyze the Data

Evaluate the
Action

6

2

Quality Improvement
Process

Implement the Plan

Generate all Potential
Solutions

Select and Plan Action

5

3

4

Basic Total Quality Management Tools

References

Abramson, L. Y., Seligman, M. E. P., & Teasdale, J. D. 1978. Learned helplessness in humans: Critique and reformulation. *Journal of Abnormal Psychology,* 87: 19-74.

Adams, J. S. 1963. Toward an understanding of inequity. *Journal of Abnormal and Social Psychology,* 67: 422-436.

Adler, N. J. 1983. Cross-cultural management research: The ostrich and the trend. *Academy of Management Review,* 8 (2) : 226-232.

Anderson, J. C., Rungtusanatham, M., & Schroeder, R. G. 1994. A theory of quality management underlying the Deming management method. *The Academy of Management Review,* 19 (3) : 472-509.

Archer, M. S. 1988. *Culture and agency: The place of culture in social theory.* Cambridge: Cambridge University Press.

Arsensberg, C. M. 1963. The old world peoples: The place of European cultures in world ethnography. *Anthropological Quarterly,* 36: 75-99.

Atkinson, P. 1990. *The ethnographic imagination: Textual constructions of reality.* New York: Routledge.

Avolio, B. & Bass, B. 1986. *Transformational leadership, charisma, and beyond.* Binghamton, NY: State University of New York School of Management.

Bacharach, S. B. & Lawler, E. J. 1980. *Power and politics in organizations.* San Francisco: Jossey-Bass.

Barksdale, H. C., Perreault, W. D., Arndt, J., Barnhill, J. A., French, W. A., Halliday, M., & J.Zif. 1982. A cross-national survey of consumer attitudes toward marketing practices, consumerism, and government regulations. *Columbia Journal of World Business,* 17 (2) : 71-86.

Barrett, R. A. 1991. *Culture and conduct.* Belmont, CA: Wadsworth.

Bass, B. 1985. *Leadership and performance beyond expectations.* New York: Free Press.

Benet, S. 1951. *Song, dance, and customs of peasant Poland.* London: Dennis Dobson.

Beyer, J.M., Ashmos, D. P. & Osborn, R.N. 1997. Contrasts in enacting TQM: Mechanistic vs. organic ideology and implementation. *Journal of Quality Management* 2 (1) : 3-39.

Bojar, A. 1992. Group identity, group interest and democratic procedures. *The Polish Sociological Bulletin,* 2: 159-166.

Bowen, D. E. & Lawler, E. E. I. 1992a. The empowerment of service workers: What, why, how and when. *Sloan Management Review,* Spring: 31-39.

Bowen, D. E. & Lawler, E. E. I. 1992b. Total Quality-oriented Human Resources Management. *Organizational Dynamics,* 20 (4) : 29-41.

Boyacigiller, N. A. & Adler, N. J. 1991. The parochial dinosaur: Organizational science in a global context. *Academy of Management Review,* 16 (2) : 262-290.

Boyacigiller, N. A., Kleinberg, M. J., Phillips, M. E., & Sackmann, S. A. 1996. Conceptualizing culture in international cross-cultural management research. In B. J. Punnett & O. Shenkar (Eds.) *Handbook of international management research* :157-208. Cambridge, MA: Blackwell.

Brannen, M. Y. 1994. *Your next boss is Japanese: Negotiating cultural change at a western Massachusetts paper plant.* Unpublished doctoral dissertation, University of Massachusetts.

Brannen, M. Y. 1996. Ethnographic international management research. In B. J. Punnett & O. Shenkar (Eds.) *Handbook for international management research* :63-81. Cambridge, MA: Blackwell.

Bromiley, P. & Cummings, L. L. 1993. *Organizations with trust: Theory and measurement.* Unpublished doctoral dissertation, Curtis L. Carlson School of Management, University of Minnesota.

Burke, W. W. 1995. Organization change: What we know, what we need to know. *Journal of Management Inquiry,* 4 (2) : 158-171.

Burns, J. 1978. *Leadership.* New York: Harper & Row.

Burrell, G. & Morgan, G. 1979. *Sociological paradigms and organizational analysis.* London: Heineman.

Bushe, G. R. 1988. Cultural contradictions of statistical process control in American manufacturing organizations. *Journal of Management,* 14 (1) : 19-31.

Butler, J. K., Jr. 1991. Toward understanding and measuring conditions of trust: Evolution of a conditions of trust inventory. *Journal of Management,* 17 (3) : 643-663.

Ciampa, D. 1992. *Total Quality: A user's guide for implementation.* Reading, MA: Addison-Wesley.

Cole, R. E. 1993. Total Quality Management: Introduction. *California Management Review,* 35: 7-11.

Coleman, J. S. 1990. *Foundations of social theory.* Cambridge, MA: Harvard University Press.

Conger, J. A. & Kanungo, R. N. 1988. The empowerment process: Integrating theory and practice. *Academy of Management Review,* 13 (3) : 471-482.

Costa, J. A. & Bamossy, G. J., (Eds.) 1995. *Marketing in a multicultural world.* Thousand Oaks, CA: Sage.

Crosby, F. 1984. Relative deprivation in organizational settings. In B. M. Staw & L. L. Cummings (Eds.) *Research in organizational behavior,* 6:51-93. Greenwich, CT: JAI Press.

Crosby, P. B. 1992. *Completeness: Quality for the 21st century.* New York: Dutton.

Crozier, M. 1964. *Bureaucratic phenomenon.* Chicago: University of Chicago Press.

Cummings, L. L. 1983. Performance evaluation in the context of individual trust and commitment. In F. Landy & S. Zedeck (Eds.) *Frontiers in Performance Evaluation*: 89-93. Hillsdale, N.J: Erlbaum.

Czarniawska, B. 1986. The management of meaning in the Polish crisis. *Journal of Management Studies,* 23 (3) : 313-331.

Czarniawska-Joerges, B. 1989. *Economic decline and organizational control.* New York: Praeger.

Daniel, S. J. & Reitsperger, W. D. 1994. Strategic control systems for quality: An empirical comparison of the Japanese and U.S. electronics industry. *Journal of International Business Studies,* 25 (2) : 275-294.

Davies, N. 1982a. *God's playground: A history of Poland, Volume 1—The origins to 1795.* New York: Columbia University Press.

Davies, N. 1982b. *God's playground: A history of Poland, Volume II—1795 to the present.* New York: Columbia University Press.

Davis, J. A. 1959. A formal interpretation of the theory of relative deprivation. *Sociometry,* 22: 280-296.

Dawson, A. 1989. Resources, regions and reform: Plans and prospects for the spatial development of the Polish economy. In R. A. Clarke (Ed.) *Poland: The economy in the 1980's*: 72-87. Westgate House: Longman.

Dean, J. W. & Bowen, D. E. 1994. Management theory and Total Quality: Improving research and practice through theory development. *The Academy of Management Review,* 19 (3) : 392-418.

Dean, J. W., Jr. & Goodman, P. S. 1994. *Toward a theory of Total Quality integration*. Paper presented at the annual meeting of the Academy of Management, Dallas, TX.

deCharms, R. 1968. Personal causation and perceived control. In L. C. Perlmuter & R. A. Monty (Eds.) *Choice and perceived control* NJ. Hillside: Erlbaum.

Deci, E. L. & Ryan, R. M. 1989. The support of autonomy and the control of behavior. *Journal of Personality and Social Psychology,* 53: 1024-1037.

Delacroix, J. 1987. *Cultural differences in international business: A minimalist proposal*. Paper presented at the annual meeting of the Western Academy of Management, Universal City, CA.

Deming, W. E. 1986. *Out of the crisis*. Cambridge, Mass.: Massachusetts Institute of Technology Center for Advanced Engineering Study.

Denzin, N. K. 1978. *The research act*. New York: McGraw-Hill.

Derr, C. B. & Laurent, A. 1989. The internal and external career: A theoretical and cross-cultural perspective. In M. B. Arthur, D. T. Hall, & B. S. Lawrence (Eds.) *Handbook of career theory*. Cambridge: Cambridge University Press.

Deutsch, M. 1985. *Distributive justice: A social-psychological perspective*. New Haven: Yale University Press.

DiMaggio, P. J. & Powell, W. W. 1983. The iron cage revisited: Institutional isomorphism and collective rationality in organizational fields. *American Sociological Review,* 48 (April) : 147-160.

Dorfman, P. 1996. International and cross-cultural leadership. In B. J. Punnett & O. Shenkar (Eds.) *Handbook of international management research*: 267-349. Cambridge, MA: Blackwell.

Dyer, W. G. J. & Wilkins, A. L. 1991. Better stories, not better constructs, to generate better theory: A rejoinder to Eisenhardt. *Academy of Management Review,* 16 (3) : 613-619.

Earley, P. C. 1993. East meets west meets mideast: Further explorations of collectivistic and individualistic work groups. *The Academy of Management Journal,* 36 (2) : 319-348.

Ebrahimpour, M. & Johnson, J. L. 1992. Quality, vendor evaluation, and organizational performance: A comparison of U.S. and Japanese firms. *Journal of Business Research,* 25: 129-142.

Erez, M. & Earley, P. C. 1993. *Culture, self-identity and work*. New York: Oxford University Press.

Erlandson, D. A., Harris, E. L., Skipper, B. L., & Allen, S. D. 1993. *Doing naturalistic inquiry: A guide to methods*. Newbury Park: Sage.

Eysymontt, J. 1989. Reform in the Polish economy. In R. A. Clarke (Ed.) *Poland: The economy in the 1980's*: 29-44. Westgate House: Longman.

Fabian, J. 1983. *Time and the other: How Anthropology makes its object*. New York: Columbia University Press.

Feigenbaum, A. V. 1986. Quality: The strategic business imperative. *Quality Progress*, 19 (February) : 26-30.

Festinger, L. 1954. A theory of social comparison processes. *Human relations*, 7: 117-140.

Fetterman, D. M. 1989. *Ethnography: Step by step*. Newbury Park: Sage.

Flynn, B. B., Sakakibara, S., & Schroeder, R. G. 1995. Relationship between JIT and TQM: Practices and performance. *Academy of Management Journal*, 38 (5) : 1325-1360.

Flynn, B. B., Schroeder, R. G., & Sakakibara, S. 1994. A framework for quality management research and an associated measurement instrument. *Journal of Operations Management*, 11: 339-366.

Fombrun, C. & Shanley, M. 1990. What's in a name? Reputation building and corporate strategy. *Academy of Management Journal*, 33 (2) : 233-258.

Ford, R. C. & Fottler, M. D. 1995. Empowerment: A matter of degree. *The Academy of Management Executive*, IX (3) : 21-31.

Freeman, R. E. 1984. *Strategic management: A stakeholder approach*. Boston: Pitman.

Geertz, C. 1973. *The interpretation of cultures: Selected essays*. New York: Basic Books.

Gehani, R. R. 1993. Quality value-chain: A meta-synthesis of frontiers of quality movement. *The Academy of Management Executive*, VII (2) : 29-42.

Gibbs, J. P. 1981. *Norms, deviance, and social control: Conceptual matters*. New York: Elsevier.

Giddens, A. 1979. *Central problems in social theory: Action, structure, and contradiction in social analysis*. Berkeley: University of California Press.

Glaser, B. G. & Strauss, A. L. 1967. *The discovery of grounded theory: Strategies for qualitative research*. Chicago: Aldine.

Goffman, E. 1959. *The presentation of self in everyday life*. New York: Anchor Books.

Gordon, G. G. 1985. The relationship of corporate culture to industry sector and corporate performance. In R. H. Kilmann, M. J. Saxton, & R. Serpa (Eds.) *Gaining control of the corporate culture*: 103-125. San Francisco: Jossey-Bass.

Gordon, G. G. 1991. Industry determinants of organizational culture. *Academy of Management Review*, 16 (2) : 396-415.

Gorlach, K. 1995. The peasant issue in contemporary Poland. *Polish Sociological Review,* 2 (110) : 139-158.

Grinyer, P. H. & Spender, J. C. 1979. Recipes, crises, and adaptation in mature businesses. *International studies of management and organization,* IX (3) : 113-133.

Hall, E. T. 1959. *The silent language.* New York: Doubleday.

Hall, E. T. & Hall, M. R. 1990. *Understanding cultural differences.* Yarmouth, ME: Intercultural Press.

Hamel, G. & Prahalad, C. K. 1994. Competing for the future. *Harvard Business Review,* 72 (4) : 112-128.

Hann, C. M. 1985. *A village without solidarity: Polish peasants in years of crisis.* New Haven: Yale University Press.

Hanss, W. 1992. A summing-up of the Warsaw seminar by a German union official. In J. Mujzel (Eds.) *Privatization and transformation in Eastern Europe: A trade union perspective:* 149-152. Warsaw, Poland: Friedrich Ebert Foundation Warsaw Office.

Harari, O. 1993. Ten reasons why TQM doesn't work. *Management Review,* 82 (1) : 33-38.

Harris, C. R. 1995. The evolution of quality management: An overview of the TQM literature. *Canadian Journal of Administrative Sciences,* 12 (2) : 95-105.

Hayek, F. A. 1978. *The pretence of knowledge.* Chicago: University of Chicago Press.

Hofstede, G. 1980. *Culture's consequences: International differences in work-related values.* Beverly Hills, CA: Sage.

Hofstede, G. 1983a. Dimensions of national cultures in fifty countries and three regions. In J. B. Deregowski, S. Dziurawiec, & R. C. Annies (Eds.) *Expiscations in cross-cultural Psychology:* 335-355. Lisse, Netherlands: Swets and Zeitlinger.

Hofstede, G. 1983b. National cultures in four dimensions. *International Studies of Management and Organization,* 13: 46-74.

Hofstede, G. 1984. The cultural relativity of the quality of life concept. *Academy of Management Review,* 9 (3) : 389-398.

Hofstede, G. 1991. *Cultures and organizations: Software of the mind.* London: McGraw-Hill.

Hofstede, G. 1992. Cultural dimensions in people management: The socialization perspective. In V. Pucik, N. M. Tichy, & C. K. Barnett (Eds.) *Globalizing management: Creating and leading the competitive organization:* 139-158. New York: John Wiley & Sons.

Hofstede, G. & Bond, M. 1988. The Confucious connection: From cultural roots to economic growth. *Organizational Dynamics,* 16 (4) : 4-21.

Homans, G. C. 1961. *Social behavior in elementary forms.* New York: Harcourt, Brace & World.

Jancarz, K. 1992. Triumphant Religion. In J. R. Wedel (Ed.) *The unplanned society: Poland during and after communism:* 205-212. New York: Columbia University Press.

Jorgensen, D. L. 1989. *Participant observation: A methodology for human studies.* Newbury Park, CA: Sage.

Juran, J. M. 1989. *Juran on leadership for quality: An executive handbook.* New York: The Free Press.

Kahn, W. A. 1990. Psychological conditions of personal engagement and disengagement at work. *Academy of Management Journal,* 33: 692-724.

Kwasniewski, J. 1984. . Translated by Margaret Watson *Society and deviance in communist Poland: Attitudes towards social control.* Oxford: Berg.

Kennedy, M. D. 1992. Transformations of normative foundations and empirical sociologies: Class, stratification, and democracy in Poland. In W. D. Connor, P. Ploszajski, A. Inkeles, & W. Wesolowski (Eds.) *The Polish road from socialism: The economics, sociology, and politics of transition:* 83-95. Armonk, NY: M.E. Sharpe.

Kiezun, W. 1978. *Elementy socjalistycznej nauki o organizacji i zarzadzaniu (Elements of sociliast management and organization science).* Warsaw: KIW.

Kloczowski, A. 1992. Onward exultation: The church's afterglow in communism's collapse. In J. R. Wedel (Ed.) *The unplanned society: Poland during and after communism:* 213-219. New York: Columbia University Press.

Kluckhohn, F. & Strodtbeck, F. L. 1961. *Variations in value orientations.* Connecticut: Greenwood Press.

Kolarska-Bobinska, L. 1989. Poland under crisis: Unreformable society or establishment? In R. A. Clarke (Ed.) *Poland: The economy in the 1980's:* 126-138. Westgate House: Longman.

Koralewicz, J. 1987. Changes in Polish social consciousness during the 1970s and 1980s: Opportunism and identity. In J. Koralewicz, I. Bialecki, & M. Watson (Eds.) *Crisis and transition: Polish society in the 1980s:* 3-25. Oxford: Berg.

Kostera, M. 1995. Differing managerial responses to change in Poland. *Organization Studies,* 16 (4) : 673-697.

Kuhn, T. S. 1970. *The structure of scientific revolutions.* Chicago: The University of Chicago Press.

Kulik, C. T. & Ambrose, M. L. 1992. Personal and situational determinants of referent choice. *Academy of Management Review*, 17 (2) : 212-237.

Kurczewski, J. 1982. The old system and the revolution. *Sisyphus*, III: 21-32.

Kurczewski, J. 1992. Shared Privacy. In J. R. Wedel (Ed.) *The unplanned society: Poland during and after communism*: 158-172. New York: Columbia University Press.

Lane, D. 1973. Structural and social change in Poland. In D. Lane & G. Kolankiewicz (Eds.) *Social Groups in Polish Society*: 1-28. New York: Columbia University Press.

Laurent, A. 1992. The cross-cultural puzzle of global human resource management. In V. Pucik, N. M. Tichy, & C. K. Barnett (Eds.) *Globalizing management: Creating and leading the competitive organization*: 174-184. New York: John Wiley & Sons.

Lawler, E. E., III. 1993. Total Quality Management and employee involvement: Are they compatible? *The Academy of Management Executive*, VIII (1) : 68-76.

Lee, S. M., Luthans, F., & Hodgetts, R. M. 1992. Total Quality Management: Implications for Central and Eastern Europe. *Organizational Dynamics*, 20 (4) : 42-55.

Lewenstein, B. & Melchior, M. 1992. Escape to the community. In J. R. Wedel (Ed.) *The unplanned society: Poland during and after communism*: 173-184. New York: Columbia University Press.

Lewis, J. D. & Weigert, A. 1985. Trust as a social reality. *Social Forces*, 63 (4) : 967-985.

Lewis, P. 1973. The peasantry. In D. Lane & G. Kolankiewicz (Eds.) *Social groups in Polish society* :29-87. New York: Columbia University Press.

Lincoln, Y. S. & Guba, E. G. 1985. *Naturalistic Inquiry*. Beverley Hills, Ca.: Sage.

Luhmann, N. 1973. *Trust and power*. Chichester, NY: John Wiley & Sons.

March, J. G. & Simon, H. A. 1958. *Organizations*. New York: John Wiley & Sons.

Marody, M. 1987. Social stability and the concept of collective sense. In J. Koralewicz, I. Bialecki, & M. Watson (Eds.) *Crisis and transition: Polish society in the 1980s*: 130-158. Oxford: Berg.

Marshall, C. & Rossman, G. B. 1989. *Designing qualitative research*. Newbury Park, CA: Sage.

Martin, J. 1981. Relative deprivation: A theory of distributive injustice for an era of shrinking resources. In L. L. Cummings & B. M. Staw (Eds.) *Research in organizational behavior*, 3:53-107. Greenwich, CT: JAI Press.

Martin, J. & Murray, A. 1983. Distributive injustice and unfair exchange. In D. M. Messick & K. S. Cook (Eds.) *Equity theory: Psychological and sociological perspectives*: 169-206. Westport, CT: Praeger.

Martin, J. 1992. *Cultures in organization: Three perspectives*. New York: Oxford University Press.

Mayer, R. C., Davis, J. H., & Schoorman, F. D. 1995. An integrative model of organizational trust. *Academy of Management Review*, 20 (3) : 709-734.

Merton, R. & Rossi, A. S. 1957. Contributions to the theory of refernce group behavior. In R. Merton (Ed.) *Social theory and social structure*. New York: Free Press.

Meyerson, D. E. 1991. "Normal" ambiguity? A glimpse of an occupational culture. In P. J. Frost, L. F. Moore, M. R. Louis, C. C. Lundberg, & J. Martin (Eds.) *Reframing organizational culture*: 131-144. Newbury Park, CA: Sage.

Mitki, Y. & Shani, A. B. 1995. Cultural challenges in TQM implementation: Some learning fom the Israeli experience. *Canadian Journal of Administrative Sciences*, 12 (2) : 161-170.

Mokrzycki, E. 1992. The legacy of real socialism, group interests, and the search for a new utopia. In W. D. Connor, P. Ploszajski, A. Inkeles, & W. Wesolowski (Eds.) *The Polish road from socialism: The economics, sociology, and politics of transition*: 83-95. Armonk, NY: M.E. Sharpe.

Morgan, G. 1980. Paradigms, metaphors, and puzzle solving in organization theory. *Administrative Science Quarterly*: 605-622.

Morris, M. H., Davis, D. L., & Allen, J. W. 1994. Fostering corporate entrepreneurship: Cross-cultural comparisons of the importance of individualism versus collectivism. *Journal of International Business Studies*, 25 (1) : 65-89.

Myant, M. 1989. Poland—The permanent crisis? In R. A. Clarke (Ed.) *Poland: The economy in the 1980's*: 1-28. Westgate House: Longman.

Myers, K. & Ashkenas, R. 1993. Results-driven quality . . . now! *Management Review*, 82 (3) : 40-44.

Myers, M. S. 1990. *Every employee a manager*. San Diego: University Associates.

Nagengast, C. 1991. *Reluctant socialists, rural entrepreneurs: Class, culture, and the Polish state*. Boulder: Westview Press.

Obloj, K. & Kostera, M. 1994. Polish privatization program: Symbolism and cultural barriers. *Industrial and Environmental Crisis Quarterly*, 8 (1) : 71-91.

Okey, R. 1986. *Eastern Europe 1740-1985: Feudalism to communism*. Minneapolis: University of Minnesota Press.

Ong, A. 1987. *Spirits of resistance and capitalist discipline: Factory women in Malaysia*, New York: State University of New York Press.

Orsburn, J. D., Moran, L., Musselwhite, E., & Zenger, J. H. 1990. *Self-directed work teams*. Homewood, IL: Irwin.

Osland, A. 1995. *Data-based dialogue and interdependence in employee involvement in Total Quality Management in Central America*. Paper presented at the annual meeting of the Academy of Management, Western Division, San Diego, CA.

Ouchi, W. G. & Johnson, J. 1978. Types of organizational control and their relationship to emotional well-being. *Administrative Science Quarterly*, 23: 293-317.

Ouchi, W. G. & Wilkins, A. L. 1985. Organizational culture. *Annual Reviews in Sociology*, 11: 457-483.

Papa, F. A. 1993. Linkage of old and new. *Management Review*, 82 (1) : 63.

Parkhe, A. 1993. "Messy" research, methodological predispositions, and theory development in international joint ventures. *Academy of Management Review*, 18: 227-268.

Parsons, T. & Shils, E. A. 1951. *Toward a general theory of action*. Cambridge, MA: Harvard University Press.

Paulhus, D. 1983. Sphere-specific measures of perceived control. *Journal of Personality and Social Psychology*, 44 (6) : 1253-1265.

Pawlik, J., (Ed.) 1996. *Statistical Bulletin*. Warsaw, Poland: Central Statistical Office.

Pearce, J. A. & Ravlin, E. C. 1987. The design and activation of self-regulating work groups. *Human Relations*, 40: 751-782.

Phillips, M. E. 1990. *Industry as a cultural grouping*. Unpublished doctoral dissertation, Anderson Graduate School of Management, University of California, Los Angeles.

Phillips, M. E. 1994. Industry mindsets: Exploring the cultures of two macro-organizational settings. *Organization Science*, 5 (3) : 384-402.

Phillips, M. E. & Sackmann, S. A. 1991. *Mapping the cultural terrain in organizational settings: Current boundaries and future directions for empirical research*. Paper presented at the Center for International Business Education and Research (CIBER) Cross-cultural collective conference, UCLA, LosAngeles, CA.

Polonsky, A. & Drukier, B. 1980. *The beginnings of communist rule in Poland*. London: Routledge & Kegan Paul.

Reykowski, J. 1992. Psychological dimensions of a sociopolitical change: The Polish case. In W. D. Connor, P. Ploszajski, A. Inkeles, & W. Wesolowski

(Eds.) *The Polish road from socialism: The economics, sociology, and politics of transition*: 83-95. Armonk, NY: M.E. Sharpe.

Reykowski, J. 1994. Why did the collectivist state fail? *Theory and Society,* 23 (2) : 233-252.

Ricks, D. 1993. International management research: Past, present and future. In *International Management Research: Looking to the Future.* New York: Walter de Gruyter.

Roney, J. 1994. *The relationship between key national culture dimensions and the organizational culture of Total Quality Management.* Paper presented at European International Business Association meeting, Warsaw, Poland.

Roney, J. & Fladmoe-Lindquist, K. 1995. Changes in perceptions of fairness in the TQM environment: Total Quality Management culture & justice in organizations. Paper presented at the annual meeting of the Academy of Management, Vancouver, B.C., Canada.

Rosaldo, R. 1993. *Culture & truth: The remaking of social analysis.* Boston: Beacon Press.

Rosati, D. K. 1991. Poland: systematic reforms and economic policy in the 1990's. In G. Blazyca & R. Rapacki (Eds.) *Poland into the 1990's: Economy and society in transition*: 20-31.

Roszkowski, W. 1991. *Landowners in Poland: 1918-1939.* Boulder, CO: East European Monographs.

Rotter, J. B. 1966. Generalized expectanices for internal versus external control of reinforcement. *Psychological Monographs,* 80 (Whole No. 609).

Rychard, A. 1987. The legitimation and stability of the social order in Poland. In J. Koralewicz, I. Bialecki, & M. Watson (Eds.) *Crisis and transition: Polish society in the 1980s*: 36-52. Oxford: Berg.

Sackmann, S. A. 1992. Culture and subcultures: An analysis of organizational knowledge. *Administrative Science Quarterly,* 37: 140-161.

Sashkin, M. & Kiser, K. J. 1993. *Total Quality Management.* San Francisco: Berett-Koehler.

Schein, E. H. 1984. Coming to a new awareness of organizational culture. *Sloan Management Review,* Winter: 3-16.

Schein, E. H. 1991. What is culture? In P. J. Frost, L. F. Moore, M. R. Louis, C. C. Lundberg, & J. Martin (Eds.) *Reframing organizational culture*: 243-254. Newbury Park, CA: Sage.

Schein, E. H. 1992. *Organizational culture and leadership.* San Francisco: Jossey-Bass.

Schneider, J. 1969. Family patrimonies and economic behavior in western Sicily. *Anthropological Quarterly,* 42 (3) : 109-129.

Schneider, S. C. 1992. National vs. corporate culture: Implications for human resource management. In V. Pucik, N. M. Tichy, & C. K. Barnett (Eds.) *Globalizing management: Creating and leading the competitive organization*: 159-173. New York: John Wiley & Sons.

Schonberger, R. J. 1982. *Japanese manufacturing techniques: Nine hidden lessons in simplicity*. New York: Free Press.

Schonberger, R. J. 1992. Total Quality Management cuts a broad swath— Through manufacturing and beyond. *Organizational Dynamics*, 20 (4) : 16-28.

Seligman, M. E. P. 1975. *Helplessness*. San Francisco: W.H. Freeman.

Seligman, M. E. P. 1981. A learned helplessnesss point of view. In L. Rehm (Ed.) *Behavior therapies for depression*. New York: Academic Press.

Seybolt, P. & Roney, J. 1994a. *Faculty empowerment: An examination of the unique properties of empowerment in the university setting*. Unpublished manuscript.

Seybolt, P. M. & Roney, J. L. 1994b. *Empowerment revisited*. Unpublished manuscript.

Silverman, S. F. 1965. Patronage and community-nation relationships in central Italy. *Ethnology*, 4: 172-189.

Sitkin, S. B., Sutcliffe, K. M., & Schroeder, R. G. 1994. Distinguishing control from learning in Total Quality Management: A contingency perspective. *The Academy of Management Review*, 19 (3) : 537-564.

Snell, S. A. & Dean, J. W., Jr. 1992. Integrated manufacturing and human resource management: A human capital perspective. *Academy of Management Journal*, 35 (3) : 467-504.

Socha, M. 1989. Wages and incentives problems. In R. A. Clarke (Ed.) *Poland: The economy in the 1980's*: 45-60. Westgate House: Longman.

Spencer, B. A. 1994. Models of organization and Total Quality Management: A comparison and critical evaluation. *The Academy of Management Review*, 19 (3) : 446-471.

Spender, J. C. 1989. *Industry recipes: An enquiry into the nature and sources of managerial judgement*. Cambridge, MA: Basil Blackwell.

Spreitzer, G. M. 1993. *The new workforce in the boundaryless organization: A conceptualization and empirical investigation of workforce empowerment*. Paper presented at the annual meeting of the Academy of Management, Atlanta, GA.

Stewart, E. C. & Bennett, M. J. 1991. *American cultural patterns: A cross-cultural perspective*. Yarmouth, Maine: Intercultural Press.

Stouffer, S. A., Suchman, E. A., DeVinney, L. D., Starr, S. A., & Williams, R. M., Jr. 1949. *The American soldier: Adjustment during army life.* Princeton, N.J.: Princeton University Press.

Sztompka, P. 1992. *Civilizational competence: The prerequisite of post-communist transition.* Unpublished manuscript, Jagiellonian University Krakow, Poland.

Sztompka, P. 1995a. *Looking back: The year 1989 as a cultural and civilizational break.* Paper presented at the annual meeting of the European Sociological Association. Budapest, Hungary.

Sztompka, P. 1995b. Trust: The missing resource of post-communist society. In B. Nedelmann (Ed.) *Kolner Zeitschrift fur Soziologie und Sozialpsychologie.* Sonderheft: Politische Soziologie.

Taguchi, G. 1990. Robust quality. *Harvard Business Review,* January-February: 65-75.

Taylor, J. 1952. *The economic development of Poland: 1919-1950.* Westport, Connecticut: Greenwood Press.

Thomas, A. S. 1996. A call for research in forgotten locations. In B. J. Punnett & O. Shenkar (Eds.) *Handbook of international management research*: 485-506. Cambridge, MA: Blackwell.

Thomas, K. W. & Velthouse, B. A. 1990. Cognitive elements of empowerment: An "interpretive" model of intrinsic task motivation. *Academy of Management Review,* 15 (4) : 666-681.

Topolski, J. 1974. Economic decline in Poland from the sixteenth to the eighteenth centuries. In P. Earle (Ed.) *Essays in european economic history 1500—1800*: 127-142. Glasgow: Clarendon Press.

Trompenaars, A. M. 1985. *The organization of meaning and the meaning of organization: A comparative study on the conceptions of organizational structure in different cultures.* Unpublished doctoral dissertation, University of Pennsylvania.

Trompennars, A. 1994. *Riding the waves of culture: Understanding diversity in global business.* Burr Ridge, IL: Irwin.

Van Maanen, J. 1973. Observations on the making of policemen. *Human Organizations,* 32: 407-418.

Van Maanen, J. 1988. *Tales of the field: On writing ethnography.* Chicago: The University of Chicago Press.

Van Maanen, J. & 'Laurent, A. 1993. The flow of culture: Some notes on globalization and the multinational corporation. In S. Ghoshal & E. l. E. Westney (Eds.) *Organizational theory and the multinational corporation*: 275-311: St. Martin's Press.

Visker, R. 1993. *Uneuropean desires: Toward a provincialism without romanticism.* Leuven, Belgium: National Fund for Scientific Research: K.U.

Wagner, R. 1981. *The Invention of Culture.* Chicago: The University of Chicago Press.

Waldman, D. A. 1993. A theoretical consideration of leadership and Total Quality Management. *Leadership Quarterly,* 4: 65-79.

Waldman, D. A. 1994. The contributions of Total Quality Management to a theory of work performance. *Academy of Management Review,* 19 (3) : 510-536.

Waldman, D. A. 1995. What is TQM research? *Canadian Journal of Administrative Sciences,* 12 (2) : 91-94.

Wallerstein, I. 1974. *The modern world system: Capitalist agriculture and the origisn of the European world economy in the 16th century.* New York: Academic Press.

Walters, E. G. 1988. *The other Europe: Eastern Europe to 1945.* Syracuse, N.Y.: Syracuse University Press.

Weick, K. E. 1989. Theory construction as disciplined imagination. *Academy of Management Review,* 14 (4) : 516-531.

Weiner, B. 1974. Achievement motivation as conceptualized by an attribution theorist. In B. Weiner (Ed.) *Achievement motivation and attribution theory.* Morristown, NJ: General Learning Press.

Wesolowski, W. & Mach, B. W. 1986. Unfulfilled systemic functions of social mobility: Part I, a theoretical scheme and part II, the Polish case. *International Sociology,*1 (1 & 2) : 19-35 & 173-187.

Wesolowski, W. & Wnuk-Lipinski, E. 1992. Transformation of social order and legitimization of inequalities. In W. D. Connor, P. Ploszajski, A. Inkeles, & W. Wesolowski (Eds.) *The Polish road from socialism: The economics, sociology, and politics of transition:* 83-95. Armonk, NY: M.E. Sharpe.

Westney, D. E. 1987. *Imitation and innovation.* Cambridge: Harvard University Press.

Whitney, J. O. 1995. *The trust factor: Liberating profits and restoring corporate vitality.* New York: McGraw-Hill.

Wilkins, A. 1983. The culture audit: A tool for understanding organizations. *Organizational Dynamics,* 12 (2) : 24-38.

Wilkins, A. L. 1989. *Developing corporate character: How to successfully change an organization without destroying it.* San Francisco: Jossey-Bass.

Wilkins, A. L. & W. Gibb Dyer, J. 1988. Toward culturally sensitive theories of culture change. *Academy of Management Review,* 13 (4) : 522-533.

Wnuk-Lipinski, E. 1987. Social dimorphism and its implications. In J. Koralewicz, I. Bialecki, & M. Watson (Eds.) *Crisis and transition: Polish society in the 1980s*: 159-176. Oxford: Berg.

Wolf, E. R. 1966. *Peasants*. Englewood Cliffs, NJ: Prentice-Hall.

Wright, L. L. 1996. Qualitative international management research. In B. J. Punnett & O. Shenkar (Eds.) *Handbook for International Management Research*: 63-81. Cambridge, MA: Blackwell.

Yin, R. K. 1994. *Case study research: Design and methods*. Newbury Park, CA: Sage.

Zimmerman, M. A. 1990. Toward a theory of learned hopefulness: A structural model analysis of participation and empowerment. *Journal of Research in Personality*, 24: 71-86.

Index

www.ingramcontent.com/pod-product-compliance
Ingram Content Group UK Ltd.
Pitfield, Milton Keynes, MK11 3LW, UK
UKHW020411010325
455677UK00029B/852